Liverpool:
City of Radicals

Liverpool:
City of Radicals

Edited by

JOHN BELCHEM and BRYAN BIGGS

the
Bluecoat.

LIVE®POOL
CITY OF
RADICALS
2011

LIVERPOOL UNIVERSITY PRESS

First published 2011 by
Liverpool University Press
4 Cambridge Street
Liverpool L69 7ZU

British Library Cataloguing-in-Publication data
A British Library CIP record is available

ISBN 978-1-84631-647-0

Typeset in Calluna by Koinonia, Manchester
Printed and bound in the UK by Bell & Bain Ltd, Glasgow

Contents

Foreword

'Radicalism'. Is it an action, belief, movement, ability, perhaps capability? Or is it a symptom as (to steal a film title) of time and place? Does it come from the individual, the time or the prevailing culture? Is necessity, once more, the prime suspect in the birth of radicalism?

Reading this collection of essays will provide both examples and proof for whichever you personally already favour. But taken together they should also underline that it is never one thing in isolation – more a convergence that brings about radical change. Pre-1911 we may have said 'cometh the hour, cometh the man'. Post-1911 and we have discovered that no person stands alone. And within that is the first lesson of radicalism. It takes time.

Just as it has taken centuries to refine the soft contortions of the Scouse accent to something that encompasses both the variegated languages that have passed through the great port city alongside the need to be able to speak without being overheard or easily understood, then so it takes time for radical ideas to be implanted, grow and become commonplace. The stories of working-class and female emancipation begin before 1911 and are still evolving a century later.

In an age when Big Society is still struggling for a foothold against Big Brother, another constant theme emerges. Whether it is the creation of the Sandon Studios, the Women's Social and Political Union or the rise and eminence of the School of Architecture: all stem from a feeling of civic indifference, a sense that the established order was, by definition, perhaps, a stultifying force.

Yet even as these stories unfold they do so around the lives and times and influences of their central characters. They reveal that radicalism comes from individual passion. So we discover Patricia Woodlock along-side Eleanor Rathbone, pre-dating Bessie Braddock and Margaret Simey. Charles Reilly is cast in a central role upon taking up the chair of Architecture, just as Tom Mann and James Larkin become principals in the industrial struggles that frightened the government enough to send a gunboat to the Mersey, an act of radicalism in itself that may have forever set Liverpool apart as a colony not a province: its own People's Republic, never again to be part of England.

But there are other recurring elements that can never be ignored: money and media. Often the two go together. Would the gunboat have been dispatched from London if the media had not been circulating revolutionary tales from Europe? Would Reilly have created the 'Liverpool Manner' in architecture without Lord Leverhulme's financial support?

It is easy to see Liverpool's growth as a port creating individual wealth not witnessed again until the advent of the Russian oligarchs. Through that wealth and its loss came the great injustices alongside the philanthropy that fuelled the Labour movement, yet also endowed our museums and galleries. It is less easy to see the rise of the so-called 'affluent worker'. The post-war white heat of technology period saw factory workers paid above subsistence levels and discovering both time and disposable income, which in turn helped drive the development of media and music. Would the Beatles and the Mersey Sound have exploded without the simultaneous growth in global media?

Even the suffragettes knew the power of attacking the right target to get the right media coverage, just as the Capital of Culture programme 2008 was put together to make sure that those same Beatles created by the global media were brought back to attract that very same media.

Among all these recurring themes, perhaps one is common to them all: pragmatism. The ability of particular individuals at particular times to sense what is not just possible but also what is probable: recognizing that, at times, stimulated by financial boom or bust, the shifts in social and political landscapes become either affordable or irresistible. The need is not for movements, structures or organisations to evolve but for people to step up and make things happen.

Without that combination of individual passion and media exposure leading to popular support, radical ideas remain just that: imagined but never implemented; conceived but never constructed.

The stories, for that is what they are, contained in this book follow another radical idea of its time: Reith's 1920s' view in establishing the BBC that it was possible to inform, educate and entertain simultaneously. They also throw some light on the radicalists who applied their pragmatism to make Liverpool what it has been and will always be: a city unafraid to speak out of turn, to ignore the status quo and to say or do what needs to be said or done; a true city of radicals.

Professor Phil Redmond, CBE
Chair, Institute of Cultural Capital
One-time radical television producer

Acknowledgements

Research into Liverpool's past, radical or otherwise, is a daunting task, but fortunately there is expert help on hand. Particular thanks are due to Maureen Watry and Katy Hooper of Special Collections and Archives in the Sydney Jones Library, University of Liverpool and to David Stoker, Roger Hull, Paul Webster and the staff of the Liverpool Record Office, who continue to make their treasures available for consultation despite displacement to a Sandhills 'satellite' during refurbishment of the Central Library in William Brown Street.

As the centenary of the remarkable conjuncture of radical activity in 1911 approached, the idea of examining Liverpool's credentials as a city of radicals across the range of cultural, creative, social, political and industrial fronts came from the Liverpool Arts Regeneration Consortium (LARC) (comprising several of the city's most prominent arts organisations). LARC has continued to provide support for publication, particularly through the Bluecoat, which has led on developing the Liverpool City of Radicals year, as has the recently established Institute of Cultural Capital (ICC), a joint initiative of the University of Liverpool and Liverpool John Moores University. Thanks are due to Cathy Butterworth for helping coordinate the 'Radical Soundings' chapter. We are also grateful to the following for their permission to reproduce images: Joey Ankarah, the Bluecoat, Liverpool Biennial of Contemporary Art, Andy Dawson, Michael Kirkham, Liverpool City Council, Liverpool Record Office, Catherine Marcangeli, the Board of Trustees of the National Museums Liverpool: Walker Art Gallery, News from Nowhere bookshop and David Sinclair. All reasonable attempts have been made to trace copyright holders where appropriate, but please contact the publisher if you are aware of any omissions in this respect. Throughout, Anthony Cond at Liverpool University Press has offered reassuring encouragement and sage advice.

List of Illustrations

Notes on Contributors

John Belchem is Professor of History and Pro-Vice Chancellor at the University of Liverpool. Much involved in the city's inscription as a UNESCO World Heritage Site and its attainment of European Capital of Culture status, he is now Director of the newly established Institute of Cultural Capital.

Bryan Biggs is Artistic Director of the Bluecoat, Liverpool's contemporary arts centre. He has written about art and its intersection with popular culture and co-edited several books including *Malcolm Lowry: From the Mersey to the World* and *Art in a City Revisited*. He is also an artist known for his drawings.

Krista Cowman is Professor of History in the School of Humanities, University of Lincoln. She has published widely on women's involvement in British politics, especially the suffrage movement. Previous work on Liverpool includes *Mrs Brown is a Man and a Brother: Women in Merseyside's Political Organisations, 1890–1920* (Liverpool University Press, 2004).

Clare Devaney is a freelance writer and communications consultant. A Cambridge graduate, she travelled extensively before returning to her native Liverpool in 2002. With a broad professional experience, she has previously published well-received academic papers and press articles on arts-led regeneration, health, housing and economic development. She is currently polishing her first novel.

Paul Du Noyer began his career on the *New Musical Express* (*NME*). He went on to edit *Q* and to found *Mojo*. He is the author of three books, including *Liverpool: Wondrous Place*, a history of his home city's music scene. He currently writes for *The Word* and runs an editorial consultancy (www.pauldunoyer.com).

Roger Hill is a director, broadcaster, performer, consultant and writer. His many professional commitments have included Assistant Director at the Liverpool Everyman Theatre, President of the National Association of Youth Theatres and presenter of the longest-running alternative music programme on UK local radio. He has been based in Liverpool since 1978.

Mark O'Brien is the author of *Perish the Privileged Orders: A Socialist History of the Chartist Movement* (Cheltenham: New Clarion Press, 2009) and *When Adam Delved and Eve Span: A History of the Peasants' Revolt of 1381* (Cheltenham: New Clarion Press, 2004). He is a Senior Research Fellow at the Centre for Lifelong Learning at the University of Liverpool.

Peter Richmond is an architectural historian who gained his PhD from Liverpool University School of Architecture. He has written books on Sir Charles Reilly and the history of the Liverpool School of Architecture as well as co-authoring a book on Shaker design. He has also published numerous papers on the history of early high-rise housing in Britain.

Kenn Taylor is a writer and project manager whose work has a particular focus upon culture, community, urbanism and regeneration. He has contributed to numerous magazines, newspapers and books, as well as working on a variety of projects for organisations including National Museums Liverpool, Metal Culture, Tate Liverpool and the Foundation for Art and Creative Technology (FACT).

John Williams is Senior Lecturer in Sociology at the University of Leicester and is a Bootle-born Kop season-ticket holder. He has written widely about football and football culture in Britain, including a number of books about Liverpool FC, most recently *Red Men: Liverpool Football Club – The Biography* (Edinburgh: Mainstream, 2010).

Introduction:
A Democratic Promenade

John Belchem and Bryan Biggs

Facing out to sea, with its back turned on England, Liverpool is a place apart, a city on the edge. In the 'industrial' north but not of it, maritime Liverpool has always had a rhythm of its own, dependent on the vagaries of wind and tide, an irregularity at odds with systematic work and time discipline, prerequisites of the industrial revolution. Imbued with a sense of independence, this foundational culture has been cherished by subsequent generations of Liverpudlians, sometimes to the despair of factory managers and labour movement organisers. Where the adjacent north of factories and mills was to the fore in the development of organised forms of radicalism, Liverpool became associated with truculence and wildcat militancy – even if in more recent times Liverpudlians have attained national leadership positions within organised labour, as general secretaries of powerful trade unions, from Jack Jones to the likes of Len McCluskey, Billy Hayes and Tony Woodley today. This perceived 'bolshiness' extends far beyond industrial relations: being argumentative, 'having an opinion', is part and parcel of the city's image and identity. What Alan Bleasdale has described as 'a city that just likes to talk' is more often categorised as a city that insists on arguing.[1]

Seaports like Liverpool have a pronounced character of their own, their shifting shorelines producing what Steve Higginson and Tony Wailey have described as 'edgy cities and "edgy" people'.[2] Crucial to its identity, Liverpool's 'edginess' is linked inexorably to the notion of the city being uncontrollable, anarchic, separate and alienated from mainstream 'middle' England. A marker of 'sonic geography', the Scouse accent announces a cherished otherness which not all visitors appreciate. 'There is a rising inflection in it, particularly at the end of a sentence that gives even the most formal exchange a built-in air of grievance', Alan Bennett noted in his critical account of Liverpudlian self-dramatisation.[3] Although repudiated by some as an external imposition, an unmerited stigma originating from the days of the slave trade and/or Irish famine, Liverpudlian 'otherness' has been upheld, and indeed inflated, in self-referential myth, a 'Merseypride' that has shown considerable ingenuity, not to mention a degree of self-pity seized upon by external critics, in adjusting to the city's changing fortunes.[4] 'Bolshie' Liverpool is also condemned for its 'self-image of put-upon miserablist isolationism'.[5]

Probably the first (and certainly most reprehensible) expression of Liverpool's 'otherness' dates back to the slave trade when Georgian Liverpool, the 'slaving capital of the world', extolled its commercial success in the infamous trade in proud defiance of the meddlesome moralism of 'outside' abolitionist opinion. Having been vilified for barbarism, philistinism and lack of civilized culture, post-abolition Liverpool recognised the need for a change of image. Reviled at the time, those who had opposed the trade were rehabilitated and revered in a major rebranding exercise, although radical abolitionists such as the blind poet Edward Rushton, a former sailor in the trade, tended to be passed over in favour of the more refined 'Humanity' men, most notably William Roscoe and his circle of merchant-scholars. Here were appropriate 'liberal' role models for the new 'Liverpolis', a Victorian version of a city state (given monumental form in St George's Hall) dedicated to commerce, culture and civilisation. As Roscoe appreciated, enlightened investment in the arts – a task which could not be entrusted to public subsidy – promised a worthwhile return to the mercantile elite in the would-be 'Florence of the north': 'If you will protect the arts, the arts will, and ought to remunerate you.'[6]

Culture continued to legitimise commerce – and distinguish Liverpool gentlemen from Manchester men – until called upon to serve another purpose when economic circumstances changed drastically for the worse in the twentieth century. As the mercantile port collapsed into interwar depression, the city's cultural resources were promoted as proxy indicator of the quality of life on Merseyside, a marketing ploy to attract much-needed (but alas short-lived) inward industrial investment. In the latest exercise to reposition the city, culture fulfils yet another and more significant role: no longer a legitimising counterweight or attractive accessory to the 'real' economy, the creative and cultural sector is acknowledged as the essential economic driver in and of itself, the very pride of 'Livercool', a successful European Capital of Culture. For all such efforts at rebranding and repositioning, however, old deep-rooted external attitudes and prejudices persist, misperceptions and misrepresentations that the city seems doomed to endure. 'I've got a theory about Scousers', the chef informs the job-seeking Liverpudlian Danny Kavanagh in Jimmy McGovern's television drama series The Lakes (1997–99): 'You're all descended from the bastard children of slave owners, so you can't help it, sitting by while others do the work.'[7]

The hapless Danny encountered another 'theory about Scousers' from the Lake District hotel proprietor, harking back to another harrowing aspect of the past, the Irish famine influx: 'Bone idle. It's not your fault you understand, it's in your genes. You're all descended from the feckless Irish. Half starved, you get on a boat, you get as far as Liverpool and say, "Sod that, I'm not going any further, this'll do".'[8] Remaining (with good justification and no little success) in the 'last seaport of the Old World', the Irish in Liverpool jostled in cosmopolitan, if not always harmonious, inter-cultural action alongside a range of other 'moving Europeans' as well as innumerable seafaring and trading groups from across the 'black Atlantic' and the oceans beyond.[9] It was this demographic mosaic that set Liverpool apart, distinguishing it from other great Victorian provincial cities. Industrial conurbations grew by short-distance in-migration, reinforcing their culture and character as regional centres, but Liverpool developed in a more dramatic and discontinuous manner. Long-distance, mainly Celtic inflows – Welsh, Manx and Scottish as well as Irish – transformed Liverpool and its 'Scouse' culture, setting it apart from its 'woollyback' English environs. Beyond the 'inland' Irish Sea – Liverpool's private Celtic empire – the great seaport looked to the oceans, adding an external dimension to the city's cultural life and its migrant mix of transients, sojourners and settlers (categories that were by no means mutually exclusive). The community mentality of the Scottie Road 'slummy' coexisted with a broader culture explored in fiction by writers such as George Garrett, James Hanley and Jim Phelan, all Liverpool-Irish seamen. Seafaring cosmopolitanism made Liverpool, the gateway of empire, particularly receptive to (un-English) foreign ideas – syndicalism, for example – and to American popular music and style. Radicalism in 'melting-pot' Liverpool was by no means restricted to conventional domestic inflexions.

The remarkable conjuncture of radical activity in 1911, the starting point of this volume, displayed how Liverpool differed from national norms. Reaching a peak in an unprecedented long, hot spell (what Juliet Nicolson has described as a 'perfect summer'[10]), the radical fervour extended from direct-action political and industrial militancy – a syndicalist-led general strike that brought the city 'near to revolution' and so alarmed the government that Home Secretary Winston Churchill sent a warship to the Mersey – to cultural and creative endeavour drawing inspiration from the American and continental European avant-garde. The opening of the Liver Building, the first major building in the UK to use reinforced concrete in its construction, transformed the Pier Head in suitably un-English style, suggesting Chicago on the Mersey. This controversial, modern edifice was crowned by two liver birds, which came to symbolise the city's resilience. Alongside artworks by Liverpool artists, the Sandon Studios Society mounted an exhibition of Post-Impressionist art at the Bluecoat, including works by Picasso, Matisse, Van Gogh, Cézanne and Gauguin, shocking conservative middle-class tastes. Defiantly non-provincial, Liverpool before the First World War was a radical and exciting 'second metropolis'.

The combination of different radical impulses in 1911 makes that year a fascinating backdrop against which to investigate Liverpool's radical make-up – culturally, socially and politically. Starting with the momentous events of a century ago, this volume of essays seeks to assess Liverpool's subsequent credentials and reputation, deserved or not, as a city of radicals. The book has been published in the context of a year of events, entitled *Liverpool: City of Radicals 2011*, which invites arts, grassroots, community, educational and other organisations and individuals to join in a programme of exhibitions, events, debates and other activities that, while drawing on a rich history, will identify and examine what – and who – is radical at the start of the second decade of the twenty-first century, and from where some of these radical threads stem.[11] Liverpool city council, for instance, is marking the centenary of the death of Robert Tressell, author of the influential socialist novel *The Ragged Trousered Philanthropists*, who died in 1911 in Liverpool where, having spent time in the workhouse, he was buried in a paupers' grave. Though his connection to the city is tenuous (he was trying to emigrate to Canada), Tressell provides a symbol of working-class resistance that fits the narrative of Liverpool as a port through which radical, emancipatory ideas flowed. Three years on from Liverpool's tenure as European Capital of Culture, this 'radicals' cultural programme suggests perhaps a confidence and maturity in the city to look more critically at itself, this time, however, through a more organic programme than what some perceived as the 'top down' approach of 2008. Like the 2011 events programme, this book aims to put Liverpool's radical reputation under long-overdue examination. While necessarily selective in its topics, the publication covers a wide cultural and political terrain in essays by ten invited writers. The final chapter, 'Radical Soundings', offers a snapshot of the city's radical prospects, with opinions from a range of contributors – including academics, activists, architects and artists – who were invited to consider the challenges the city faces and to say what they thought might constitute its radical future.

In the one hundred years that followed 1911, the city experienced many events, upheavals and innovations that contributed to its reputation for radical thought and actions, as it went from second city of empire, through decades of decline into the 'shock city' of post-imperial, post-industrial Britain, to its recent reinvention as cultural 'Livercool', the latest (but already dated?) rebranding exercise put under timely critical scrutiny by Clare Devaney in her chapter 'Scouse and the City'. Significantly, it is business rather than culture that is the concern of the newly established embassy in London of the 'People's Republic of Merseyside', a sadly ironic reincarnation of the unique London Office established at the height of Liverpool's Victorian 'city state' prosperity.[12]

In line with this roller-coaster history, and its underlying economic realities and constraints, most forms of radical culture and activity have been uneven and discontinuous, notably in the performative arts, as Roger Hill shows. Written in suitably unconventional style as a dialogue of self-interrogation, his chapter, 'The Revolution Will Not Be Dramatised', argues that the radical is to be found only at certain moments of conjuncture and in other dramatic contexts beyond theatre – in film, television, live art and spectacle. In some instances – as, for example, in the chapter 'Rebuilding the Temple', Peter Richmond's study of Liverpool's early architectural pre-eminence and promise – radicalism was soon to collapse into conservatism. Given the city's troubled twentieth-century history, much radical activity has been communal, defensive and compensatory, offering solace, solidarity and humour in the face of adversity. Even in better times, however, as in the brief period of 'branch-plant' prosperity in the years following the city's 750th anniversary in 1957, new cultural expressions continued to respect the Liverpudlian imperative of entertainment (and accessibility). Echoing Liverpool-born poet Paul Farley's view that 'Liverpool isn't about dissonance', Paul du Noyer argues in 'The Heavens Above and the Dirt Below', his chapter on the city's music, that the renowned 'Merseysound' and much that followed was melodic and tuneful rather than necessarily innovative.[13] Liverpool's literary voice – the subject of a recent comprehensive study – has tended to be characterised by melancholic ambiguity: the city is both 'special' and yet doomed, a place celebrated but which leading characters are often fated to abandon. Significantly, the most radical and innovative inflexions have been expressed by novelists such as Malcolm Lowry and J. G. Farrell in settings and cultures far removed from their Merseyside origins, distant from what Lowry described as 'that terrible city whose main street is the ocean'.[14]

Whether among stay-put locals or naturalised incomers to the city, the most persistent commitment to radicalism has been at individual level – hence this volume's title 'City of Radicals' rather than 'Radical City'. Significantly, it was individuals rather than mass movements that left their mark, individuals often, though, working to effect radical change within institutions or among groups. In the second half of this period in particular it was in creative fields – in arts, cultural and sport – that the efforts of individuals reverberated beyond the city: from the Beatles changing the face of popular music to the innovations of managers, players and fans of Liverpool Football Club, as articulated in John Williams's chapter 'The Liverpool Way, the Matchless Kop and the Anny Road Boys'. In a city that Roger Hill describes here as 'built on the rock of the family', radicalism was also a mission carried from one generation to the next within families, as highlighted here by Mark O'Brien's study of 'Liverpool 1911 and its Era: Foundational Myth or Authentic Tradition'. As the example of the Bamber family shows, radicalism was not an exclusively male preserve, despite the overtly masculine character of the port and its labour market. By no means restricted to such formidable and well-known figures as Eleanor Rathbone (descendant of the foremost philanthropic radical-Liberal Unitarian merchant family of the nineteenth century) and 'Battling' Bessie Braddock (née Bamber), Krista Cowman's study, 'Women and Radicalism', looks at an array of pioneering women, socialist and/or suffragette, whose role in Liverpool radicalism extended far beyond the merely supportive. As this chapter shows, radicalism transcended gender and class, with middle-class women to the fore in the Edwardian years (and beyond) defying the spatial codes and conventions of the time.

A noteworthy feature of middle-class 'progressive' radicals in the early twentieth century was their involvement in a range of activities (beyond the specialisms that prevail today), a pattern personified by Charles Reilly, described here as socialist and socialite. Head of the School of Architecture at the University of Liverpool (and unrestrained critic of the Liver Building), he had considerable impact on other cultural areas, in theatre and in art, for instance, as well as an influence beyond the arts, hence his appearance in several chapters here. Similarly moving between different interests, Littlewoods' founder John Moores extended his business entrepreneurialism into both football and art. These culture brokers from the middle classes (acting in latter-day Roscoe mould) were not necessarily radical figures in terms of new thought, and in Moores's case certainly not politically (he was a Conservative councillor for a period), but we can regard their work as having radical effect. Both Moores and Reilly are considered key figures by Bryan Biggs in his chapter 'Radical Art City?', which locates the radical in art at key moments across a century, connecting the Post-Impressionists' presence in the city in 1911 to Liverpool's globally connected visual arts offer today.

From its foundational expression in 1911, radicalism in Liverpool has been particularly associated with two distinctive locales: the waterfront, with its casual labour market and cosmopolitan mix of transients, sojourners and settlers; and the cultural artery running along the sandstone ridge into Liverpool 8, the 'Bloomsbury' of what was then the second city of empire. Much has changed in the ensuing period. As the 2001 census revealed, Liverpool, having fallen far down the urban hierarchy, is now one of the least ethnically diverse of British cities (asylum dispersal apart), with small numbers of post-1945 'new Commonwealth' migrants; and the mechanised container docks, no longer a major source of employment, are now far distant from the city centre, with scrap metal having replaced manufactured goods as the main export trade. The new history marking the 800th anniversary in 2007 of the granting of letters patent to found the borough, questioned whether Liverpool, once the most multicultural and un-English of provincial cities, now has a sufficiently cosmopolitan and bohemian complexion to attract the highly mobile 'creative classes' regarded as the key drivers of economic growth in the post-industrial city.[15]

The cultural spine now links two universities, two cathedrals and a host of cultural and other institutions, but the Edwardian aspiration for 'a great boulevard avenue running along the ridge'[16] has not materialised. As pre-war progressive potential dwindled, and the bourgeoisie decamped to the suburbs in greater numbers, cultural activity took diverse, radical and more-inclusive forms amid decaying Georgian splendour. In the 1950s, Richard Whittington-Egan relished the 'poetic justice' of the former townhouses of slave traders being transformed into after hours drinking clubs run by 'coloured stowaways' where it was now 'the negro who exploited the thirsty white'.[17] Once favoured by privileged bohemians, Liverpool 8 continued throughout the 1960s, up until its recent gentrification, as a febrile bohemian hang-out for the city's impoverished 'Beat', poetry and art crowd, as referenced here by Bryan Biggs and Roger Hill. The epicentre of Liverpool's distinctive cultural radicalism, Liverpool 8, as John Cornelius has observed, is 'not so much a place as a state of mind':

> an unpunctuated state of mind that wrapped up the pubs the shops the art college the cathedral the early mornings the late nights the dawn chorus the clubs the police vans the architecture the poets the musicians the prostitutes the students the semi-famous the famous the down and out ...[18]

In the century following 1911, workplace radicalism extended from the waterfront to the new outlying industrial estates, where the local labour force, accustomed to the independence of casual and maritime labour,

were confronted with 'alien' factory discipline and managerial preroga-
tives. Exacerbated by the large size of new plant on Merseyside and high
levels of external ownership and control, this 'culture clash' led to frequent
disputes, sometimes over pay but more often over sets of issues such as
discipline and dismissal and redundancy, manning levels and work alloca-
tion, including, as Krista Cowman shows, gender equality in the workplace.
In more recent years, efforts to retain residual workplace independence
have led to conflicts in postal, rail, fire and other 'uniformed' service
sectors, where Liverpool workers have been to the forefront in resisting
managerial imposition.

As Liverpool workers have continued to uphold the struggle for some
workplace autonomy, labour historians have charted – and celebrated,
as here in Mark O'Brien's contribution – an unbroken tradition of class
solidarity back to 1911. Placed within a wider cultural history of the city,
John Belchem's nuanced analysis of the general strike in his chapter
'Radical Prelude: 1911', acknowledges its long-term inspirational importance but draws attention to fracture, ambivalence and disappointment
in the immediate aftermath. As with the cultural and creative activity of
'radical' Liverpool in the years before the First World War, the progressive
potential of class-based Liverpool labour was not to be realised, *at least in
the short term*. Beyond the ritual clashes on the streets, the ethno-sectarian
formations – both Orange and Green – remained firmly entrenched,
offering collective mutuality and support, through pub, parish and informal
networks, to those of the requisite faith, reaching into parts beyond the
confines of trade unions and the Labour movement. 'Black' Liverpool,
however, remained apart, as trade unions and other formations sought
(as with the seamen who initiated the strike wave in 1911) to protect the
wages of whiteness. Later than in other cities, Labour came gradually to
the fore in the interwar period and beyond, but in Liverpool inflexion, best
personified by Bessie Braddock and her husband Jack, the party machine
combined close attention to local welfare with a right-wing influence at
national and ideological levels, a stance briefly, but defiantly, overturned
in the Militant years of the 1980s. Synonymous with Liverpool politics of
that era, this Trotskyist group that entered (and was subsequently expelled
from) the city's ruling Labour group may stake a claim to the radical, yet
opinion remains fiercely divided in the city and beyond, and though several
writers here reflect on Militant's impact, the degree to which they may be
regarded as radical – ideologically and tactically – deserves a fuller study
that is beyond the scope of this book.[19]

Subsequent disillusion with New Labour is one of the factors prompting the recent emergence of grassroots action on Merseyside, particularly in deprived areas of the city. This is a radical 'bottom-up' addition to Liverpool's distinguished history of voluntary and philanthropic activity[20] and is an echo of earlier community-focused initiatives, begun in the 1960s and 1970s, such as the Scotland Road Free School (whose legacy stretches back to the Liverpool Anarchist–Communist Sunday School and the influence of Spanish anarchist and 'Modern School' theorist, Francisco Ferrer, who visited Liverpool at the start of the century) or the *Liverpool Free Press*, part of the mushrooming of alternative presses in the UK that grew out of the late 1960s counter-culture, or housing co-ops and tenants' groups. As both Clare Devaney and Kenn Taylor show in their respective chapters, a plethora of grassroots groups, mainly neighbourhood based, have been stirred into activism to protest at detrimental governmental and official policies and/or to remedy the deficiencies and inadequacies of municipal, 'Corpy' or 'top-down' provision – be it welfare, housing or culture. Whether committed to radical resistance or radical transformation, these neighbourhood activist groups, like the football fans studied by John Williams, bring a characteristically Liverpudlian, innovative and practical edge to their local pride and to their intensely 'conservative' loyalty to place. As in the footballing rivalry between red and blue, localism of this order has served to reinforce a wider sense of shared 'Merseypride' within the imagined Scouse community. Some deconstructed forms of local territorial affiliation, however, are less positive, particularly as recently reported in the media, serving to perpetuate external misrepresentation of Liverpool – for example, in the infamous and internecine gang wars between those sharing the same L11 postal district: the likes of the Croxteth 'Crocky Crew' and the Norris Green 'Nogga Dogz'.[21]

Strongly held external opinions of Liverpool – expressed through both journalism and creative writing – are hardly a recent phenomenon. The pocket-sized *Mersey Minis* series of collected extracts from writers' experiences of Liverpool – ranging from the life-changing to the appalling, and stretching back to Melville, Dickens and Henry James – demonstrates a fascination visitors have had with the city over many years.[22] African Americans, descended from victims of the infamous triangular trade, relished being 'truly free' as they strolled through the streets, conscious of the irony that 'the victims of the oppressions of the American Republic find freedom and social equality upon the shores of monarchical England'. Having formerly been 'steeped in the guilt of negro slavery', early Victorian Liverpool, William Wells Brown was pleased to record, 'is now to the hunted negro the Plymouth Rock of Old England'.[23]

A much later inversion of the normal flow of Atlantic attitudes, the American Beat poet and countercultural icon Allen Ginsberg's oft-quoted, and invariably misquoted, declaration of Liverpool as 'at the present moment the centre of the consciousness of the human universe'[24] is a reminder of the city's hyperbolic appeal to visiting cultural commentators. Such comments delight the locals as much as they appear incredulous to sceptical outsiders, for whom the city will forever remain a symbol of all that is wrong with Britain, rather than the vital, if at the same time contradictory, contrary and bolshie place it actually is. The city is quick to defend its honour when negative utterances are made, such as actor and playwright Steven Berkoff's account of his dispiriting experience of the city's 'vandalised soul',[25] just as it will embrace plaudits like psychogeographer Iain Sinclair's appreciation of the 'breathing space ... like being in Europe' of the city's 86 bus journey along Smithdown Road: 'the privilege of being chauffeured around town, in comfort, for a few coins.'[26] Eulogies like these quickly become adopted as part of Liverpool's self-mythologising propensity. So we learn that, as well as being the 'centre of the creative universe',[27] Liverpool is the 'Pool of Life',[28] that the city has produced more number one hits and has more comedians per square mile than any other city, has more Georgian buildings than Bath, and more museums, galleries and equestrian statues than anywhere in the UK outside London.

These claims, real or inflated, should not be conflated with the radical. Yet the city is proud to use those of its sons and daughters who have had an impact beyond Merseyside – if not necessarily in ways that are obviously radical – in how it projects an image of itself to the world, as a city that does things differently. Visitors arriving today at the city's airport, for instance, are met by a statue of a 'narky' radical, John Lennon, the Beatle who described the avant-garde as another name for 'bullshit' before adopting some if its strategies and using his pop star status to raise consciousness about pressing political issues and counter-cultural alternatives. Visitors arriving by rail at Lime Street are greeted by more bronze sculptures (by the same artist)[29] of two other local icons: vociferous MP for the city Bessie Braddock and comedy legend Ken Dodd. Representative of a bygone age, the politician is a reminder of old Labour politics, in a city that did not elect a Labour council until 1955. The comedian, who continues to perform, is a British institution, though still something of an outsider: his surreal material (not to mention his marathon shows) perhaps too much for the entertainment establishment to embrace quite as wholeheartedly as it has 'family-friendly' Morecambe and Wise or the Two Ronnies. It is perhaps appropriate that in Liverpool the radical also finds voice in humour, which emerged as the city's response to its psychological, economic and structural problems. Verbal wit and surreal wordplay came to the fore, distinguishing Scouse humour from the slow-building, anecdotal, character-based northern monologue and the fast patter of cockney dialogue.[30] Roger Hill discerns a 'surreal ethos' as part of the city's psyche, a claim borne out by several radical individuals discussed in his and other chapters.[31]

An idiosyncratic combination to grace the concourse at the city's principal railway station, Bessie and 'Doddy' can be described – like Lennon at the airport named in his memory – as awkward, yet characteristically Scouse radicals. Today ships in the Mersey estuary sail past more metal statues – made of iron rather than bronze – Antony Gormley's *Another Place*, a congregation of silent, naked, cloned figures spread out along the distant shore. It is a haunting presence at the maritime entrance to a city that once ruled the waves (just as its merchants perhaps waived the rules), yet few passengers make this sea journey now. Over a century ago, however, immigrants and emigrants arriving or departing at Liverpool's landing stage witnessed something quite different, experiencing what Walter Dixon Scott described as a 'democratic promenade':[32] the coming together of business and pleasure, a rich diversity of people, from the city's wealthy merchants to its casual poor, from Europeans heading to a new life across the seas to sailors from around the globe dropping anchor on Merseyside, among them those taking or bringing with them radical voices that would resonate across a century.

Notes

1 '"We Are a City that Just Likes to Talk": An Interview with Alan Bleasdale', in Michael Murphy and Deryn Rees-Jones (eds), *Writing Liverpool: Essays and Interviews* (Liverpool University Press, 2007), pp. 184–93.

2 Steve Higginson and Tony Wailey, *Edgy Cities* (Liverpool: Northern Lights, 2006), p. 13.

3 Alan Bennett, *Writing Home* (London: Faber, 1994), pp. 144 and 289. Philip Boland, 'Sonic Geography, Place and Race in the Formation of Local Identity: Liverpool and Scousers', *Geografiska Annaler: Series B, Human Geography*, 92 (2010): 1–22.

4 John Belchem, *Merseypride: Essays in Liverpool Exceptionalism*, 2nd edn (Liverpool University Press, 2006).

5 Mick Hume, 'We're all Scousers now? Count me out', *The Times* (27 May 2005).

6 William Roscoe, *On the Origin and Vicissitudes of Literature, Science and Art, and their Influence on the Present State of Society*, a discourse delivered at the opening of the Liverpool Royal Institution, 25 Nov. 1817, quoted in John Willett, *Art in a City* (London: Methuen, 1967; repr. Liverpool University Press, 2007), p. 27.

7 Quoted in Philip Smith, "'I've Got a Theory about Scousers": Jimmy McGovern and Linda La Plante', in Murphy and Rees-Jones, *Writing Liverpool*, p. 210.

8 Ibid.

9 John Belchem, *Irish, Catholic and Scouse: The History of the Liverpool-Irish, 1800–1939* (Liverpool University Press: 2007).

10 Juliet Nicolson, *The Perfect Summer: Dancing into Shadow in 1911* (London: John Murray, 2006).

11 Liverpool City of Radicals 2011. <www.cityofradicals.co.uk/ >.

12 'It's business, not Beatles, as Liverpool sets up embassy', *Guardian* (22 Jan. 2011); W. O. Henderson, 'The Liverpool Office in London', *Economica*, 13 (1933): 473–79.

13 Paul Farley in conversation with Mark Haddon, *Guardian* (3 Apr. 2010), pp. 12–13: 'Liverpool isn't about dissonance. It's hung up on tunes. Believe me, I've tried dissonance. But I keep coming back to the music.'

14 Murphy and Rees-Jones, 'Introduction: Sounding Liverpool', *Writing Liverpool*, pp. 1–28. Lowry describes Liverpool as 'that terrible city' in a letter of 1936 to John Davenport, included in Harvey Breit and Margerie Bonner (eds), *Selected Letters of Malcolm Lowry* (London: Jonathan Cape, 1985), p. 13. The extent to which Lowry's birthplace continued to haunt his writing, produced mainly in Mexico, then Canada, is explored in Bryan Biggs and Helen Tookey (eds), *Malcolm Lowry: From the Mersey to the World* (Liverpool University Press, 2009). Farrell's postcolonial, historically set *Empire Trilogy* starts in Ireland during its struggle for independence before moving to India and Singapore.

15 John Belchem, 'Celebrating Liverpool', in John Belchem, *Liverpool 800: Culture, Character and History* (Liverpool University Press, 2006), p. 57.

16 Stuart Hodgson (ed.), *Ramsay Muir: An Autobiography and Some Essays* (London: Lund Humphries, 1943), p. 24.

17 See the section headed 'Crime Dossier' in Richard Whittington-Egan, *Liverpool Roundabout* (Liverpool: Philip, Son & Nephew, 1957), pp. 275–323.

18 Preface to reprint edition of John Cornelius, *Liverpool 8* (Liverpool University Press: 2001).

19 For a useful account of the emergence of Militant and controversies during their period in office, see Jon Murden, 'City of Change and Challenge: Liverpool since 1945', Belchem, *Liverpool 800*, pp. 448–63. On the financial and political context, see Michael Parkinson, *Liverpool on the Brink: One City's Struggle against Government Cuts* (Hermitage: Policy Journals 1985). For strident criticism of one of the most controversial aspects, see Liverpool Black Caucus, *The Racial Politics of Militant in Liverpool: The Black Community's Struggle for Participation in Local Politics, 1980–1986* (Liverpool and London: Merseyside Area Profile Group/Runnymede Trust, 1986). For stout defence of Militant, see Peter Taaffe and Tony Mulhearn, *Liverpool: A City that Dared to Fight* (London: Fortress, 1988).

20 See the publication marking the centenary of Liverpool Charity and Voluntary Services: Roger Morris and Hilary Russell (eds), *Rooted in the City: Recollections and Assessments of 100 Years of Voluntary Action in Liverpool* (Liverpool Charity and Voluntary Services, 2010).

21 Philip Boland, 'The Construction of Images of People and Place: Labelling Liverpool and Stereotyping Scousers', *Cities*, 25 (2008): 355–69.

22 Deborah Mulhearn (ed.), *Mersey Minis*, 5 vols (Liverpool: Capsica, 2007).

23 Quoted in David Seed (ed.), *American Travellers in Liverpool* (Liverpool University Press: 2008), p. xiv.

24 Ginsberg visited Liverpool in 1965 and famously described the city as 'at the present moment the centre of the consciousness of the human universe. They're resurrecting the human form divine there – all those beautiful youths with long, golden archangelic hair'. The comment has led to much controversy and analysis. See Simon Warner, 'Raising the Consciousness? Re-visiting Allen Ginsberg's Liverpool Trip in 1965', in Christoph Grunenberg and Robert Knifton (eds), *Centre of the Creative Universe: Liverpool & the Avant-Garde* (Liverpool University Press, 2007).

25 Steven Berkoff, recounting his return to the city in 1966, when he performed at the Liverpool Playhouse at a fundraising event for the theatre. The feature, 'The Leavings of Liverpool', appeared in the weekend *Guardian* (4 May 1991), pp. 4–6.

26 Iain Sinclair, 'Further', in the first issue of *Corridor8* (July 2009), p. 46.

27 Misquoting from Ginsberg, Tate Liverpool used this as the title of its 2007 exhibition *Centre of the Creative Universe: Liverpool & the Avant-Garde*.

28 Carl Gustav Jung's description of Liverpool in a dream of 1927, recalled in *Memories, Dreams, Reflections* (London: Collins and Routledge & Kegan Paul, 1963), pp. 223–24.

29 Liverpool sculptor Tom Murphy has somewhat cornered the market in Liverpool commemorative public statues with (as well as Braddock, Dodd and Lennon) Bill Shankly among his popular bronzes. Unlike the 'radicalism' of many of his subjects, his style is, however, resolutely traditional.

30 Jeffrey Richards, *Stars in Our Eyes: Lancashire Stars of Stage, Screen and Radio* (Preston: Lancashire County Books, 1994).

31 Surrealist-inclined Scousers include Lennon, Adrian Henri, George Melly, Roderick Bisson, the characters in Alan Bleasdale's *Boys from the Black Stuff*, as well as others not discussed here like comedian and writer Alexei Sayle, Liverpool surrealist painter George Jardine and cartoonists Brian O'Toole, Mal Dean and Bill Tidy. See also Paul Morley's chapter 'Liverpool Surreal' in Grunenberg and Knifton, *Centre of the Creative Universe*.

32 Walter Dixon Scott, *Liverpool 1907* (Neston: Gallery Press, 1979), p. 39 (originally published as *Liverpool* (London: Adam and Charles Black, 1907)).

I

Radical Prelude: 1911

John Belchem

While firmly under the political control of Archibald Salvidge's Tory electoral machine, Edwardian Liverpool was a vibrant place, enlivened by social networks in which radicals, progressives and bohemians were often to the fore. Ramsay Muir, Professor of Modern History at the university, attributed the 'remarkable vitality' of pre-war Liverpool, its 'ardour of youth and experiment', to the propensity for social interaction: 'In Liverpool one knew people of an immense variety of types, and I found this very stimulating'.[1] Various venues facilitated varying degrees of social, cultural and political contact. Starting from the sandstone ridge, the city's 'high' cultural spine, there was the Bloomsbury-like sociability of Sandon Terrace, home first of the University Club and then of the Sandon Studios (prior to the move into the Bluecoat), premises favoured by progressive 'New Testament' academics, Romani scholars and the artistic avant-garde as well as by wealthy ship owners and merchants with cultural and scholarly tastes. A little further down the hill was the more bohemian 'Latin quarter' around the artist Albert Lipczinski's 'Schloss' on the corner of Knight Street and Roscoe Street, where fellow artists, academics, actors and trade union activists intermingled.[2] Lower still (in topographical terms) were more explicitly 'political' and working-class milieus: the Clarion Café, which opened above 'a stale and musty newspaper and barber's shop' in Williamson Street before moving into Lord Street;[3] the International Club in Canning Place, where local syndicalists like Fred Bower, the 'rolling stonemason', spread the socialist message among various nationalities;[34] and hostelries such as the American Bar in Lime Street, 'known, like its genial hostess, throughout the Seven Seas ... as a refuge for the returned sailor or the weary and harassed agitator.'[5] Originally peripatetic, the Rodewald Concert Club, established in 1911 (as was the Liverpool Repertory Theatre), provided chamber music, classical and contemporary, 'with long intervals between items "to permit of free social intercourse"' in congenial venues such as Carlton Restaurant, Bear's Paw and the Compton.[6]

To what extent were radical elements the dominant cultural force within and between such networks in 1911, a formative year in Liverpool's reputation for radicalism? By looking at cultural and creative activity as well as political and industrial militancy, this chapter offers a rounded approach to understanding and assessing 'radical' Liverpool. An exercise in cultural history, it provides a starting point (and benchmark) by which to gauge the city's trajectory throughout the twentieth century and beyond.

Housed in fine Regency premises in Sandon Terrace, the University Club provided the ideal ambience for Muir to lobby support among mercantile and civic luminaries for the campaign to secure independence for the federal University College. Having begun in inauspicious manner in the early 1880s, 'in a disused lunatic asylum in the midst of a slum district', the university became fully independent in 1903, a symbolic advance redolent of the heightened Edwardian sense of civic pride and mission. Muir's head of department, the redoubtable (but research-inactive) Professor Mackay, leader of the 'New Testament' group of progressive academics, best articulated the new vision: 'Through its University Liverpool was to be a new Athens saving the country from its materialism by the clearness of its thought, the fineness of its work and the beauty of its buildings.'[7]

Newly appointed members of staff such as Charles Reilly, Professor of Architecture, were soon inducted into the University Club and the New Testament, so named to imply (not without arrogance) 'that all outside it belonged to the Old'.[8] Socialite and socialist, Reilly, a cultural 'live wire', enjoyed the energizing mix of academics, artists and bohemian types who attended the Club and lived in its environs, 'a sort of Bloomsbury area' of handsome Georgian houses, recently vacated by suburban-fleeing merchants. By contrast, he detested his new working environment in a depressing building, inherited from the University College, approached by 'mean streets' up through the Brownlow Hill 'ghetto'. Harsh and ugly, the Victoria Building represented the worst features of its age: an interior of 'pastrycook's architecture', with repetitive interior detail moulded in 'coarse, glutinous, jelly like stuff', and an external appearance in 'colours of mud and blood' that rendered the building akin to a 'less prosperous' Prudential Insurance office.[9] These surroundings notwithstanding, Reilly proved a true pioneer in architectural education: through the Liverpool School, he succeeded in establishing architecture as an academic subject in its own right while offering a path to professional qualification. Reilly, Muir acknowledged, 'created out of nothing the greatest architectural school in England; and to architecture he added the first serious study of

town-planning'.[10] Through his close working relationship with the indus-
trialist W. H. Lever, developed over regular visits to Port Sunlight, Reilly
secured the funds that led to the appointment of S. D. Adshead to a chair
in Civic Design. As the British leader in the field, Liverpool attracted a
number of international conferences on town planning, although some
delegates in 1911 were somewhat shocked by their encounter with the
barefoot denizens of the city centre: 'Several of the German ladies were
much distressed at seeing the neglected appearance of a percentage of the
children who clustered around ... Having learned town-planning from
Germany, Liverpool should next learn much more of efficient mothering.'[11]

Reilly and Adshead were natural allies in the progressive cause, seeking
an end to anything that smacked of the Victorian 'picturesque' in the built
environment. They led the vociferous, lengthy and ultimately successful
campaign to prevent placement of a statue of the late Edward VII in front of
St George's Hall, a proposal that would have necessitated cutting through
the high-podium wall at the south end. 'We could not sit by and see the
severity of the noblest classical monument in Europe cut about to make a
setting for a new statue and keep quiet', he recorded in his autobiography.[12]
The controversy intensified when amended but not significantly different
plans were put forward by distinguished architects of national renown.
Reilly resumed the attack with iconoclastic fervour. As Alan Powers has
observed, Reilly

> was not afraid to criticise an established figure such as Norman Shaw over
> his proposals to alter the plinth of St George's Hall in 1910–11, seeing in this
> issue a focus of the differences between the old picturesque generation and
> his own generation's greater respect for civic decorum. Reilly was undoubt-
> edly intemperate in this affair, but the abiding feeling is his need symboli-
> cally to kill off the old king and begin a new regime.[13]

Aided by Lever's funds and his growing reputation, Reilly was to travel
extensively, most notably to the United States, trips that deepened his
understanding of Beaux-Arts architecture and brought a new perspective
to the vision of a neo-classical Liverpool – 'cleaner, more straightforward,
larger scale classic instead of the complicated stuff with which our streets
are filled'. In place of Edwardian opulence, Reilly's work (in what was to
become known as the 'Liverpool manner') came to favour a restrained
classicism of the American kind. This direct exposure to America was in
marked contrast to the career of W. Aubrey Thomas, architect of the Liver
Building, a 'skyscraper' of transatlantic inspiration. Thomas is not known
to have visited New York or Chicago: indeed, he belonged to the Merseypride breed of self-sufficient Liverpudlians. As Peter De Figueiredo notes,

he chose to spend his professional career outside the architectural establishment (he was never a member of the Royal Institute of British Architects (RIBA)) and entirely in Liverpool.[14] A natural eclectic who combined
shrewd business sense with a keen interest in technology, Thomas worked
creatively with Mouchel and Partners, structural engineers and British
agents for the French Hennebique system, to exploit the possibilities for
reinforced concrete. Begun in 1908, construction was remarkably rapid,
each of the ten main storeys being erected at an average rate of nineteen
working days. A triumph of radical architecture, the building acquired two
finishing touches in 1911: first, the arrival of the Liver Birds to adorn the
domes – 'What more appropriate terminal could be had for these noble
towers than the figure of the fabled liver of proportional height and stately
mien to harmonise with the building?' the *Daily Post* opined;[15] and then
the installation of the four dial electric clock, the largest in the world. On
Coronation Day, 22 June, the clock in the western tower was set in motion
by Mark Lewis, chair of the Royal Liver Friendly Society at the precise
moment that the crown was placed on the new monarch's head, prompting
the suggestion that it be called 'Great George'.[16] The name was not to stick.
It was the Liver birds, not royal affiliation, which gave the building its
identity. A place, however, was found for royalty: after more than a decade
of debate and controversy, the statue of Edward VII was installed in 1921 in
front of the Cunard Building next to the Liver Building.

The success of the School of Architecture under Reilly came to serve
as consolation for the failure of ambitious plans to place Liverpool at the
forefront of education across the arts. Unlike Reilly, Mackay and his disciples were enthusiasts for the late Victorian arts and crafts movement and
had succeeded in linking applied art to the chair in architecture, 'adding
"artiness" to architecture'. Having assumed the applied art section, housed
in corrugated iron sheds in the university quadrangle, concerned itself
with mere 'decorative crafts', Reilly was pleasantly surprised to discover
its staff included artists of the highest calibre. Colourful personalities,
they contributed much to the ambience of the University Club: 'It was a
Bohemian place, frequented by painters such as Augustus John and David
Muirhead', Ramsay Muir recorded: 'Its good fellowship was a real enrich-
ment of the university's life, and helped to save it from becoming a mere
knowledge-shop.'[17] Thus there was considerable dismay in progressive
circles when the university agreed to amalgamate its art classes with the
proposed Municipal School of Art in 1905. Gerard Chowne and Herbert
McNair led a revolt and established an independent art school and atelier
in Sandon Terrace, premises recently vacated by the University Club. A

couple of years later, when the Terrace was demolished, Sandon Studios moved into the former city centre premises of the Blue Coat School where, thanks to the new owner, Lever, it was soon to be joined by Reilly and the University School of Architecture.

Cultural clashes of various kinds account for this upheaval. At a basic political level, the city council, having proudly welcomed the advent of an independent university, did not wish to diminish its own sense of civic importance. The council, Reilly observed, 'was getting a little nervous of the new University, that child with such predatory habits which was growing up in their midst'. By insisting that painting and sculpture were a municipal preserve, the council established a divide that widened over time, much to the dismay of Reilly and colleagues, with their aspirations for

> a complete Faculty of Fine Arts, the first in any English university if not anywhere in the world ... Augustus John was to be brought back to Liverpool – we were all feeling the loss of him pretty deeply – and appointments like Epstein and Elgar were to be made to other Chairs ... It might have altered the whole course of art in this country.[8]

As municipal assertion intensified, the New Testament vision for the arts was perforce abandoned: the chair of Architecture continued (as it does to this day) to stand in lieu of any appointment in Fine Art.

As the university withdrew, the Sandon Studios stood forward to continue the 'brave fight for what we called in those days "free art" in contradistinction to South Kensington and Royal Academy art'.[19] In acquisition and exhibition, as in education, the city council eschewed any embrace of the experimental. Liverpool was to establish its cultural credentials (and avoid any suggestion of provincial parochialism) by emulating the metropolitan artistic establishment. Conventional works from Royal Academicians and the like dominated the annual autumn exhibition in the Walker. Profits from this commercial exercise were the only funds available to the Gallery, money which, the Sandon Studios bemoaned, was 'misspent in the acquisition of the mediocre and in the depreciation of the valued in art'.[20] Visiting the Walker in 1911, George Bernard Shaw ridiculed local municipal policy in a telling contrast with the arch civic rival:

> Comparing Manchester's sense of civic responsibility in this respect with that of Liverpool, he said the former had become an artistic town as a means of getting relief from the horror of its surroundings (laughter). They gave £2,000 a year for the acquisition of pictures, while Liverpool not only gave nothing for that purpose but put a magnificent collection in the cellar for the greater part of the year, and put up a commercial exhibition in order to pay expenses.[21]

As proud Liverpolitans, members of the Sandon Studios were appalled by the city's failure to recognise and encourage local artistic talent. There were vociferous protests when the commission for frescoes in the Town Hall, funded by proceeds from the Pageant in 1907 celebrating Liverpool's 700th anniversary, was awarded to a London studio: 'It is as ridiculous in our view that the destiny of Liverpool Art should be at the mercy of "the butcher, the baker, and candlestick maker", as it would be to place in the hands of an artist the control of the tramway system.'[22] The controversy over 'Art and the Municipality' intensified amid the outrage that greeted Augustus John's portrait of the retiring Lord Mayor in 1909. Devoid of due municipal dignity, it displayed what the local press described as 'Mr John's barbarities as draughtsman, colourist, and spreader of paint'.[232] Having taught several members of the Sandon Studios back in the Art Sheds, John was the radicals' cynosure; a position confirmed when his application for membership of the antiquated Liverpool Academy was rejected. Reilly relished an oil sketch of three nude women on rocks that he purchased from John, 'very useful later on for shocking the more Philistine and tiresome of the Liverpool ladies when they called on my wife or came to dinner'.[24]

Given the heated polemics in the preceding years, the relative absence of public comment on the remarkable Post-Impressionist exhibition staged by the Sandon Studios Society at the Bluecoat in early 1911 – discussed here by Bryan Biggs – seems somewhat surprising. In 1908, the Sandon Studios had been the first to exhibit a Monet outside of London. Another provincial first, the 1911 exhibition, based on Roger Fry's sensational show in London, included forty-six works of the French school: five Picassos, eight Gauguins, three Matisses, two Derains, three Vlamincks, two Rouaults, two Van Goghs and a Cézanne; with additional works by Sandon Studios artists, including two by Lipczinski.[25] While largely ignored by the press and civic establishment, the Sandon Studios Society represented much more than a *salon des refusés*: based in the Bluecoat, soon to be renamed Liberty Buildings by Lever following his success in a libel action, it was the city centre 'club' for radical progressives. Here was temporary refuge from what Miss Horniman described in opening the exhibition as the 'ugliness and dullness' of life: the purpose was less to promote a specific form of radical art than simply to shock the boringly conventional middle class (*épater les bourgeois*), content with 'hideous clothes', 'comfortable hygienic homes' and boredom alleviated 'by betting on everything'.[26] The Sandon offered a dynamic alternative to the Artists' Club in Eberle Street, that congenial venue for 'happy badinage' among those wishing to prosper in the commercial and professional life of the city, 'as sculptors modelling the characters of captains of industry, architects in the building and structures of finance, engravers making lines of impress on the City's life'.[27] The Sandon Studios Society aspired to a more creative cultural mission among the local middle class:

> We want to stimulate the artistic and intellectual life of Liverpool by bringing together those who are interested in something more than fashion and football and bridge and the share market. We want the amateur musical enthusiast to meet the rising professional and the young composer, the collector of taste to meet the promising artist. We want all the bright, appreciative people to meet the clever and original. This ought to give pleasure to them all and make for mutual development quite apart from the actual entertainment at which they meet.[28]

Writing from the stuffy confines of the Athenaeum, Robert Gladstone, chairman of the Mersey Docks and Harbour Board (and an active classical scholar), declined to mix with such company: 'As I am socially a recluse, and artistically a Philistine, I regret to be obliged to confess that the project of the Sandon Studios is altogether outside (or above) my sphere.'[29]

While leading commercial figures kept their distance, an eclectic mix of artistic, academic and political radicals passed through the doors, including suffragette artists – 'Bohemian feminists' within the Women's Social and Political Union – such as Ethel Frimstone.[30] Through his links to Lipczinski, Fred Bower introduced trade union leaders to the Sandon set. 'Lippi' painted portraits of Tom Mann and Jim Larkin, Bower's schoolboy sectarian sparring partner, from whom he borrowed copies of the *Clarion* and the *Labour Leader* to wrap around a socialist address placed under the foundation stone of the Anglican cathedral to remind posterity that 'within a stone's throw from here, human beings are housed in slums not fit for swine'.[31] Encouraged by Bower, Lippi took Larkin and Mann down to the Sandon: on one memorable occasion Tom Mann stood on a chair in the Dining Room and sang 'The Red Flag' to be followed by ballads by Augustus John and George Harris 'with a sensational rendering of "The Jabberwocky"'. As the historian of the Society recorded with pride:

> It is memorable that at Liberty Buildings, by the generosity of Sir William Lever, a tycoon if ever there was one, such men as Bower, Larkin and Mann, John, Lipczinsky [sic] and Harris, and those who held the ivory cards of the Wellington Assembly Rooms, and actors and actresses of the Playhouse and the Professors and their wives from the University could gather together more or less amicably.[32]

There was no place here, however, for the 'wage slaves' whom Mann and Bower rallied in the general strike of 1911. Even in radical inflexion, culture came at a price that by no means all could afford: annual subscription to the Sandon cost two guineas (£2.10); admission to the Post-Impressionist exhibition was one shilling (5p), well beyond hard-pressed working-class budgets.

Earmarked for demolition by futurists who viewed the site as the ideal location for the Liverpool station on a projected monorail link to Manchester, the old Bluecoat building survived under Lever's proprietorship to develop into a prototype arts centre, with the Sandon Studios Society and Reilly's School of Architecture as principal tenants. Revised plans for a Faculty of Fine Arts based in the Liberty Buildings were abandoned, however, after the First World War, when Lever withdrew his patronage for the proposed Lancashire Society of Arts.[33] The Schloss was also forced to close its doors after the war when Lipczinski was arrested as a dangerous character: 'One war had ended, but another had begun', Reilly observed: 'The only things against him were that he had a few socialist friends – who has not? – and wore a black hat and had a square black beard.' Previously Reilly had negotiated Lippi's release from internment at the outbreak of the war and then aided his finances by arranging for him to paint a group portrait of the New Testament professors. However, he was unable to prevent the imprisonment and subsequent deportation to Poland of Lippi and his much-admired Irish–Scottish wife 'Doonie', a former model for Augustus John and Reilly's long-term lover: 'With the break up of the life that centred around them and their strange studio ended a happy little coterie, a sort of Latin Quarter centre in the heart of Liverpool, which as far as I know has never been replaced.'[34]

The pre-war progressive fervour (and subsequent dissipation) extended from the visual to the performing arts. Reilly, Muir and other academics were to the fore in establishing a permanent repertory theatre in 1911, 'the first permanent theatre in Great Britain to be established, owned and controlled by a large body of local citizens'.[35] According to the *Westminster Gazette*, there were '1,100 shareholders representing all classes of local society, even down to what we snobbishly call the lower middle-class'.[36] The old Star music hall was converted for the purpose by Adshead with interior decoration by members of the Sandon Studios, although work was delayed by the industrial strife of the summer: Williamson Square became the 'chief battleground between the strikers and the police. The two streams seemed to meet there as by some instinct and our piles of bricks came in handy'.[37] As in the visual arts, there was a clear determina-

tion to reject provincial subservience to the metropolis. Here the Philharmonic led the way through an efficient subscription system enabling it to
schedule, *The Times* observed, 'a large collection of intensely interesting
music which Londoners, with all their myriad concerts, may go through a
whole season without hearing, and some of which we have never heard'.[38]
For the theatre, the priority was to escape the commercial inanities of
'rubbish' from London sent round the provinces by the touring system.
Reilly, however, had higher aspirations:

> The management should begin to feel that the Repertory theatre stands to
> the town in a similar position to the University. It is the duty of the latter
> to provide Liverpool with a seat of learning where any reasonable subject
> can be studied and explored, and with its great variety of Chairs, from Civic
> Design to the Chemistry of Oils, Fats and Waxes, it must be admitted the
> University has interpreted its obligations in this respect pretty thoroughly.
> Liverpool's one producing theatre, responsible for a great art to a million
> people, must do the same ... It should, in short, be a complementary
> civilizing force to the University as well as a place of entertainment.[39]

As soon became apparent, such highbrow tastes took no account of
commercial reality: 'Professor Reilly would be quite happy', it was observed,
'if the stage was darkened and only vague moanings could be heard, and
if the auditorium contained only two persons – Professor Reilly and the
Official Receiver'. After a promising beginning under Basil Dean, the
post-war Playhouse ceased to be 'in any real sense a pioneer theatre' Reilly
rued: 'No School of Authors has grown up round it, nor has it promulgated
any particular range of ideas in expression or presentation.'[40]

As well as commitment to the arts, the Liverpool progressive elite was
characterised by another enthusiasm: Gypsy lore. Here the inspirational
force was John Sampson, the university's first librarian, renowned for his
velvet jackets, sardonic conviviality (most notably in the University Club)
and mastery of Romani, in which language he wrote love letters (as well
as poems) to the beautiful 'Doonie'. Augustus John was a kindred spirit,
relishing encounters with Gypsies in North Wales and beyond, having
been instructed in Romani dialect by Sampson. It was Sampson's congenial
influence that led one of the scholarly businessmen who patronised the
University Club, the fifth-generation sugar-refiner R. A. Scott Macfie, to
devote his entire leisure time to punctilious editing of the *Journal of the
Gypsy Lore Society* (for which John occasionally provided illustrations).[41]
'Gypsies' were not an uncommon sight on Edwardian Merseyside, although
few matched Macfie's exacting standards of Romani authenticity. The

winter camp caravans in Pighue Lane contained about fifty persons, 'many of whom are half-bred Gypsies and only a few pure Romanicals', the most interesting being a woman 'celebrated for having poisoned 5 husbands'.[42] Across the water, the Birkenhead camp close to Green Lane station was 'a depressing place – no grass, no hedges, no trees; but lots of mud in wet weather ... Good Gypsies, but tamed by too long residence in one place'.[43] Hence Macfie's unbridled delight at the unexpected arrival in 1911 of a band of thirty or so coppersmith Gypsies from eastern Europe with 'strange dark faces of exotic beauty, a blaze of scarlet gowns and yellow gold'. 'The sight of a lifetime' for members of the Gypsy Lore Society, these 'real Roma' consti- tuted a radical presence within Liverpool's cosmopolitan demographic:

> Many kinds of foreigner tread the streets of Liverpool, and thus, when Uncle Kola and his tribe appeared on the banks of the Mersey from nowhere in particular the little boys put him down as a new species of 'Dago', and did not embarrass him with unwelcome attention ... Kola is, in fact, a ruler ... Us and all that we value, with the single exception of money, he despises even more cordially than we despise him. Like a drop of oil in a glass of water he and his tribe live in our midst untouched, strangely aloof and alien, a wonderful spectacle of *Imperium in Imperio*.[44]

Once the coppersmiths settled in Birkenhead, Macfie visited on a daily basis. Dressed for the part as 'Andréas', he quickly gained acceptance by the humour and skill with which he resisted their intense importuning, haggled over their exorbitant prices (although for craftsmanship of the highest order using fifteenth-century methods) and grappled with 'their puzzling Rumanian dialect'. He was even invited to become godfather to one of the children: 'Thanks to a most amiable Irish priest, who refrained from asking whether I was a Catholic, the ceremony passed off well, and in the evening the godmother made it perfectly clear to me that I was now one of the family with the privilege of supplying her with unlimited cigarettes!'[45] In August, however, 'Andréas' was forced to abandon his daily visits. For the first time in the lengthy history of the family firm, there was a strike at the sugar refinery.

A paternalist employer, Macfie was despondent about the unprece- dented industrial militancy of 1911:

> The strike in our works is a very sad event. We have hitherto been old-fashioned enough to treat our men as friends & personal dependents – keeping them long after they ceased to be useful, employing their children and grand-children, and finally giving them small pensions. To get into our works used to be considered a provision for life. Now, I fear, we shall be

compelled to look upon everything in a 'business-like way' – which means almost brutally. I do not like it, and I do not believe the men will; but it seems to be inevitable.[46]

From his perspective, workers had nothing to gain (indeed the reverse) from union-imposed pay and conditions (which led to his previously non-unionised carters having 'to start half-an-hour earlier in the morning, & accept about a shilling a week less than they are getting!'); conciliation boards ('the very thing they most disliked'); or from the introduction of state national insurance.[47] Macfie's analysis was undoubtedly partisan and tendentious, but the tension he identified between external (seemingly progressive) imposition and Liverpudlian (no nonsense) autonomy persisted throughout the strife of 1911.

In collective bargaining, as in popular politics and protest, Liverpool deviated from national organisational (and 'respectable') norms, prompting Ramsay MacDonald, a leading figure in the Independent Labour Party, to observe in 1910: 'Liverpool is rotten and we had better recognize it'.[48] Liverpool, indeed, played a backward role in the forward march of Labour. Trade unionism came late to its maritime, dockland and casual labour markets. In these difficult settings, organisation tended to develop in the wake of militant action and 'unofficial' strike waves, to be followed thereafter by structural tension between bureaucratic national union leaders and local 'rank and file' members. While leaders and officials sought union recognition and incorporation in national agreements, to which end they were prepared both to discipline and decasualize the membership, the rank and file (often with syndicalist support, as in 1911) protested against impositions and innovations which infringed local custom and autonomy. For all its ills, casualism was a cherished symbol of independence for the Liverpool worker, the best guarantee of freedom from irksome work discipline, from the tyranny of the factory bell.

There were also ideological aspects to the independent streak, aided by Liverpool's receptivity to ideas from across the seas. 'No-one telling us what to do' was the motto of the anarchists whose numbers in Liverpool, although by no means large, were second only to those in London. Inspired by visits from the Spanish anarchist pedagogue (and executed martyr), Francisco Ferrer, Liverpool libertarians established an International Modern School in opposition to the compulsion, repression and regimentation of state (and faith-based) education. Although housed in the rooms of the Independent Labour Party (ILP), the School failed to engage with wider traditions of independent working-class education, hindered first by its own ideologically sectarian mind set and then by the 'scare' following the Sidney Street siege in London. As the anarchist panic spread in January 1911, the *Post and Mercury* labelled Liverpool as 'the most active centre … anarchist schools have been opened where the children are practised in revolutionary songs and brought up in the ways of violence.' The School was promptly evicted from ILP premises.[49]

There has been much debate about the extent of syndicalist influence on the remarkable series of overlapping industrial disputes in Liverpool throughout the summer months of 1911. Like the anarchists, syndicalists rejected orthodox electoral politics and craft-based moderate trade unionism: they looked instead to direct action, co-ordinated by all-embracingindustrial unions through sympathetic and general strikes, as the most effective means of class conflict and the organisational nucleus of a new social order. Outside the mainstream of British labour history, syndicalism had a particular resonance in Liverpool where influential foreign inflexions of the creed were frequently encountered. The footfall of syndicalist literature brought back by seamen, the port also offered safe (and welcoming) haven for members of the American Industrial Workers of the World (IWW), better known as 'Wobblies', escaping repression across the Atlantic – Fred Bower, a leading local syndicalist, had first encountered their ideas while working in the United States. The Spanish anarcho-syndicalist movement was another source of inspiration, particularly within the International Club where Lorenzo Portet, foreign languages teacher and close friend of Ferrer, 'acted as a link between emerging Liverpool syndicalists and the development of a revolutionary industrial movement in Spain'.[50]

Encouraged by the charismatic presence of the syndicalist Tom Mann at the head of the co-ordinating strike committee, Liverpool workers were united in unprecedented class-based industrial militancy in 1911, a direct action 'strike wave' that brought the city 'near to revolution', prompting the government to dispatch a gunboat to the Mersey.[51] Liverpool, indeed, experienced a composite form of 'general strike' involving seamen, ships' stewards and catering staff, dock labourers, carters, tugboatmen, coalheavers, ancillary waterfront workers (such as cold storage men and boiler scalers), coopers, brewery workers, oil-mill workers, refinery workers, railwaymen, tramwaymen, electric power station workers, scavengers (dustmen and street cleaners) and others (women and children included). Seen in retrospect, the solidarity of 1911 has been imbued with mythic force, the defining inspirational point of reference, as Mark O'Brien shows, for Liverpool's radical heritage. As with cultural and creative activity of the pre-war years, however, the progressive potential of Liverpool labour was not to be realised, at least in the short term.

After the 'false dawn' of the 1870s and the limitations of the 'new unionism' of the late 1880s, trade union leaders such as Havelock Wilson of the seamen and Jimmy Sexton of the dockers sought above all to transform the workplace militancy of 1911 into permanent and recognised organisation within their particular 'non-craft' sectors. Sexton, the first (and sole) Labour member of Liverpool council, regarded employer recognition as crucial for the successful resolution of disputes and improvement in conditions by negotiation, accompanied by social reform (but not secular education) achieved through constitutional means. An able if uninspiring administrator, Sexton managed to ensure the survival of the National Union of Dock Labourers in the unpropitious period before 1911 but his cautious ways and means came under challenge. Blessed with dazzling oratory and 'presence', Toxteth-born Jim Larkin was the very antithesis of Sexton in style, attitude and philosophy. Following his appointment as national organiser for the National Union of Dock Labourers (NUDL), a post that conveniently took him away from Liverpool, Larkin distanced himself ever further from Sexton as he sought to extend the benefits of organised labour beyond dock workers to include all 'unskilled' labour. From his Irish base, Larkin, the syndicalist revolutionary, moved beyond trade union reformism, home rule and 'mere political reform', a trajectory seemingly in line with the mood of 1911 but which was to bring him into conflict with Liverpool's distinctive Catholic labour movement a couple of years later.[52]

Still smarting from 'libellous' attacks by Larkin and others, Sexton found himself sitting alongside the syndicalist Tom Mann in the strike committee in 1911. The memory was so painful that he chose virtually to exclude these events from his autobiography other than to condemn 'the blunder of calling out the butcher, the baker, the candlestick maker, who were in no way concerned in the originating dispute'.[53] The success of the general transport strike in Liverpool in 1911 was not of Sexton's making, but the consequent concordat with employers on union recognition and working practices on the waterfront was more readily achieved and consolidated, Eric Taplin concludes, because of Sexton's work over the preceding years, permitting Liverpool to become the best organised port in the country. The 'clearing house' scheme introduced in 1912 confirmed the union's control of access to the waterfront: indeed, it may have brought more benefits to the dockers than to employers[54] But once again Sexton came under attack as the scheme, predicated on decasualisation, coincided with the beginnings of National Insurance, a further step in bureaucratic intrusion, prompting fears that the police, tax-gatherers and other interfering bodies would make use of the clearing house registers. Heart sick of vilification by militants and syndicalists, Sexton sought vindication through his play 'The Riot Act', based on the events of 1911 and performed at the Repertory Theatre in 1914. Mann was thinly disguised as the 'fanatic' Maddocks, an advocate of 'solidarity' with no understanding of the 'one essential item – discipline', while other characters were portrayed as 'irresponsibles' in the Larkin mould.[55] For once, dockers thronged the gallery in the Playhouse but, as its historian notes, the most strident criticism came from another quarter, militant suffragettes:

> The one woman character lied, was disloyal, had a 'past', made open love to her employer, – and was a suffragette. Here, it was alleged, was an attack on the whole movement. So suffragettes rose in the stalls, protested and were forcibly ejected; or they addressed the audience from the boxes and were ejected from there.[56]

Criticism of Mann extended from the trade union to the political wing of the labour movement. Bruce Glasier, a leading figure in the ILP, was dismayed when Mann arrived in Liverpool seeking 'some new jumping off ground to afford him a fresh start as an agitator. Since returning from Australia, he has been unable to "catch on" either in the Socialist or Trade Union movement: and this strike is just the thing for him. He has played himself out in all reputable lines of agitation.' From his Wirral base, Glasier undertook detailed inquiries that led him to question the achievements claimed by Mann: the dockers had 'given away more than they gained'; the vaunted 'solidarity' in support of the sacked tramwaymen (the one group not to gain concessions) was 'mere bluff' and would not have materialised 'had not the Shipping Companies "locked out" the dockers and this they did for their own convenience seeing as long as the Railway Strike lasted they would not get goods transported to or from the ships by rail'. Glasier's conclusion was damning: 'Altogether it would seem as if the Dockers Strike was made merely a means of enabling Mann to "boom" himself – as I suspected from the outset.' For advocates of the parliamentary path to socialism in the ILP, militant strike action was not the means to secure a labour breakthrough in 'rotten' Liverpool. 'I agree with MacDonald', Glasier wrote in his diary, 'the strike weapon is like war of all kinds – a reactionary resort ... one does not feel that any social advance is really achieved by rehabilitating war ... So with strikes'.[57]

Mann's presence and oratory undoubtedly contributed to the spread of the strike during the second phase in August when the focus shifted from the waterfront to the railway, but it was the provocative behaviour of the authorities that heightened the tension, ushering in a period of virtual 'class war'. On 'Red Sunday', 13 August 1911, some eighty to ninety thousand assembled in front of St George's Hall to support striking transport workers. According to the official report, violence broke out in a side street behind the Empire Theatre, initiated by 'roughs from the adjoining Irish district'. This served as sufficient cause for troops and police reinforcements from Birmingham and Leeds, previously concealed, to be sent out to clear the plateau: their ill-disciplined baton charges left hundreds injured, hence the subsequent designation, 'Bloody Sunday'. Outrage at this 'unnecessary display of force' intensified as the unrepentant (now 'gung-ho') civic authorities instituted a Committee of Public Safety, requisitioned more troops and welcomed the arrival of a naval gunboat in the Mersey. In defiant response, there was a dramatic strengthening of the 'general' strike with movements of essential goods controlled by Mann's strike committee through the issue of permits.[58]

Rank-and-file syndicalists sensed the revolutionary potential, insisting that 'the culminating object of the workers should be the capture of the means of production', but, as Robert Holton notes, Mann's objectives were more pragmatic, based on securing improved wages and conditions and union recognition: 'Mann's syndicalism was limited in the short-term to the creation of "industrial solidarity". This was intended as the first step towards fuller industrial unionism, committed to revolutionary industrial rather than Parliamentary methods.'[59]

As the classes polarized, Mann was demonised by the employers and authorities. 'Tom Mann, the strike leader, is practically dictator in this town, & nothing can be done without his permission,' Macfie protested:

> At times we have had no trams, no tunnel railway & only partial electric light. The pubs still close at 2 p.m., and business is suspended. Many liners are unable to sail, and there is a warship in the Mersey. Special constables are enrolled by the thousand to carry food through the streets in the early morning, and the power stations are manned by volunteers.[60]

Having settled with his own workers, Macfie was soon counting the cost of action elsewhere: 'we can get no coal today, and expect none this week; and the dockers are on strike, and the carters too, so that we can neither get raw sugar, nor send away refined.' He came to hope that Mann might suffer a similar fate to that of the Protestant demagogue John Kensit, victim of a lethal attack a few years back: 'Everybody is losing at a dreadful rate, and I am murderous enough to wish that the man who threw a file at Kensit would pitch a planing machine at Tom Mann. All orators should be locked up – they spread a paralytic disease of reason.'[61]

'Is the City to be Paralysed?' the Tory *Courier* demanded, rallying its readers with unconcealed middle-class pride to undertake demeaning but essential manual labour:

> The middle-class has always furnished the brains of the country. By its members, the professions, the commerce, and the industry of the country are directed and carried on.

> Now there is a splendid opportunity for the middle-class to render another signal service to their native land.

> Let them show that their trained capacity can be devoted as well to lower as to higher services – that they have skill and muscle as well as brains.[62]

University students replaced striking workmen at the Lister Drive Power Station, playing their part, the Vice-Chancellor noted approvingly, 'in averting serious danger from the city and in helping to maintain public order and safety'.[63] The press proudly announced the establishment of Liverpool Civic Service League,

> a permanent organization of Citizens willing to assist the Authorities in preserving the health, safety and well-being of the City in time of need ... all persons who have recently given their services as Special Constables, Workers at Lister Drive Power Station, or as Members of the Civic Service Corps established by the Lord Mayor, shall be entitled to become Members.[64]

Dale, the Vice-Chancellor, declined an invitation, however, to join the Anti-Socialist Union of Great Britain.[65]

Working-class solidarity was symbolised by ecumenical attendance at the funerals of Michael Prendergast (a Catholic docker) and John Sutcliffe (a carter, an occupation dominated by Protestants), killed when police and troops opened fire as five prison vans containing men sentenced for offences during the strikes came under attack.[66] (A few months later Liverpool was the first city to introduce motorised 'Black Marias' in an effort to prevent 'objectionable scenes' on the streets as 'wretched women' routinely impeded the progress of horse-drawn prison vans, communicating with prisoners inside and 'flinging imprecations' at the driver and the constable at the rear.[67]) Syndicalists heralded a new era of class solidarity above the old sectarian divisions. In Dingle Ward, Bower averred, 'they were going to put up another colour – orange on the one side, green on the other, and red down the middle'.[68] However, as public sanction was withdrawn from the authorities and the police after 'Bloody Sunday', there was an outbreak of lawlessness, a veritable orgy of looting and old-style sectarian violence that rendered Liverpool, in the words of the *Review of Reviews*, 'A Nightmare of Civilisation'.[69] Observers agreed the violence was provoked not by the strikers, whether organised trade unionists or not, but by these denizens of the local culture of 'rowdyism', described interchangeably in official reports as idle, hooligan and Irish, the 'horde of rowdy loafers with which Liverpool is unfortunately infested, who will not work, and avail themselves of disturbances of this kind to loot and rob when occasion offers'. Amid universal condemnation of the 'hooligan', the *Transport Worker*, edited by Tom Mann, sought to inject a sense of context, drawing attention to the demoralising aspects of Liverpool's casual labour market: the 'hanging about waiting for a job, the tramping from place to place in search of work ... the intermittent nature of the work when it is obtained, etc, all has a terrible effect on a person who perhaps does not belong to the highest category – small blame to him that he becomes what he does. Society is to blame'.[70]

Much concerned by the violence and 'bitter feeling' in Liverpool, the government decided to intervene. T. P. O'Connor, the veteran Irish Nationalist MP for the Scotland Division, and Colonel Kyffin-Taylor, Conservative MP for Kirkdale (and committee member of the Protestant Reformation Society), were appointed to a Conciliation Committee, assisted by D. J. Shackleton, the Home Office labour adviser. O'Connor was the driving force, running considerably over budget for expenses, as he brokered deals with employers and trade unionists from rooms in the Adelphi Hotel. It was O'Connor too who encouraged the Committee to extend its remit from industrial to sectarian conciliation by picking up the proposals recommended by the inquiry into the 1909 riots. Chaired by Lord Derby, a 'conciliation conference' amended and strengthened the proposals drafted but not implemented in 1910 to regulate meetings, processions, emblems, music and weapons. Thanks to these new powers (hailed in the press as 'A New Eirenicon'[71]), the last stages of the Home Rule crisis before the First World War were uncharacteristically riot free in Liverpool. The peaceful nature of the carefully stage-managed monster anti-Home Rule demonstration in 1912, relocated by Salvidge on Derby's instructions from the city centre to Sheil Park, pointed to a new dispensation.[72]

The continued resonance of confessional affiliation among organised workers is perhaps best personified by George Milligan, whose collection of 'essays, letters and lyrics from the worker's own point of view', *Life through Labour's Eyes*, was published in 1911. Former barman, then quay porter and specialist checker for the White Star Line, Milligan was an active member of the NUDL who played the vital role in organising non-union dockers in the north end. Swept along by the strike wave of 1911, this group of predominantly Irish workers, previously denied union recognition by the big liner companies, was at first reluctant to adhere to the call of the strike committee for a return to work, believing that more could be achieved by continued militant action. Having been co-opted onto the committee, Milligan, acting as Sexton's lieutenant, managed to persuade them of the advantages of co-ordinated discipline.[73] A devout Catholic, Milligan was fervently anti-socialist, but militant and fearless in defence of his fellow dockers' rights. In his essays and other writings in the *Mersey Magazine*, he looked back beyond the 'new individualism' and the 'new materialism' of the Reformation to a medieval 'golden age' when 'the material welfare of the Church and of the worker fell together'. Hence the priority was to 'Christianise the Labour Movement', to banish the twin evils of secularism and socialism.[74] He was taken to task in local socialist publications such as *Liverpool Forward*, which vehemently repudiated his contention that the forward march of Labour was hindered by association with the ILP and other socialist bodies.[75] Shortly afterwards, the Dublin transport strike of 1913 led by Jim Larkin prompted a major culture clash between Merseyside socialists and the Liverpool-Irish-Catholic labour movement.

Aided by James Connolly and Big Bill Haywood, Larkin's efforts to arouse sympathetic support in Liverpool were ridiculed in the local Catholic press, disparaging the preponderance of 'middle-class Socialists, Suffragettes, and curiosity mongers ... not overflowing with friendliness to sane trade unionism'. Sympathetic strikes, Milligan insisted, were 'not compatible' with 'the ethics of striking from a Catholic trade unionists point of view'. There was much contention over the welfare of children sent across from Dublin to escape the privation of the strike. Much to the annoyance and concern of Liverpool-Irish Catholics, they were jealously guarded by middle-class socialists in Wallasey, denied proper spiritual (and ethnic) guidance. When the children were finally sent back, the opposing parties almost came to blows on the Liverpool landing stage, the socialists apparently insulting the Catholic priests in attendance while the Catholics drowned out the attempt to raise a cheer for Larkin.[76]

As this episode encapsulated, the terms Irish, Catholic and working-class had acquired synonymic force in the north end, strengthened in opposition to secular (often middle-class) socialism. By embracing this conjuncture, the Irish National Party was able to prevent a switch to Labour, to badge itself as *the* party of the Liverpool-Irish workers, committed to workers' rights, housing reform, denominational education and Irish independence. Over the decades since the election of Laurence Connolly in 1875, the INP had been carried forward by a radicalising dynamic, driven as much by progressive change in the composition of its council members as by mounting frustration at the Liberals' failure to deliver home rule. On retirement from the council, members from established middle-class professions and occupations (doctors, lawyers and rich businessmen like Connolly) tended to be replaced by those with a more popular style: butchers, shopkeepers, penny-a-week insurance collectors, undertakers and others who attended to the daily needs of the Liverpool-Irish.[77] In areas of Irish Liverpool under INP control, poor law relief 'discretion' was applied in 'generous' fashion. Eleanor Rathbone was scathing of such flagrant confessional favouritism in her 1913 *Report on Condition of Widows under the Poor Law*:

> The Orangeman or Welsh Nonconformist of Everton or Kirkdale cannot be expected to relish the knowledge that if misfortune and an untimely death should oblige his widow and children to appeal for help, they will in all probability receive just half as much out of the public purse as they would have done if they had been Irish Roman Catholics living in a slum near the Vauxhall Road.[78]

Protected by the 'Nat-Labism' of the INP, the north end was a milieu (or 'habitus') of solidarity and security, consolidated by the associational culture and collective mutuality based on the pub and the parish, inclusive cradle-to-grave 'welfare' extending across socio-economic and gender divisions. There were limitations: accepting the Catholic church's teachings on marriage, the much-abused mother of Pat O'Mara, a 'Liverpool Irish Slummy', was unable to turn to the priest and the parish at times of greatest need, when compelled to leave her drunken and violent husband.[79]

Viewed from the outside, the Liverpool-Irish enclave smacked of immobility and a culture of poverty, inhabited by those, described by Frederic D'Aeth, as 'the despair of the social reformer'.[80] Socialists were incredulous of what they considered the self-enclosed horizons, the 'mental and physical starvation', of 'Irish slummies' whose lives (even when re-housed) extended no further than 'the sad blot called Paddy's Market'. A correspondent to the *Liverpool Forward* described his impressions of 'A Day in the Slums':

> what appalled me most was not the open ashpits, not the endless gin shops, not the beautiful and costly Roman Catholic churches, not the stuffed and broken windows, not the stinking refuse in the gutters, but the grave content amongst a people who are living their lives without knowing what life is.[81]

Despite such unpropitious circumstances and against the advice of George Milligan, Labour decided to challenge the INP by running Joseph Cleary, secretary of the Warehouse Workers Union, in a by-election in Great George Ward in 1913. He polled a derisory seventy-two votes.[82]

The socialist message had as yet failed to make significant advance across the sectarian divide among Protestant workers, whose 'marginal privilege' was underwritten by the Tories. Here too there were inclusive forms of mutuality open to all of the faith. Notorious for his role in inflaming sectarian violence, George Wise sustained his popularity among Protestant workers through his tontine society that offered sickness, unemployment and death insurance, and by provision of a range of leisure and recreational facilities, including the George Wise Cycling Club, the largest in the city.[83] Committed to social reform (even 'municipal socialism'), Toryism in Liverpool had a distinctive inflexion and style. The Working Men's Conservative Association was at the hub of an interlocking associational network – party, popular and Orange sectarian – which facilitated ready interaction between the classes. Local notables continued to monopolise political positions – there was no working-class Conservative councillor before 1914 – but, as need arose, they were able to mingle at ease within the network, displaying the common touch that soon became a distinguishing (and essential) characteristic of local Tory leadership, a style perfected in Archibald Salvidge's electoral machine, perhaps the most remarkable example of British 'boss politics'.[84]

For 'Salvidge of Liverpool' (as he was always known) 1911 was a critical year. Immune to the blandishments of Westminster, he declined the invitation to transfer to the capital to bring the national organisation of the Conservative Party up to Merseyside standards.[85] Revelling in the bustle and manipulation of the municipal machine, he was to play a key role in bringing the strikes to an end in 1911: astutely repudiating the vindictive intransigence of the Tramways Committee, he promoted a compromise, accepted by Mann, by which strikers would be reinstated whenever men were required.[86] Chastened by the extent of violence on the streets, and the invocation of class solidarity, he looked to a more secure foundation for popular Toryism through (much-needed) structural change in the Merseyside economy. He placed himself at the forefront of the 'Wake Up Liverpool' campaign, a prescient initiative, launched in autumn 1911, to promote industrial diversification beyond the maritime–mercantile base. New investment in the Lister Drive Power Station, the symbolic battleground of the summer strikes, held out the promise of 'a new and bright industrial future', ushering in a period of prosperous class unity:

> We have had enough in Liverpool of the wreck and ruin wrought by the class-war mongers, with their wild-cat vapourings, and we do not want any more of their impudent dictation ... We preach not a class war, but a class unity by which alone our people can prosper. Industrial development means more and better paid work for the toiling masses and a chance for

their children to join the aristocracy of labour and earn an honest and sturdy independence ... the extension of industrial training is the best of all possible remedies for the social conditions which have too often been the smirching of the fair fame of Liverpool. We want to get rid as far as possible of casual labour and give more of our working classes an opportunity of entering those skilled employments which are after all the very backbone of our industrial system and the prosperity of which is the surest guarantee of peace and comfort all round.[87]

As the Tories adjusted to new circumstances and the INP continued to enjoy a form of home rule in the north end, the radical advance of 1911 failed to progress. An air of militancy still prevailed at the municipal elections in the autumn, exceptional circumstances which prompted Tories and Liberals to enter an electoral truce while Labour issued a manifesto written, according to Glasier, by an 'anarchistic crack-head'. 'A mere piece of "class war" jingo without a single suggestion of constructive policy', the manifesto continued the dictatorial posturing of the summer, 'making socialism repellent to the people': if elected, the thirteen candidates 'must be subject to the will of the Trades Council! The Trades Council! – a lot of Tom Mann, S.D.P. and Clarion blockheads'.[88] Labour added six sets to that held by Sexton but advanced no further. In 1912–13, indeed, Labour lost every contest, overwhelmed (in some instances, humiliated, as noted above) by the continued popular resonance of the city's ethno-sectarian affiliations.[89] Studies of these persistent formations have mapped the disputed borders between 'orange' and 'green' – the second anniversary of the 1909 riots was marked by the enforced removal of the last remaining Catholic resident from the Netherfield Road – but the inviolable boundary that kept 'black' distant and apart awaits investigation.[90]

Such class solidarity as was forged in pre-war 'radical' Liverpool is perhaps best understood in terms of the making of a 'white' working class. The determination to exclude cheap 'coloured' labour brought sharply dressed ships' stewards and catering staff, who otherwise kept themselves apart from deck hands and those who toiled in the stokeholds, into united action with Havelock Wilson's National Sailors and Firemen's Union, unaccustomed 'unity' that secured the first significant gains in the 1911 strikes.[91] Deploying hysterical racist discourse to condemn the 'beastly' morals of the 'Chinaman', Sexton, the dockers' leader, joined forces with INP councillors to oppose the inflow of 'alien' Asiatic labour, the 'yellow peril': 'He comes here like an international octopus, spreading its tentacles everywhere, and he undermines and corrupts the morals, and pulls down the wages of the English people.'[92] For all its impeccable ILP socialist credentials, *Liverpool Forward* gave strong support to the efforts to remove what it called cheap 'Ching-Ching' labour.[93] In a series that brought new meaning to the sobriquet 'Black Spot on the Mersey', the Catholic press sought to deflect attention away from the proverbial binge-drinking and violent disorder of Scotland Road, main thoroughfare of Irish Liverpool, by highlighting the 'no-go' cosmopolitan area around Mill Street and Beaufort Street in Toxteth, characterised by 'lodging-houses for negro, lascar and other foreign seamen, mulatto children, drunken men and women, and street fights. These streets are not considered desirable beats by the police, many of whom have come to grief in the perambulations therein'.[94] The International Club established by local socialists included members from a range of nationalities, but, as was pointed out to Fred Bower, no black African:

> 'Couldn't you give the platform a little more colour?' our secretary asked me. 'How so?' I replied. 'Why,' he said 'you've got no coon.' Off I set, jumped on the first tram car, got down to the purlieus of the docks, and soon ran up against a son of Africa. 'Say, have a drink?' I called to him. Sure, he would. 'Would he like to come to a meeting?' 'Anything for a shilling'.[95]

Their fascination with Gypsies notwithstanding, similar attitudes prevailed among the progressive elite – although Augustus John seems to have enjoyed underworld pleasures incognito among the opium dens of 'sailortown'.[96] (Macfie, by contrast, was horrified to encounter an underground subculture up on the ridge: 'I have discovered some extraordinary things about sexual perverts in Liverpool', he wrote to an Oxford colleague: 'there are certain pubs & restaurants, kept by people of their own persuasion, which they frequent. One was right at the back of Hope Place!'[97]) A register of Merseypride, celebration of cosmopolitanism and diversity in the 'second city of empire' with its 'abnormally mixed' population, was undermined by racist discourse, even in the measured prose of Ramsay Muir, with its characteristic concern for the image of the city and its ability to attain national standards of efficiency and welfare:

> There is no city in the world, not even London itself, in which so many foreign governments find it necessary to maintain consular offices for the safeguarding of their exiled subjects. It should, however, be noted that this amazingly polyglot and cosmopolitan population, consisting to a considerable extent of races which are backward in many ways, and maintaining itself largely by unskilled labour, vastly increases the difficulty of securing and maintaining the decencies of life.[98]

Having relished its Edwardian 'fizz', Muir left Liverpool before the First World War, dismayed that plans to establish 'a weekly paper of a new type' to 'focus all this ferment of life and to keep it fermenting' were abandoned, hindering his hope that 'Liverpool might become a place of really vivid intellectual life'.[98] The university's response to the events of 1911 was to strengthen its commitment to social science and social work. 'The troubles of last summer strengthened my conviction that two things are essential if we are to mend what is amiss', the Vice-Chancellor wrote to the Earl of Derby, outlining proposals for new premises for the Men's University Settlement: 'a knowledge of facts that can be gained only by skilled and systematic investigation; a sympathy with suffering that can only be the outcome of personal relations. These are the two lines along which the Settlement works.'[99] Here was an outcome far short of the social and cultural revolution that 1911 seemed to have promised.

Notes

1 Stuart Hodgson (ed.), *Ramsay Muir: An Autobiography and Some Essays* (London: Lund Humphries, 1943), p. 73.

2 R. F. Bisson, *The Sandon Studios Society and the Arts* (Liverpool: Sandon Studios Society/Parry Books, 1965), pp. 99–100. See also David Bingham's eagerly awaited biographical study, *1911: Art and Revolution in Liverpool – The Life and Times of Albert Lipczinski* (Bristol: Sansom & Company, 2011).

3 *Sphinx*, 13.15 (1906): 232–37.

4 Fred Bower, *Rolling Stonemason: An Autobiography* (London: Jonathan Cape, 1936), pp. 184–85.

5 James Sexton, *Sir James Sexton, Agitator: The Life of a Dockers' MP* (London: Faber & Faber, 1936), p. 214.

6 'Rodewald Concert Society: Golden Jubilee, 1911–1961', p. 7.

7 Charles Herbert Reilly, *Scaffolding in the Sky: A Semi-Architectural Autobiography* (London: George Routledge and Sons, 1938), p. 77. P. E. H. Hair, 'The Real MacKay', in P. E. H. Hair (ed.), *Arts Letters Society: Miscellany Commemorating the Centenary of the Faculty of Arts at the University of Liverpool*, Liverpool Historical Studies (Liverpool University Press, 1996), pp. 183–212.

8 Quoted in T. Kelly, *For Advancement of Learning: The University of Liverpool 1881–1981* (Liverpool: Liverpool University Press, 1981), p. 127.

9 Reilly, *Scaffolding in the Sky*, pp. 68–74.

10 Hodgson, *Ramsay Muir*, p. 79. Peter Richmond offers a more qualified assessment in his contribution to this volume, noting Reilly's talents as a promoter rather than innovator of architectural education.

11 *Post and Mercury* (17 July 1911).

12 Reilly, *Scaffolding in the Sky*, p. 138.

13 Alan Powers, 'Liverpool and Architectural Education in the Early Twentieth

Century', in J. Sharples, A. Powers and M. Shippobottom (eds), *Charles Reilly and the Liverpool School of Architecture, 1904–1933* (Liverpool University Press, 1996), p. 10.

14 Peter de Figueiredo, 'Symbols of Empire: The Buildings of the Liverpool Waterfront', *Architectural History*, 46 (2003), pp. 237–41.

15 *Daily Post* (27 May 1911).

16 *Post and Mercury* (23 June 1911).

17 Hodgson, *Ramsay Muir*, p. 49.

18 Reilly, *Scaffolding in the Sky*, pp. 124–25.

19 Ibid., p. 134.

20 William Rothenstein, Frank Rutter *et al.*, *The Sport of Civic Life or, Art and the Municipality* (Liverpool: C. W. Sharpe, 1909), p. 12.

21 *Post and Mercury* (30 Dec. 1911).

22 Sharpe, *Sport of Civic Life*, p. 4.

23 *Post and Mercury* (6 Oct. 1909). See also Matthew Vickers, 'Civic Image and Civic Patriotism in Liverpool', University of Oxford DPhil thesis (2000), chap. 7: 'Carthage, Venice and the Liverpool School of Painters'.

24 Reilly, *Scaffolding in the Sky*, p. 89.

25 Bisson, *Sandon Studios Society*, pp. 61–62; John Willett, *Art in a City* (London: Methuen, 1967; repr. Liverpool University Press, 2007), p. 61.

26 'Post-Impressionist Pictures and Others', *Manchester Guardian* (6 Mar. 1911).

27 Artists' Club (Liverpool), *Story of the Artists Club Liverpool. By Percy Corkhill* (Liverpool: 1949), p. 5.

28 *Sandon Bulletin* (Mar. 1912), quoted in Bisson, *Sandon Studios Society*, p. 76.

29 Bisson, *Sandon Studios Society*, p. 59.

30 Krista Cowman, *Mrs Brown is a Man and a Brother: Women in Merseyside's Political Organisations, 1890–1920* (Liverpool University Press, 2004), p. 80.

31 Bower, *Rolling Stonemason*, pp. 120–22.

32 Bisson, *Sandon Studios Society*, pp. 99–100.

33 W. S. MacCunn, *Bluecoat Chambers: The Origins and Development of an Art Centre* (Liverpool University Press, 1956), pp. 3–12.

34 Reilly, *Scaffolding in the Sky*, pp. 185–202.

35 *The Times* (6 Nov. 1911).

36 Quoted in *Daily Post* (31 Oct. 1911).

37 Reilly, *Scaffolding in the Sky*, p. 151.

38 *The Times* (23 Sept. 1911).

39 Reilly, *Scaffolding in the Sky*, p. 159.

40 Ibid., 140–61; Hodgson, *Ramsay Muir*, pp. 79–80; G. W. Goldie, *The Liverpool Repertory Theatre, 1911–1934* (London: Liverpool University Press/Hodder & Stoughton, 1935), chaps 3–5.

41 This section is based on material in University of Liverpool, Special Collections: GLS, A31 and A32, letterbooks of R. A. Scott Macfie.

42 Macfie to Prietz, 3 Feb. 1911.

43 Macfie to Ferguson, 28 Mar. 1911.

44 Macfie wrote a booklet about the visit under the pseudonym Andréas (Mui Shuko), *Gypsy Coppersmiths in Liverpool and Birkenhead* (Liverpool: Henry Young & Sons, 1913).

45 Macfie to Ferguson, 1 June 1911; 12 July 1911; 10 Aug. 1911.

46 Macfie to Mrs Willett, 3 Aug. 1911.

47 Macfie to Bartlett, 20 Aug. 1911; Macfie to Shaw, 22 Aug. 1911; Macfie to Urban, 23 Sept. 1911; Macfie to Spalding, 25 Sept. 1911.

48 Quoted in Sam Davies, *Liverpool Labour: Social and Political Influences on the Development of the Labour Party in Liverpool, 1900–1939* (Keele University Press, 1996), p. 19.

49 Matthew Thomas, '"No-one Telling Us What to Do": Anarchist Schools in Britain, 1890–1916', *Historical Research*, 77 (2004): 405–36.

50 Robert J. Holton, 'Syndicalism and Labour on Merseyside, 1906–14', in H. R. Hikins (ed.), *Building the Union: Studies on the Growth of the Workers' Movement: Merseyside, 1756–1967* (Liverpool: Toulouse Press, 1973), pp. 121–52.

51 Eric Taplin, *Near to Revolution: The Liverpool General Strike of 1911* (Liverpool: Bluecoat, 1994); H. R. Hikins, 'The Liverpool General Transport Strike, 1911', *Transactions of the Historic Society of Lancashire and Cheshire*, 113 (1961): 169–95.

52 Eric Taplin, *The Dockers' Union: A Study of the National Union of Dock Labourers, 1889–192* (Leicester University Press, 1986), chaps 5 and 6.

53 Sexton, *Sir James Sexton, Agitator*, pp. 213–16.

54 Taplin, *Dockers' Union*, chaps 7 and 8.

55 P. J. Waller, *Democracy and Sectarianism: A Political and Social History of Liverpool, 1868–1939* (Liverpool University Press, 1981), pp. 251–64.

56 Goldie, *The Liverpool Repertory Theatre*, pp. 92–93.

57 University of Liverpool, Special Collections: GP/2/1/18 Bruce Glasier Diary, 1911. See entries for 26 June and 5 Sept.

58 For the official account of events, see National Archives, Kew: Home Office Papers, HO45/1065410658/212470: Strikes, Liverpool Railway Strike, 1911. Tom Mann, *Tom Mann's Memoirs* (London: Labour Publishing, 1923; repr. London: MacGibbon & Kee, 1967), chap. 19.

59 Holton, 'Syndicalism and Labour on Merseyside', p. 139.

60 Macfie to Ehrenborg, 22 Aug. 1911.

61 Macfie to Bartlett, 20 Aug. 1911.

62 *Courier* (18 Aug. 1911).

63 University of Liverpool, Special Collections: S2337, Letter-book of the Vice-Chancellor, 1911–12: letter from Dale to John Shannon, Liverpool and Vicinity United Trades and Labour Council, 23 Aug. 1911.

64 See the handbills and press cuttings in Liverpool Record Office: Town Clerk's News-Cuttings, Feb.–Nov. 1911, 352CLE/CUT1/36.

65 Dale to Wilson, 18 Nov. 1911.

66 Sutcliffe died on the eve of his wedding. See *Daily Express* (21 Aug. 1911). Hikins, 'The Liverpool General Transport Strike', p. 191 draws attention to cross-faith attendance at the funerals.

67 *Courier* (14 Dec. 1911).

68 'Red Riot Sunday', *Daily Post and Mercury* (26 Sept. 1911).

69 Quoted in Waller, *Democracy and Sectarianism*, p. 256.

70 HO45/10654-10658/212470. 'The Hooligan', *Transport Worker* (Oct. 1911).

71 *Courier* (14 Nov. 1911).

72 John Bohstedt, 'More Than One Working Class: Protestant–Catholic Riots in Edwardian Liverpool', in John Belchem (ed.), *Popular Politics, Riot and Labour: Essays in Liverpool History, 1790–1940* (Liverpool University Press, 1992), pp. 213–14; Dan Jackson, '"Friends of the Union": Liverpool, Ulster and Home Rule, 1910–1914', *Transactions of the Historic Society of Lancashire and Cheshire*, 152 (2003): 101–32.

73 'The North-End Liverpool Dockers', *Transport Worker* (Sept. 1911).

74 George Milligan, *Life Through Labour's Eyes: Essays, Letters and Lyrics from the Worker's Own Point of View* (London and Edinburgh: Sands & Co., 1911) contains extracts from the *Mersey Magazine*, no copies of which seem to have survived. Milligan also contributed regularly to the *Liverpool Catholic Herald*.

75 *Liverpool Forward* (18 Apr. 1913; 25 Apr. 1913).

76 *Liverpool Catholic Herald* (1 Nov. 1913; 13 Dec. 1913; 7 Feb. 1914).

77 John Belchem, *Irish, Catholic and Scouse: The History of the Liverpool-Irish, 1800–1939* (Liverpool University Press, 2007).

78 Eleanor F. Rathbone, *Report on the Condition of Widows Under the Poor Law in Liverpool: Presented to the Annual Meeting of the Liverpool Women's Industrial Council, on December 11th, 1913* (Liverpool: Lee and Nightingale, 1913), pp. 24–33.

79 Pat O'Mara, *The Autobiography of a Liverpool Irish Slummy* (London: Martin Hopkinson, 1934).

80 Fredric D'Aeth, 'Liverpool', in Mrs Bernard Bosanquet (ed.), *Social Conditions in Provincial Towns* (London: Macmillan, 1912), p. 38.

81 *Liverpool Forward* (1 June 1912).

82 *Liverpool Forward* (21 Nov. 1913) and *Liverpool Catholic Herald* (22 Nov. 1913).

83 Bohstedt, 'More Than One Working Class', pp. 195–210.

84 Waller, *Democracy and Sectarianism*, chaps 11–16.

85 Stanley Salvidge, *Salvidge of Liverpool: Behind the Political Scene, 1890–1928* (London: Hodder & Stoughton, 1934), chap. 8.

86 Waller, *Democracy and Sectarianism*, p. 257.

87 'Now is the Time!', *Express* (25 Oct. 1911).

88 Glasier Diary, 19 Oct. 1911.

89 Waller, *Democracy and Sectarianism*, p. 265.

90 Frank Neal, *Sectarian Violence: The Liverpool Experience* (Manchester University Press, 1987); Andy Shallice, 'Orange and Green Militancy: Sectarianism and Working-Class Politics in Liverpool, 1900–1914', *Bulletin of the North West Labour History Society*, 6 (1979–80): 15–31.

91 Taplin, *Near to Revolution*, p. 16; Waller, *Democracy and Sectarianism*, p. 252.

92 Quoted in Gregory B. Lee, *Troubadours, Trumpeters, Troubled Makers: Lyricism, Nationalism and Hybridity in China and its Others* (London: C. Hurst & Co., 1996), p. 206.

93 *Liverpool Forward* (27 Mar. 1914; 1 May 1914). See also Ken Lunn, 'The Seamen's Union and "Foreign" Workers on British and Colonial Shipping', *Bulletin of the Society for the Study of Labour History*, 53 (1988): 5–13.

94 *Liverpool Catholic Herald* (10 Jan.–14 Feb. 1902).

95 Bower, *Rolling Stonemason*, pp. 184–85.

96 Bisson, *Sandon Studios Society*, p. 14.

97 Macfie to Winstedt, 25 Jan. 1911.

98 Ramsay Muir, *A History of Liverpool* (London: Williams and Norgate for the University Press, Liverpool, 1907), p. 305. Liverpool was lauded in 1911 as 'the most famous and the most frequented emporium of cosmopolitan traffic the world has known in ancient or modern times'; the landing stage was 'one of the most cosmopolitan spots on earth'. See W. T. Pike (ed.), *Liverpool and Birkenhead in the Twentieth Century* (Brighton: W. T. Pike & Co., 1911), pp. 11–13 and 69.

99 Hodgson, *Ramsay Muir*, p. 81.

100 Dale to the Earl of Derby, 21 Oct. 1911.

Rebuilding the Temple: Modernism with Ancestry in the Liverpool School of Architecture

Peter Richmond

With the completion of the Royal Liver Building in 1911, Liverpool acquired not only what many consider to be its most famous and iconic building, it also added to the city's long list of buildings that employed innovative methods of construction and use of materials. The frame of the building used a system of ferro-concrete – concrete reinforced with steel – and was one of the most ambitious uses of this relatively new type of construction resulting in a monumental building that was the tallest office block of its day. The building, however, was not universally admired, and Charkes Reilly, the professor of architecture at the university described it as 'the childishly gigantic and irregular Liver pile'.[1] Liverpool was no stranger to the innovative in terms of its architecture: stretching back as far as the early nineteenth century it had pioneered the use of cast iron. The partnership of Thomas Rickman – a Quaker pharmacist turned accountant turned architect – and Thomas Cragg – proprietor of the Mersey Iron Foundry – produced a number of remarkable domestic and ecclesiastical buildings that employed cast iron wherever the opportunity arose, not only in the structure but also in detailing such as the window and door frames. In the cases of St George's Church, Everton (1813), St Michael's, Aigburth (1814) and St Philip's, Hardman Street (1816) the churches had external skins of stone, with the interiors, including the roof, external buttress copings, parapets, windows and finials all expressed in cast-iron. From these three buildings Rickman and Cragg developed an industry in prefabricated cast-iron churches that they shipped out of the ports of Liverpool and Bristol to America and Australia. The designers recognised the merit of mass production and the economy that could be achieved through the use of a single mould – a practice that would gain prominence in the modernist movement a century later.

It was, however, in the field of commercial architecture that Liverpool was at its most innovative and groundbreaking, particularly with regard to the construction of the system of docks and dock buildings. Foremost in this area was Jesse Hartley, who had been appointed Dock Engineer in 1824 and who set about expanding the dock system, with Brunswick Dock (1827–32) followed by Clarence Dock (1832) designed specifically to handle the new steamers that were starting to replace sail. But it is without doubt the Albert Dock (1843–47) that stands as his masterpiece. The idea for an enclosed dock dated back as far as 1803, but had been rejected in 1811. With the combined forces of Liverpool's spectacular growth of trade and Hartley's appointment and personal determination, however, the scheme was revived. The startling simplicity and originality of the design drew the inevitable contemporary criticism and it would take more than a century before the radical nature of Hartley's design philosophy would be appreciated by the likes of Sir Nikolaus Pevsner, the eminent architectural historian and critic, who in 1969 wrote that 'For sheer punch there is little in the early commercial architecture of Europe to emulate it'.[2]

Other architects would use apparently conventional architectural styles but combine them in innovative ways. When Liverpool staged competitions for new law courts and a concert hall in the mid-nineteenth century the winning designs for both buildings were submitted by a young unknown architect, Harvey Lonsdale Elmes. Elmes's original designs for both buildings had been conventional Greek Revival; however, with the decision to combine the concert hall and law courts in one building, Elmes rose to the challenge and the designs he produced in 1840–41 are altogether more inventive, drawing together Roman and Greek influences. The classical design is supplemented by a state-of-the-art Victorian heating and ventilation system designed by Dr Boswell Reid, which combines efficiency and economy in its ability to circulate air around the building.

Cast iron continued to be used, with perhaps the most important example being Peter Ellis's Oriel Chambers, Water Street, completed in 1864. The building has a cast-iron frame and is remarkable in a number of respects; not least it being one of the earliest attempts to break away from the classical tradition of commercial architecture. The use of large expanses of glass surrounded by extremely slender cast-iron frames that form the oriel windows covering the Water Street and Covent Garden elevations allowed for the maximum entry of light through the top and sides of the windows as well as the front. This design feature, however, proved to be extremely controversial and the building was lambasted in the architectural press with the *Builder* describing it as a 'large agglomeration of protruding plate-glass bubbles ... Did we not see this vast abortion – which would be depressing were it not ludicrous – with our own eyes, we should have doubted the possibility of its existence. Where and in what are their beauties supposed to lie?'³ The condemnation would have a devastating effect on Ellis's career as an architect and he designed only one other documented building, at 16 Cook Street, Liverpool in 1866. However, his presciently modern designs have since been reassessed by numerous modern commentators, with Pevsner describing Oriel Chambers as one of the most remarkable buildings of its date in Europe.

By the end of the nineteenth century, Liverpool was at the height of its commercial power, secure in its position as the second city of the Empire. As Tony Lane noted, 'London apart, Liverpool produced more wealthy families than any other English city. At its peak in the years 1890–1899, Liverpool produced as many millionaires as Greater Manchester, West Yorkshire, West Midlands, Tyneside and East Anglia combined'.⁴ The effect of such wealth was that Liverpool had by the turn of the century amassed an enviable architectural stock, and it would seem only natural that the leaders of the city's cultural community should wish to include among the chairs to be endowed at the newly established university one dedicated to the study of architecture.

Early Years of the Liverpool School of Architecture

In 1885, the university invited William Martin Conway to become Roscoe Professor of Art at the newly established University College. Conway's brief tenure in the post is not considered to have been a great success and he resigned his position in 1888 to be replaced by R. A. M. Stevenson, who also remained in post a short time, resigning in 1892. Upon his resignation, Stevenson suggested that the chair should be reassigned to a specific artistic discipline such as a Life School or a School of Architecture. After some deliberation it was decided that the chair should be renamed the Roscoe Chair of Architecture and in 1895 the City of Liverpool School of Architecture and Applied Arts was inaugurated, with Frederick Moore Simpson as the first holder of the newly assigned chair. The School started its life with its educational principles rooted in the stylistic ideology of the Arts and Crafts movement and its programme of instruction combined architectural training along with classes in metalworking, enamelling etc. While the School was neither the first to provide an architectural course in Britain (although it was the first non-metropolitan one) nor the first full-time course, what made it innovative in the history of architectural education was its alliance with the ideas of the Arts and Crafts philosophy combined with its adoption of an integrated teaching programme – one that briefly became the teaching norm adopted by other institutions such as the Central College of Arts and Crafts in London and the Royal College of Art. A physical manifestation of this integrated system can be seen in the decorative work undertaken by members of the School on the Philharmonic Hotel, Hope Street (1898–1900) in collaboration with the architect Walter Thomas.

In the early years of the twentieth century a combination of events led to the demise of the integrated system that had operated within the School – the newly established Municipal School of Art had the financial and administrative power to insist upon the transfer to them of the applied art section of the School – while the architecture element within the course had by this time secured its future in a degree from a university that had recently received its Royal Charter. These events coincided with Simpson's resignation from the university, and his successor, Charles Herbert Reilly, upon his appointment in 1904, was responsible solely for the School of Architecture. As Quentin Hughes notes of this move:

> With the appointment of Reilly, for better or for worse, the school became a school for architects, rather than a 'school of architecture'... It was to be tied firmly to the RIBA and, academically controlled by rigid examination, would soon receive exemption, first from the intermediate examination of the institute and later from its final examination.[5]

Reilly and the Liverpool School of Architecture

On his appointment to the Roscoe Chair, Charles Reilly was just thirty years of age, and while he possessed a first-class degree in engineering from Cambridge, experience in the offices of London architects John Belcher and Stanley Peach together with teaching experience from the evening classes at King's College, London, he had built little and was not well known in architectural circles. He quickly set about establishing himself within the university and wider circles of the city and liked to portray himself as a new broom sweeping away the outmoded Arts and Crafts of the Simpson era. In his autobiography, written some thirty years later, he recalls himself 'at once ... putting away the Gothic casts and putting the Renaissance and classical ones into positions of greater prominence'.[6] This 'clean break' with Simpson's regime is not strictly accurate. Simpson had gradually been moving towards a Beaux-Arts classicism as the model for teaching within the School, and a pamphlet he published as early as 1895 shows him to be an admirer of both the French and American models of architectural training.[7] As Christopher Crouch notes, 'That Simpson ultimately planned a School of Architecture modelled upon the American is without doubt. His respect for the course at Columbia University is further reinforced through his acknowledgment of the receipt of "much valued information" from its Professor, William Ware'.[8] Many of the initiatives claimed by and subsequently credited to Reilly had in fact been set in place before his appointment. As Crouch goes on to state

> It is implied that Reilly's vision of architectural education was at odds with past practice at the School, and that he was responsible for the linking of the School with formal architectural structures … the Architectural Degree scheme was initiated in 1901, and it is this restructuring of the course, this formalizing of architectural education at the expense of the applied arts, that marks the end of the aesthetic and educational experiment … By the time of Reilly's appointment, holders of the School's Certificate in Education had been exempt from the RIBA's Intermediate examination for two years … Reilly's importance to the development of the 'old' course was minimal, the structure that enabled him to create a flourishing Beaux-Arts school were already in place.[9]

Reilly's importance as a modernising figure therefore owed less to the 'novelty' of the design philosophy he was advocating, despite his best efforts to present it otherwise. Where he did bring a radical new impulse to the School of Architecture was in the means by which he promoted the School. In contrast to Simpson, who was a quiet and scholarly figure, Reilly was an extrovert with little or no pretension to scholarship. What he did possess was an instinctive understanding of public relations, a sociable and forceful personality, an interest in internationalism and an innate ability to seize upon every opportunity in order to promote himself, the School of Architecture and his students. Early examples of Reilly's promotional activity can be seen in the letters he wrote to the local and national press and to professional journals, drawing attention to the School's curriculum[10] as well as his thoughts on various architectural issues of the day. These were quickly followed by a more formal means of advertising the work of the School and its students in the form of the *Portfolio of Measured Drawings*, the first of which was published in 1906, with a second edition appearing in 1908. These included studies undertaken by students of some of Liverpool's finest classical buildings and helped reinforce the classical ethos of the School's teaching programme in the minds of the wider architectural community. A further series entitled *The Liverpool Architectural Sketchbook* followed in 1910, 1911, 1913 and 1920, and provided an interesting chronicle of the School's architectural stance during the middle period of Reilly's tenure. Reilly's promotional activity would continue through his tenure in the Roscoe Chair and he would go on to write for a variety of publications as disparate as *Tit-Bits* and *Country Life*.

While reaching out to the architectural community, Reilly also understood that in order to strengthen both his own position and that of the School in the university, he needed to increase student numbers. Following his first trip to the United States in 1909, he returned with a case full of promotional material he had collected from various American schools of architecture where the process of curriculum advertising was at a more advanced stage. In a letter to the Registrar from May 1909, Reilly states that

> Since visiting America and making a collection of the prospectuses of the American Schools of Architecture I have come to the conclusion that it would be well to somewhat alter the form of our own prospectus. The alteration I wish to make is the omission of the detailed regulations governing the various courses ... and the inclusion in their place of illustrations of the actual work of the students in each year. These illustrations will explain at a glance the character of the work done and be more convincing to architects than any number of printed pages.[11]

Reilly instinctively understood that a picture painted a thousand words. The effect of the improved publicity material was that Liverpool started to attract increasing numbers of able students locally, nationally and internationally. Consequently the Beaux-Arts design philosophy favoured by Reilly and taught in the School was exported throughout the then extensive reach of the British Empire, strengthening Reilly's desire to portray Liverpool as *the* leading British school of architecture.

The Department of Civic Design

Arguably the most important initiative with which Reilly was involved in the University of Liverpool was the part he played in the founding of the Department of Civic Design, the first of its kind in the world. As with his work in the School of Architecture, many of the theories behind the department were already current in the wider architectural community but it was the way in which Reilly harnessed and used them to further his own ambitions that make him a radical force in early planning history. There was a general feeling that some system of urban planning needed to be formulated in order to contain the increasing spread of the cities. The debate over the siting of the new Liverpool Cathedral had raised issues regarding the formulation of a planned environment along Beaux-Arts lines that culminated in a 'City Beautiful Conference' being held in the city in 1907. The City Beautiful movement had been popularised by Charles Mulford Robinson in his 1901 book *The Improvement of Towns and Cities* and was a term current in the general early planning debates. In the early years of the new century Reilly and a number of other leading figures in the city, such as Philip Rathbone, a member of the influential Liverpool banking and merchant dynasty, were delivering speeches and lectures on the theme of the 'City Beautiful', leading to calls in the press for the formation of a 'City Beautiful Society'.

The staging of the City Beautiful conference in June 1907 was a promotional triumph for Reilly and while he only succeeded in gaining coverage in the *Builder*, it was his paper on 'Urban and Sub-urban Planning' that received all the attention. Reilly's paper was in line with his developing theories regarding Beaux-Arts architecture. Reilly considered the Beaux-Arts buildings he was encouraging his students to design on paper as being the most appropriate style suited to an urban pattern, and he envisaged them translated onto a monumental city scale. 'Reilly's contribution combined the wider national and international issues of city planning and made it pertinent to Liverpool, thus at the same time increasing the city's importance through the nature of his comparisons.'[12] By contrast, the Garden City apologists had a diametrically opposing view, rooted in the Arts and Crafts tradition. As Crouch notes, 'It is clear that apart from the desire for rational planning which united the two approaches, what separated them was the conception of the city as a domestic environment, in opposition to the city as an expression of a collective civic culture'.[13] This division would become increasingly apparent as time moved on and planning theory was put into planning practice.

The foundation of the Department of Civic Design could not have come about without the financial support of Sir William Hesketh Lever (later Viscount Leverhulme) – the soap magnate. Reilly had met Lever shortly after his arrival in Liverpool, and while they did not immediately gel, over time they forged a close and productive working relationship. Lever shared many characteristics with Reilly: both were extroverts with a keen sense of publicity and self-promotion. In 1908, Lever had helped the School to relocate from their previously rather inadequate accommodation on the university campus into the Blue Coat building on School Lane, which he had recently acquired, and when Reilly approached him with his plans for the establishment of a department dedicated to the study of 'Civic Design' he agreed to fund both the founding of a chair and the production of a journal – *Town Planning Review* – which would be used to promote and disseminate current planning theory and projects. Things progressed quickly and the first Lever Professor of Civic Design – as the chair was named – Stanley Adshead, was appointed in 1909.

The formation of the department was important for Reilly for a number of reasons. First, the appointment of Adshead,[14] who was an old friend and colleague of Reilly's from his London days, meant he had another ally in the university to help him support his ambitions to turn the School into a leading light in the field of architectural training. Adshead and Reilly shared a similar approach to architecture and planning with an emphasis on the aesthetic qualities of buildings and their arrangement. Secondly, the department and the journal provided Reilly with an ideal conduit through which to expound his Beaux-Arts enthusiasms. As Crouch notes:

> It is possible to read the early editions of *Town Planning Review* as an ideolog-ical text. By this I mean that it is possible to look at the issues discussed within its pages as a reflection of a set of values pertinent to those who ran the journal. If it is acknowledged that *Town Planning Review* was as much a mouthpiece for the Liverpool School as it was an objective journal examining the nature of town planning, then through an analysis of its pages it should be possible to determine the relationship between the Liver-pool School and the rest of the architectural and planning community.[15]

Lastly, the foundation of the Lever Prize Competition, which formed part of the department's endowment, provided another avenue through which Reilly's students could rehearse the Beaux-Arts theories they were being taught in the School. Similarly, the competition was envisaged by Lever as a source of ideas for projects he was planning to implement, as was the case of the first prize winner –Ernest Prestwich, with his scheme for the redesign of the central area of Port Sunlight. Unlike Prestwich, future prize winners did not see their schemes built; however, they all displayed a coherence that stemmed from the teaching programme of the School of Architecture and added to the general ambition to keep the School and the department at the forefront of the developing planning ideological debate.

Moves Towards Modernism

The development of modernism in Britain has been presented, depending upon the writer's outlook, as either constituting the importation of an alien European style – inappropriate to the 'true' national style – or as the rehabilitating and revitalising element of a decadent British design philos-ophy. Pevsner, in books such as *Pioneers of Modern Design* (1936) and *The Sources of Modern Design* (1968), suggested that Britain's influence in the development of twentieth-century architecture lay primarily in the work of William Morris and the proto-modernist phase pre-1900. By Pevsner's account, it then became dormant until the arrival of European émigrés in the early 1930s. Reilly and the Liverpool School were considered implicit in this failure to embrace European modernism, with the emphasis of the School heavily skewed towards the American Beaux-Arts model. As writers such as Alan Powers have stated:

> The common view in the past has been that Reilly's lack of awareness of European proto-modernism in the pre-1914 period implicated him in the 30 wasted years between the completion of Glasgow School of Art and the construction of the Boots D10 building by Owen Williams in 1930 ... This view identifies the future modern style and traces its gradual and inevitable dissemination around the world. To concentrate on America, as Reilly did so emphatically in the 1920s, was arguably to unbalance English architecture.[16]

This view considered the intervening years as being neatly split by the First World War, and did not recognise any sense of continuity between the pre- and post-war periods. For Reilly, the period he spent during the war as an inspector for the Ministry of Munitions brought him into contact with the ideas formulated by the ministry's head of design, Raymond Unwin, with regard to mass production and standardisation as demonstrated by the Office of Works architects Frank Baines and R. J. Allison on munitions workers' estates such as New Hall, Woolwich. These ideas would become evident in Reilly's writings after the war and would help to inform the School's teaching throughout the 1920s.

The general design philosophy of the School remained largely as it had been prior to the war. As Myles Wright notes, 'In the 1920s Reilly's students were rigorously drilled in the Classic Orders and in Classical designs'.[17] Certainly the work published in the Sketch Book of 1920 demonstrates this to be the case. While Reilly was able to continue to expound classicism as the best style for Liverpool, developments on the Continent neverthe-less began to exert some influence on the work produced in the School as the 1920s progressed, albeit still interpreted through the classical idiom. As Powers notes, 'The ethos of Liverpool in the 1920s remained Classical, although it was possible through the Beaux-Arts method to retain the principles and change the details towards a cooler or perhaps more Art Deco character'.[18] Indeed, the classical Beaux-Arts language proved to be more flexible than writers such as Pevsner were willing to give it credit for and an examination of *The Book of the Liverpool School of Architecture* (1932), published in order to display a catalogue of the School's work to date, illustrates the variety of styles employed by students in the School, and how they were ciphered through the classical training of the 1920s. These ranged from the monumental classicism of the Egyptian State Telegraph and Telephone Building, Cairo (1927) by Maurice Lyon and the American Beaux-Arts of Herbert J. Rowse's Martin's Bank headquarters, Water Street, Liverpool (1927–32) to the 'Jazz Moderne' of Harold E. & H. Hinchcliffe Davies's, Clock Inn, Liverpool (c.1930). The book also contains photographs and a short essay on the design for the new School of Architecture that had been designed by Reilly, his deputy Lionel Budden and former pupil J. E. Marshall. The design demonstrates just how far down the modernist road both Reilly and the School had travelled. In the essay accompanying the illustrations, Stanley C. Ramsey notes:

> He [Reilly] is at the present moment with Professor Budden and his other colleagues initiating ... what purports to be a very important ... contribution to 'Modern' architecture. I am here using the word 'modern' to mean the beginning of a new epoch as something distinct from the traditional – and yet ... Behind these fresh and sometimes startling presentations of design ... is the quiet force of a traditional culture ... the new modern note at Liverpool ... is modern with a difference ... It is, if I may so phrase it, 'Modernism with ancestry'.[19]

Reilly retired from the Roscoe Chair in 1933 on the grounds of ill health and was succeeded by his long-standing deputy and former student, Lionel Budden. By the time of his retirement, projects such as the new school of architecture and the numerous articles he was writing for the professional and national press illustrate his by now complete commitment to modernism. While some have criticised Reilly for staying with American Beaux-Arts as his preferred teaching style for too long through the 1920s, other commentators see a link between the classical training of the early generation of British modernists and their subsequent design philosophy. Anthony Jackson sees Amyas Connell's groundbreaking – at least in British terms – house High and Over (1930) as relying heavily on Connell's own classical training. The Liverpool-trained modernist Edwin Maxwell Fry's work can also be seen in the same light. For Jackson this was due to the fact that '[the] aspiring modern architect with a Beaux-Arts training, wishing to obey Le Corbusier's exhortations, had no need to change his method but only his formula'.[20]

Reilly's successor, Lionel Budden, was a contrasting character to Reilly, being a measured and scholarly figure who had supported Reilly at the School for many years. Budden was not ambitious to take up the chair and had, with Reilly's support, suggested that Walter Gropius be invited to apply for the position. Gropius along with Erich Mendelsohn briefly taught in the

School at the end of 1933, having fled Nazi Germany; however, he declined the post and instead took up a professorship at Harvard. The ideological shift that had taken place during the latter years of Reilly's time continued, but the full-blown modernism of the visiting European lecturers was still not seen as being entirely compatible with the Beaux-Arts axial symmetry of the School's training methods. Nevertheless, there was a sense of a change of mood taking place. Sir Peter Shepheard, a student at the time, later noted that this seemed to come from the students themselves: 'We threw away our watercolours and started going to Germany to do line drawings'.[21] The traditional Beaux-Arts training continued to provide a solid grounding for the modern design elements that were being introduced in the early years of the 1930s. Wesley Dougill recognised this when he reviewed the School's end of year show in 1932:

> Much of the Liverpool School depends on the thorough grounding in traditional forms which the students receive in the earliest years of the course. It is not until they have reached the latter half of the third year that their work is preponderating modern. Thus there is a virtual absence of half-baked designs carried out in a style which at once presupposes a scientific and advanced knowledge of construction and materials ... which junior students cannot possibly have attained.[22]

Budden, like Reilly before him, continued to encourage refugee European architects to come to the School. When approached in 1942 by the British Council with a proposal to offer a Polish School of Architecture sanctuary at Liverpool, there began a fruitful period of collaboration and cross-fertilisation of ideas between the two institutions. The time the staff and students of the Polish School spent at Liverpool up to the end of the war and beyond

> proved to be a most successful way of exchanging ideas on professional problems, as by this means the subject is considered from various points of view and thus a balanced judgment is achieved. In this way each programme of an architectural exercise, after being worked out by the students, is the subject of a criticism-lecture delivered ... by the British or Polish lecturers. In this respect a very important task carried out by the Teaching Staff of the Polish School of Architecture should be mentioned. It consists of a thorough study of the methods of training employed in the Liverpool School of Architecture.[23]

This brief period proved to be successful for both parties, with 'Astragal' noting in the *Architects' Journal* that 'So far as I am concerned, all arguments about which is the best school of architecture in this country today have been settled. If the work of the students, rather than their number, is to be the criterion, the Polish School of Architecture ... at Liverpool, is hands down the winner'.[24]

It was into this environment of cultural exchange that arguably Liverpool's most illustrious graduate entered the School. Sir James Frazer Stirling (1924–92) completed his first year in 1941 before being called up to serve in the army, returning to his studies in 1947. While his time at Liverpool overlapped only slightly with the Polish School, he would have re-entered a school that had become a hybrid of the best of the Liverpool and Polish teaching and design methods. As Rob MacDonald notes of this period in the School,

> Eclecticism was the rule and Modernism was only one of the options ... the Polish School ... occupied one of the studios and its staff were all committed modernists. They were all precise draughtsmen producing minimalist black line drawings, derived from Le Corbusier. Jim bought a book of their work and he was certainly influenced by their work.[25]

As well as the Polish influences, Stirling also drew inspiration from the city of Liverpool itself and in particular the dock system, together with the work of Le Corbusier. His final-year thesis design – a project to replace the heart of the ancient market town of Newton Aycliffe in County Durham with a single monolithic structure combining various building functions within a unified complex – displays all of these influences. Stirling would later note that the Beaux-Arts system, upon which much of the teaching of the School was still founded, together with that of the Bauhaus, both based upon pedagogic practice, were 'for us now equally unfortunate. There surely must be another way driving down between them'.[26]

Much of Stirling's subsequent work can be interpreted as this 'middle way' via his quoting of admired modernists, such as in his Leicester University Engineering Faculty building (1959), the Florey Building, Queen's College, Oxford (1966–71) and the unrestrained historicism of the Staatsgalerie, Stuttgart (1977–84), a design that David Thistlewood describes as being 'interpretable as a sustained, beneficial effect of the Polish communitarian spirit and strong sense of responsibility towards a deeply rooted culture'.[27] It is a mark of the decline of the autonomous power of provincial cities such as Liverpool that they were unable to retain architects of Stirling's calibre and ambition in the years immediately following the Second World War. It meant that Stirling, on graduation, left the city to practise in London. His work for Runcorn New Town, Cheshire (1967–77) – which was demolished in the early 1990s – and the Tate Gallery Liverpool, Albert Dock (1980–87) are the only examples of his work in the Liverpool city region. Liverpool can, however, claim Stirling in the long list of its architectural innovators and radicals, in the sense that it was both the Liverpool School of Architecture and the physical and spiritual essence of the city that formed – and continued to inform – his architectural philosophy.

Modernism with Ancestry?

The success of the Liverpool School of Architecture as a radical force in the cultural life of twentieth-century Liverpool is debatable. Certainly its position as a major port with links to North America made it a fertile ground for the importation of ideas such as the American Beaux-Arts. Simpson, from as early as the mid-1890s, and then Reilly were quick to seize upon the possibilities of Beaux-Arts theory as a means of promoting their individual agendas for the School. If Simpson had been somewhat thwarted in his ambitions to develop the School along Beaux-Arts lines by a certain cultural isolation in the broader Liverpool artistic community, Reilly was far more fortunate in the timing of his appointment. Allied to this were Reilly's personal qualities and his innate understanding of the value of the new promotional opportunities available to him via his contact with the big American schools of architecture. The real importance of the Beaux-Arts style for Reilly was its flexibility, providing him with an envelope that harked back to a classical golden period while also being able to absorb the technological innovations of early modernism – a flexibility that would prove useful for many years within the School, even up to the generation of students of which Stirling was a member. Ideologically, it also set him firmly against the still-raging arguments over national style and the picturesque of the Arts and Crafts – representing instead to Reilly a fitting symbol of a universalised metropolitanism that appealed to his socialist inclinations as well as to his taste for all things urban.

   Reilly's natural inclination towards internationalism marked him out from a number of his contemporaries who continued to call for a national style based on gothic forms. For Reilly, Beaux-Arts was an amorphous representation of urbanity and sophistication. It solved the dual problems of the 'national style' debate as well as allowing for a cultural universalism that fitted neatly with his desire to discard the old notion of the architect as an individual master. Reilly would increasingly argue for a move towards the idea of an anonymous, less-personal architecture. This would be translated into the teaching programme of the School and allowed for a consistency of quality of design that would see the Liverpool School dominate the prestigious Rome Prize from its inception in 1912.[28] The downside of this emphasis on stylistic consistency could be a lack of originality of approach; but for Reilly this was a price worth paying. He believed that the technical abilities of students trained in his system would triumph over the vagaries of quality and style displayed by office-trained architects. At its most rudimentary, as Reilly himself noted in his paper entitled 'The Training of Architects', written in 1905, the idea was not to encourage genius, but to make 'mediocrity as respectable and sober in architecture as it generally manages to be elsewhere'.[29] Reilly was so successful in implanting the notion of the Liverpool School's position at the forefront of the Beaux-Arts revolution that the style he taught and promoted so heavily throughout his tenure in the Liverpool chair was widely referred to in the professional and general press as the 'Liverpool Manner'.

The founding of the Department of Civic Design was a major development both for the field of planning in general and the promotion of the reputation of the School of Architecture in particular. Just as Simpson had developed the conceptual links between the Arts and Crafts and the Beaux-Arts in the 1890s, Reilly, with the help of the department and its journal *Town Planning Review*, was able to make links between the Beaux-Arts as practised at Liverpool and the nascent Modern Movement. As Crouch notes:

> The cultural views of the Beaux-Arts practitioners were to be reinforced by the immediate post-war rationalization in the construction of municipal housing estates, where economic necessity meshed with the Liverpool School's pre-war rejection of Garden Suburb architecture in favour of a set of planning precepts based on the formal relationship of the part to the whole. The School of Architecture at Liverpool was to play an important role in the dissemination of European Modernism in the 1930s. Why was this? It can only be the case that the rationalizing, technologically based view of architecture that Reilly inculcated at Liverpool was immediately receptive to the underlying ideology of European Modernism.[30]

We can only speculate as to what further influence the School may have had on the national and international architectural stages in the post-Second World War period had Walter Gropius accepted the invitation to the Roscoe Chair in 1933. It is tempting to place too heavy an emphasis upon the ability of individuals such as Reilly to influence wider cultural flows in an environment such as Liverpool. We might ask why it was that the energy he tapped into and used so successfully to promote both himself and the Liverpool School seemed to disappear. The period after the Second World War saw a gradual decline in Liverpool's fortunes, with a slow ebbing away of commercial, maritime and political power. The prosperity and attendant self-confident environment that had given rise to a century and a half of radical architectural activity – culminating in the foundation of the Liverpool School – came to an end. The city entered a long period of what might be termed architectural conservatism, with little outstanding modern architecture being built throughout the remainder of the twentieth century. Why was this the case? Economic factors most certainly played a central role, and as Liverpool's pre-eminent position as an economic powerhouse ground to a halt its architectural energy also stalled. Architecture is the most economically dependent of all the arts and it is generally the case that architectural innovation and experimentation go hand in hand with economic vitality. The pre-war pioneering energy that had helped turn Liverpool into a national and international centre for architectural innovation, training and practice, would, in the latter half of the century, go on to find an outlet in other forms of artistic expression within the city that relied more for their impetus upon the individual, rather than patronage, money and power.

If economic prosperity was the driving force behind the innovative approach Liverpool took in its architectural philosophy throughout the nineteenth and early twentieth centuries and which it subsequently lost during the post-war decline, what of the much vaunted 'renaissance' the city has undertaken in the last ten years? Have the billions of pounds of public and private investment brought about a new era of innovative quality architecture to equal that of the previous period? Certainly the city centre has been transformed, and where once there was dereliction and cleared sites left undeveloped since the 1940s there are now shops, galleries, offices and apartment blocks. The city is undoubtedly cosmetically improved and a much greater sense of activity is evident compared with the low point of the mid-1980s. However, not everyone is convinced by the approach that has been taken in reshaping and rebuilding our major city centres. Writers and critics such as Owen Hatherley in *A Guide to the New Ruins of Great Britain* (2010) and Anna Minton in *Ground Control: Fear and Happiness in the Twenty-First Century City* (2009) detect in the architectural and planning agendas of the past quarter-century a gradual move towards a triumph of style over content and a privatisation of previously public spaces.

For Hatherley, the policies pursued by both Conservative and Labour governments have led to a homogenising of our urban environments. The suburbanisation of swathes of Liverpool city centre by the Militant administration in the 1980s, with the development of estates of bungalows and

low-density housing estates, are in his eyes both wasteful and inappropriate. The ubiquitous waterfront developments, beloved of the Thatcher
government, consisting of identikit architecture, reflect nothing of their
setting in terms of history or geography. Tony Blair's cultural policy of
promoting 'Cool Britannia', and the desire on the part of British cities to
create 'iconic' buildings in the hope of capturing something of the illusive
magic that Bilbao's Guggenheim Museum performed for that city, have led
to a situation where architecture is 'branded'. Buildings attempt to 'shout'
louder than others through the application of fashionable detailing in a
vain attempt to be noticed – as if to suggest that iconic status can somehow
be conferred by the architect rather than achieved by general consensus. As
Hatherley notes:

> 'showpiece' buildings, such as Daniel Libeskind's Imperial War Museum
> North, Michael Wilford's Lowry, Capita Percy Thomas's Cardiff Millennium
> Centre, Norman Foster's Sage Gateshead or Hamilton Architects' atrocious
> Liverpool Pier Head Terminal, appear to have been designed from the
> outside in, shapes and logos waiting around for appropriate functions to
> be conjured out of them. If form once claimed to follow function, then here
> form was the function – to be eye catching, to attract tourists, to get the
> cameras snapping. If Modernism was about revealing structure, showing
> the workings, and attempting to transcend the divide between architect
> and engineer, now the architect draws a shape and asks the engineer to
> make it stand up.[31]

Minton has similar concerns but focuses more upon the psychological
effects the gradual privatisation of our public spaces has had upon British
life, suggesting that it has made us a fearful, insular society, and consequently a much less happy one compared with our European neighbours.
She traces this trend from the Thatcherite model developed in the London
docklands in the 1980s and 1990s and which was subsequently used as the
template for urban spaces across the country. In the opening paragraph to
her book's first chapter, 'Docklands: The Birth of an Idea', she states:

> This book was conceived in a boom and written in a bust. It is about the
> emotional impact of an environment created during the 1990s, a period
> when Britain's unregulated economy built an architecture of boom and
> bust. Apartments in gated developments, security, private streets and plazas
> are its motifs, sitting side by side with enclaves of poverty. In the 1980s,
> when I was growing up, this cityscape, fuelled by the soaring value of
> private property, or 'real estate', as the Americans would say, barely existed
> in Britain. Now, a generation later, this way of doing things, which was
> pioneered in London's Docklands, has taken root in towns and cities

around Britain, changing the physical fabric, the culture and the government of the places we live in. It's an approach that owes a lot to American ideas, yet has a peculiarly British twist.[32]

The model developed in London can be see in Liverpool's own dockland developments, where the quasi-gated communities stretching along the main road leading out to the south of the city turn their backs on the nineteenth-century buildings across the road. Here we see the stark contrast of a 'tale of two cities', the privately owned and controlled dockland estates on the one side, the rather more chaotic and eclectic old city on the other. More recent concerns over the transfer of previously publicly controlled space into the hands of private developers can be seen in the Liverpool One development completed in 2008 by the Grosvenor Group, the property company owned by the Duke of Westminster. For some, the development represents another example of the move towards an urban environment controlled and owned by a few and the loss of a multi-levelled and complex landscape, while for others it is an example of rejuvenation and progress, taking as it did a largely underused and poorly conceived part of the city centre and adding value.

Liverpool One's architectural quality is at best variable. The building that might have stood out as the keynote for the scheme – César Pelli's One Park West – was cut down and emasculated in response to conservationist fears that its planned height might somehow impact upon the UNESCO World Heritage site status that had been awarded in 2004. Similar protests on the part of conservation groups, both public and private, have impacted on other proposals and helped delay, cancel or severely alter the original design. The history of the attempts to develop the Mann Island site adjacent to the group of Edwardian buildings on the Pier Head that includes the Royal Liver Building illustrates this conflict perfectly. Will Alsop's 'The Cloud', which caused enormous consternation among conservation groups, may or may not have been a successful addition to the waterfront, and certainly the buildings that have been built in its place are not without their critics as well as their admirers. Ironically, the building so revered by many of those conservationists who resisted new development on the Mann Island site – the Royal Liver Building – was, as I have already noted, reviled by numerous contemporaneous commentators. Who knows what will be the fate of the generation of buildings that have been erected in the city in the early years of this new century? It is only with the passage of time that we can fully understand and appreciate a building in both its architectural and historical contexts.

Notes

1 Charles Herbert Reilly, 'A Note on the Architecture of Liverpool', in Alfred Holt (ed.), *Merseyside: A Handbook to Liverpool and District* (University Press of Liverpool, 1923), p. 55.

2 Quoted in Joseph Sharples, *Liverpool: Pevsner Architectural Guides* (London and New Haven, Conn.: Yale University Press, 2004), p. 103.

3 *Builder* (22 June 1866).

4 Tony Lane, *Liverpool: Gateway of Empire* (London: Lawrence & Wishart, 1987), pp. 54–55.

5 Quentin Hughes, 'Before the Bauhaus', *Architectural History*, 25 (1982): 110.

6 Charles Herbert Reilly, *Scaffolding in the Sky: A Semi-Architectural Autobiography* (London: George Routledge and Sons, 1938), p. 71.

7 Frederick Moore Simpson, *The Scheme of Architectural Education* (Liverpool: Marples, 1895).

8 Christopher Crouch, *Design Culture in Liverpool, 1880–1914: The Origins of the Liverpool School of Architecture* (Liverpool University Press, 2002), p. 104.

9 Ibid., p. 118.

10 See, for example, 'Architectural Education at the University of Liverpool', *Builder*, 95 (Oct. 1908): 341.

11 Letter from Reilly to the University Registrar, 21 May 1909, quoted in Peter Richmond, *Marketing Modernisms: The Architecture and Influence of Charles Reilly* (Liverpool University Press, 2001), p. 44.

12 Crouch, *Design Culture in Liverpool*, p. 155.

13 Ibid., p. 158.

14 Adshead was supported by a group of part-time lecturers, each of whom brought a specialism with them, including H. Chaloner Dowdall, a barrister who lectured on civic law, John Brodie, City Engineer, landscaper Thomas Mawson and Patrick Abercrombie, editor of *Town Planning Review*.

15 Crouch, *Design Culture in Liverpool*, p. 170.

16 Alan Powers, 'Liverpool and Architectural Education in the Early Twentieth Century', in J. Sharples, A. Powers and M. Shippobottom (eds), *Charles Reilly and the Liverpool School of Architecture, 1904–1933* (Liverpool University Press, 1996), pp. 14–15.

17 Myles Wright, *Lord Leverhulme's Unknown Venture* (London: Hutchinson Benham, 1982), p. 63.

18 Powers, 'Liverpool and Architectural Education', p. 15.

19 Stanley C. Ramsey, 'Charles Herbert Reilly', in Budden (ed.) *The Book of the Liverpool School of Architecture* (Liverpool University Press, 1932), pp. 27–28.

20 Anthony Jackson, *The Politics of Architecture: A History of Modern Architecture in Britain* (London: Architectural Press, 1970), p. 20.

21 Quoted in Powers, 'Liverpool and Architectural Education', p. 17.

22 Wesley Dougill, 'Work of the Schools: Liverpool, *Architects' Journal* (6 July 1932): 12.

23 Boleslaw Szmidt, 'Polish School of Architecture in Liverpool', *Art Notes*, 8.1 (1944): 2–3.

24 'Astragal', *Architects' Journal* (14 Mar. 1946).

25 Quoted in Jack Dunne and Peter Richmond, *The World in One School: The History and Influence of the Liverpool School of Architecture, 1894–2008* (Liverpool University Press, 2008), pp. 54, 58.

26 James Stirling, 'Reflections on the Beaux-Arts', *Architectural Design*, 48 (1978): 88.

27 David Thistlewood, 'Modernism with Ancestry', Liverpool School of Architecture Centenary Review, *Architects' Journal* (11 May 1995): 60–65.

28 For a full account of the Rome Prize, see Louise Campbell, 'A Call to Order: The Rome Prize and Early Twentieth-Century British Architecture', *Architectural History*, 32 (1989): 131–51.

29 Charles Herbert Reilly, *The Training of Architects* (London: Sherrat and Hughes, 1905).

30 Crouch, *Design Culture in Liverpool*, p. xiii.

31 Owen Hatherley, 'A Guide to the New Ruins of Great Britain', *Guardian* (16 Oct. 2010).

32 Anna Minton, *Ground Control: Fear and Happiness in the Twenty-First Century City* (London: Penguin, 2009).

Further Reading

'Astragal', *Architects' Journal* (14 Mar. 1946).

Bennett, Mary, *The Art Sheds, 1894–1905* (Liverpool: Walker Art Gallery, 1981) (catalogue).

Budden, Lionel (ed.), *The Book of the Liverpool School of Architecture* (University Press of Liverpool, 1932).

Campbell, Louise, 'A Call to Order: The Rome Prize and Early Twentieth-Century British Architecture, *Architectural History*, 32 (1989): 131–51.

Cherry, Gordon E., *Pioneers in British Planning* (London: Architectural Press, 1981).

Crouch, Christopher, *Design Culture in Liverpool, 1880–1914: The Origins of the Liverpool School of Architecture* (Liverpool University Press, 2002).

Dougill, Wesley, 'Work of the Schools: Liverpool', *Architects' Journal* (6 July 1931): 9.

Dunne, Jack, and Peter Richmond, *The World in One School: The History and Influence of the Liverpool School of Architecture, 1894–2008* (Liverpool University Press, 2008).

Hatherley, Owen, *A Guide to the New Ruins of Great Britain* (London: Verso, 2010).

Hughes, Quentin, 'Before the Bauhaus: The Experiment at the Liverpool School of Architecture and Applied Arts', *Architectural History*, 25 (1982): 102.

— *Liverpool* (London: Studio Vista, 1969).

— *Seaport: Architecture and Townscape in Liverpool* (Liverpool: Bluecoat Press, 1993).

Jackson, Anthony, *The Politics of Architecture: The History of Modern Architecture in Britain* (London: Architectural Press, 1970).

Kelly, Thomas, *For the Advancement of Learning: The University of Liverpool, 1881–1981* (Liverpool University Press, 1981).

Lane, Tony, *Liverpool: Gateway of Empire* (London: Lawrence & Wishart, 1987).

Maxwell Fry, E., *Autobiographical Sketches* (London: Elek, 1975).

Minton, Anna, *Ground Control: Fear and Happiness in the Twenty-First Century City* (London: Penguin, 2009).

Powers, Alan, 'Architectural Education in Britain, 1880-1914', Cambridge University PhD thesis (1982).

Reilly, Charles Herbert, 'A Note on the Architecture of Liverpool', in Alfred Holt (ed.), *Merseyside: A Handbook to Liverpool and District* (London, 1923).

— *The Liverpool Architectural Sketch Book* (University of Liverpool School of Architecture, 1910).

— *The Liverpool University Architectural Sketch Book* (London: Architectural Review, 1920).

— *Portfolio of Measured Drawings* (University of Liverpool School of Architecture, 1910).

— *Scaffolding in the Sky: A Semi-Architectural Autobiography* (London: Routledge, 1938).

— *The Training of Architects* (London: Sherrat & Hughes, 1905).

Richmond, Peter, *Marketing Modernisms: The Architecture and Influence of Charles Reilly* (Liverpool University Press, 2001).

Sharples, Joseph (ed.), *Charles Reilly and the Liverpool School of Architecture, 1904–1933* (Liverpool University Press, 1996).

— *Liverpool*, Pevsner Architectural Guides (New Haven, Conn. and London: Yale University Press, 2004).

Simpson, Frederick M., 'Architectural Education and a School of Architecture', *Builder*, 71 (1896): 539.

— *The Scheme of Architectural Education* (Liverpool: Marples, 1895).

Szmidt, Boleslaw, 'Polish School of Architecture in Liverpool', *Art Notes*, 8.1 (1944): 2–3.

Stirling, James, 'Reflections on the Beaux-Arts', *Architectural Design*, 48.11–12: 88.

Thistlewood, David, 'Modernism with Ancestry', Liverpool School of Architecture Centenary Review, *Architects' Journal* (11 May 1995): 60–65.

Wright, Myles, *Lord Leverhulme's Unknown Venture* (London: Hutchinson Benham, 1982).

3
Radical Art City?

Bryan Biggs

Among Liverpool's many claims, the one that it has more museums and galleries than anywhere in the UK outside London may well be true, and certainly during the Liverpool Biennial there is a staggering amount of exhibitions and art interventions within and beyond its wealth of mainstream venues. The main programme of the 2010 edition of the UK's largest visual art festival took place at thirty sites and involved over 350 artists from all round the globe, and when the 500 or so other artists showing in a further sixty venues participating that year in the Independents – the 'fringe' section of the Biennial – are added, together with impressive audience figures, the city's boast as the most vital and important centre for the visual arts outside the capital does not seem exaggerated, at least not during this ten-week period every two years. Glasgow may claim a more vibrant and internationally connected artists' community and art school, while other cities, including Newcastle, Bristol, Manchester, Sheffield and Nottingham can boast significant regional scenes. But all envy Liverpool's concentration of galleries and festivals and how it has positioned itself in the pantheon of international biennials, as well as developing fruitful ongoing exchanges with its twin cities like Cologne and Shanghai. And the strength of Liverpool's visual arts offer was certainly a determining factor in winning the European Capital of Culture 2008 designation.

Any claim, however, that the city may have on the *radical* in art cannot be subject to such crude competitive measurement. And it would be ludicrous to try and position Liverpool as having art historical significance comparable to the major twentieth-century cultural centres where radical art has been created, avant-garde movements forged or reputations made – cities like Paris, New York or London, with their interconnections of commerce, media, the art world and, increasingly today, celebrity. With the scope of this study spanning a century too, locating the very idea of the radical becomes problematic. The changing nature of art across this period, with the ruptures of modernism and postmodernism, demands examination of the radical not just in terms of formal experimentation and aesthetics, but of the relational also – the significant shifts in the way art is produced, defined, theorised, mediated, disseminated, discussed, experienced, collected or otherwise consumed. And, in recent decades, how art has been appropriated for instrumentalist purposes by a range of agencies, including governmental, with agendas that encompass education, social cohesion, health and well-being, tourism, nation- or city-branding and urban regeneration, requires new strategies of the artist intent on developing a radical practice with which to negotiate this new landscape. Such options might include community participation, interventions into the public realm, activism, interdisciplinary work with other art forms or engagement with technology. In tandem with these shifts in practice, different theoretical frameworks have emerged, such as Nicolas Bourriaud's Relational Aesthetics, as the language for discussing concepts of the radical has had to change.

While the prevalence of an avant-garde would constitute the notion of the radical in art in 1911, and indeed for a large part of the rest of the twentieth century, today the radical is as likely to be located beyond the gallery or even outside the art world altogether, as artists contest and negotiate a highly sophisticated, networked world in which everything, including contemporary art, is subject to instant commodification. In such a globalised environment, the local takes on new significance, and within visual art it is the biennial, traditionally based on the model of Venice, with its international pavilions, that has become a predominant site through which to consider the local within the new global relationships. And a new generation of biennials, including Liverpool's, has provided a platform for a critical re-evaluation of this type of art expo. Despite the international standing that its Biennial has brought to Liverpool's art scene, however, the city can much less claim to be a hub of radical art practice, a place reflecting a particular zeitgeist comparable with, say, those cities whose energy created an art world buzz outside of the major centres, like the Glasgow painters in the 1980s, or those of the Leipzig School who made such an international impact in the first decade of our new century. I will attempt to show, however, that Liverpool's art *has* witnessed moments of genuine innovation, some of them having an impact beyond the narrow context of art world endorsement, and that its arts infrastructure today provides a framework within which the radical can flourish. The study will identify occasions across the past century when there seemed the possibility that Liverpool could transcend the parochial and connect to something bigger:

first, and looked at in some detail, 1911 and the exhibition of 'radical' art from the Continent hosted at the Bluecoat by the Sandon Studios Society, whose efforts helped lay the foundations for a pioneering arts centre; secondly, the establishment of the John Moores painting competition in 1957 and the renaissance in art it ushered in during the 1960s, articulated in John Willett's seminal study *Art in a City*, with its prescient view of Liverpool's potential to develop a fruitful civic relationship with modern art; and, finally, the extraordinary growth of the visual arts infrastructure that followed in the wake of the Tate's arrival in 1988, including initiatives like FACT and the Liverpool Biennial. In doing this, I will interrogate, as Tate Liverpool's exhibition *Centre of the Creative Universe* set out to do,[1] the extent to which Liverpool's reputation as a vital contemporary art centre is the result of its indigenous scene, and how much rests on it being receptive to progressive ideas from outside.

Radical Roots

In 1911, between 4 March and 1 April, it was possible to see in Liverpool eight paintings and drawings by Gauguin, five by Picasso, three each by Matisse and Vlaminck, two each by Van Gogh, Derain and Rouault, and one each by Cézanne, Denis and Signac. Included in an exhibition of modern art at the Bluecoat, it was only the second time this group of artists – dubbed Post-Impressionists by English art critic and artist Roger Fry – had been shown together in this country, and the first alongside British artists. The exhibition was a smaller selection from Fry's controversial exhibition that arguably marked the birth of modern art in Britain, *Manet and the Post-Impressionists,* at the Grafton Galleries in London the previous winter, though significantly Manet was left out of the Liverpool show. Of the forty-four British artists also exhibiting – members of the Sandon Studios Society (the artists' group initiating the exhibition) – thirty-one were locally based, several with studios in the Bluecoat. The non-residents included eminent names like Augustus John (semi-permanent in the city at the time), Philip Wilson Steer and Henry Tonks. The Liverpool artists included Albert Lipczinski, Edward Carter Preston (father of well-known potter, Julia Carter Preston) and Henry Carr.

George Bernard Shaw is recorded as saying in Liverpool that 'the corruption of taste and the emotional insincerity of the mass of the people had gone so far that any picture which pleased more than ten per cent. of the population should be immediately burned'.[2] And it is hardly surprising that the Post-Impressionist exhibition in Liverpool 'outraged the civic authorities and the conventional public',[3] which in reality would have been limited to a cultured middle-class audience, since it is doubtful that, with admission of one shilling, attendance extended to the 'lower classes'. Its critical reception is largely undocumented apart from a favourable review in the *Manchester Guardian*, which praised the Sandon artists as well as the Post-Impressionists, offering a sympathetic understanding of what they were trying to achieve:

> We speak of likeness to nature, but the fact is, we come into a picture gallery, not with nature in our minds, but with eyes prejudiced by the art we have seen before, whether it is in an almanac or in the National Gallery. We have, then, in such a show as that at Liverpool, to readjust the focus of our eyes before we can judge with fairness the result of a new point of view on the part of the artist. The result is curious in the extreme ... Whether these pictures are great or not, or whether or not we admire them, is not quite the point. It is more pertinent to urge that they succeed very considerably in their task of simplifying expression; that they are not mere puerility or charlatanry.[4]

While Virginia Woolf later declared – partly in reference to Fry's exhibition – that 'On or about December 1910, human character changed',[5] the reaction to its showing in London a few months before Liverpool's had been generally hostile. But although evidently shocking to bourgeois tastes and undoubtedly having a profound effect on British art, we need to ask just how radical was the exhibition? Several of the Post-Impressionists were long dead and the most recent work on display was already two years old. The term itself was 'of purely British origin, coined to cover their ignorance of several art movements in France which were bracketed together in this country'.[6] With the Post-Impressionists' link back to, rather than radical break from, the Impressionists, whose work they considered too naturalistic and devoid of emotion, Fry's artificial grouping appears in hindsight less radical than what was happening elsewhere in Europe. At the same time as the Sandon exhibition, Futurism, for instance – with its embrace of the dynamism, speed and violence of the new technological century – was having its first public showing in Milan, with works by Boccioni, Carrà and Russolo. Also in 1911, in St Petersburg, the second exhibition of the group Soyuz Molodyozhi (Union of Youth) included Malevich and Tatlin, who during Russia's turbulent years would revolutionise art through Suprematism and Constructivism, and, in Munich, Kandinsky, Macke and Marc formed the Expressionist painting group Die Blaue Reiter (The Blue Rider). In contrast to these radical groupings, Post-Impressionism was a diffuse construct, part of Fry's attempt to educate his fellow countrymen on the important shifts taking place in painting in Continental Europe, notably in France, and was necessarily didactic given Britain's backwardness in relation to these movements. The exhibition did, however, contain one genuinely radical painting, Picasso's portrait of his dealer Clovis Sagot, painted at the start of his Analytical Cubism period (1909–12), accompanied by four drawings.

The Liverpool showing can be regarded as more daring than its first manifestation in London for two reasons: first, Manet and other artists considered more acceptable to British tastes, brought in as a 'sweetener' to temper the anticipated outrage of the show in London, were left out of the Liverpool selection (the exhibition catalogue states that the Sandon 'invited works by Post-Impressionists' but it is not known if they or Fry made the selection), and, secondly, British artists were included, something that Fry was keen to see happen, though the extent to which he had a hand in this is also unclear, the British work being selected by a hanging committee of the Sandon. This work would have undoubtedly looked pedestrian in the company of Picasso *et al.*, but nevertheless it was the first time in Britain that dialogue, through an exhibition, between these European and home-grown art works was possible.

Seeing a Matisse landscape in Liverpool so early in the century, and work by a twenty-nine-year old Picasso, who together with Braque was revolutionising art through Cubist experimentation, must have had an impact. The Sandon organised a debate towards the end of the exhibition, which, according to the *Liverpool Courier*, represented 'an almost unqualified condemnation of the "new" art', with the conservative director of the Walker Art Gallery, E. R. Dibden, declaring 'It will not be long before most of these things are relegated to the lumber-room, the attic, or the refuse destructor', and the Revd T. W. M. Lund suggesting 'a gigantic hoax. It is the most stupendous joke ever perpetrated'.[7] Sandon members, however, were passionate in their defence of the show they had brought to Liverpool, George Harris arguing that Post-Impressionism 'was a revolution certainly, and respectable people objected to revolutions'; a Mr Abercrombie (brothers Patrick and Lascelles were both members) claimed the work was not outrageous *enough*; and, chairing the proceedings, J. G. Legge (Director of Education and Chairman of the Sandon's General Committee) concluded that 'The real effect of these artists would be in stimulating a fresh departure in art'.[8] The exhibition clearly 'delighted those who took a serious interest in painting',[9] namely the artists and art lovers who hosted the exhibition. And it is an examination of this group of people, how they came together, the creative energy they generated and their legacy on art in Liverpool – rather than looking at the 1911 exhibition in isolation – that will reveal the extent to which this period in the city's cultural life can be regarded as radical.

The 1902 Education Act compelled the Education Committee of Liverpool Corporation to take over the university's Applied Art section, fusing it in 1905 with the Applied Art School to establish a Municipal School of Art. Municipally controlled art education following the South Kensington System (the norm for art teaching established in the second half of the nineteenth century) was regarded as conservative and constraining by the university students housed in what were known as the Art Sheds, who were used to the freedoms taught by staff that included Augustus John, recently graduated from the Slade and working in Liverpool. So, under the direction of painter Gerard Chowne and designer J. Herbert MacNair (Charles Rennie Mackintosh's brother-in-law and a member – with Charles and their respective spouses, Frances and Margaret MacDonald – of 'The Glasgow Four'), students and staff set up their own art school at Sandon Terrace, next door to the Municipal School of Art on the site now occupied by the Liverpool Institute for Performing Arts' car park, overlooking the Anglican Cathedral. Sandon Terrace Studios attracted one hundred members within its first year, and ran evening as well as daytime classes, open to amateurs too. A prime mover was Fanny Dove Hamel Lister, later Mrs Calder, who raised essential funds from private sources, as she was to do throughout her association with the Sandon. When evicted from their premises, the artists of the Sandon Studios Society (as it was now called) occupied spaces at the recently evacuated Queen Anne period Blue Coat School in the heart of the city – the oldest city centre building – in 1907, establishing a creative community there that continues to this day, even though the Sandon is no more. It was here that their number exhibited alongside the Post-Impressionists in 1911 and again in 1913, by which time there was less hostility in Britain to these modernist trends, Arnold Bennett noting 'the school which was guffawed at last year in England, was treated with marked respect by *The Times* this year, and which in a few years more will be worshipped in England as ignorantly as it is now condemned'.[10] Sandon members again debated the merits of the modern movement, the Society's fifth *Bulletin* balancing an article of informed praise for the 1913 show with another poking gentle fun at the Post-Impressionists' 'second coming'.[11]

There were not to be exhibitions of such significance at the Sandon again, but instead of seeing these shows as isolated occurrences, they are manifestations of an attitude among a young generation of artists (mostly

under the age of thirty-five) who opposed official art and resisted its municipal bureaucratisation, strenuously challenging the Liverpool Academy
and the moribund state of the city's principal public venue, the Walker Art
Gallery. Open to new ideas from the Continent and connected to progressive art circles in London, the Sandon also had a mischievous streak,
publishing scurrilous pamphlets such as *A Bushel of Chaff* (1912), a scathing
satire on various local worthies, including politicians, a bishop, a newspaper
editor and the curator of the Walker, accompanied by cruel caricatures by
George Harris. Interestingly, F. T. Marinetti's *Futurist Manifesto* of three
years earlier was also included, though it has been suggested this was to
annoy people rather than providing evidence that the Italian's ideas had
taken root on Merseyside.[12] The Sandon's attack on officialdom began with
its 1909 pamphlet *The Sport of Civic Life or, Art and the Municipality*, whose
main feature was an essay by painter and writer on art William Rothenstein. In it he argued for greater participation in civic life by the artist,
then seemingly regarded as 'little more than a parasite, waiting on the
caprices of the rich rather than expressing the essential culture of his own
time',[13] and advocated nurturing the city's indigenous art while having the
confidence to attract significant artists and cultural movers and shakers
to the city. These were themes echoed over half a century later in *Art in a
City* by John Willett, who traces the journey that Rothenstein's ideas for
a 'University of the Arts' took. They informed Charles Reilly's scheme to
develop the Bluecoat as an arts centre, based on the two resources already
there, the Sandon artists and the University School of Architecture, which
he headed. Reilly's plan, backed initially by William Lever (the first Lord
Leverhulme), who acquired the premises, renaming it Liberty Building,
became 'the emasculated ancestor' of the present Bluecoat.[14] Much of the
Sandon's youthful energy and radicalism dissipated with the outbreak of
the First World War. However, a new constitution meant that its focus
had broadened beyond just visual art to include music, theatre and other
areas of the arts, and opened its membership to those *interested* in the arts,
not just practitioners. Largely a story of voluntary effort in the face of civic
indifference (despite the backing of the Lord Mayor, Corporation funds
were not forthcoming), the Sandon members were instrumental in raising
the money to purchase the building after Leverhulme's death and establishing a new organisation, the Bluecoat Society of Arts, in 1927, which
continues today as simply the Bluecoat.

What comes across in studies of the development of the Bluecoat
as a centre for the arts is the collision of the worlds of the amateur and
high art, the coming together of voluntary effort, collective enthusiasm

and the drive of passionate individuals.[15] Long before the proliferation of arts centres across the country, often set up with Arts Council and local authority funding, offering cultural amenities for local populations, the Sandon supporters established what is arguably the first combined arts centre in Britain. The roots of this were there in 1911. If this is not radical in itself, there is a strong argument for claiming that the Bluecoat's transformation from school to working arts building represents an early, perhaps even the first, example of arts-led urban regeneration.

This focus on a building as a resource and, from 1927, an asset, housing a creative community, distinguishes the Sandon from other progressive groups that flourished as provincial equivalents of Bloomsbury (though none of these could compare to the London group's breadth of influence on developments in literature and visual art, as well as feminism and economic theory). The Sandon's impact on cultural, social and intellectual life locally would arguably have been less had it not had the foresight to seek patronage to secure the building, with its distinctive and historically significant architecture and its favourable city centre location. While the Bluecoat over time became increasingly connected to the life of the city, today attracting some 700,000 visits a year, the Sandon was a club for a cultured elite for much of its existence. The musician, writer and entertainer George Melly fondly recalls as a child being brought to fancy dress parties dressed as Mickey Mouse in the 1930s,[16] by which time the Sandon was hardly a hotbed of the avant-garde, the artists dominated more by the New English Art Club than Picasso's late Cubism or other progressive trends. As Maud Budden warns the would-be bohemian, Augustus, in her 1933 poem, 'In Search of Sin: A Cautionary Tale for the Youth of Liverpool':

> Then, trembling to his very core,
> He staggered through the Sandon Door
> And stood in eager, wild suspense
> Prepared for scenes of decadence.
> But oh, the sad and bitter Truth!
> Alas for Roseate Dreams of Youth!
> The sights that met th'expectant Gus
> Were Utterly Innocuous.
> The pictures hung upon each wall
> Did not repel nor yet appal:
> And seeming just what you or I
> Would, if we had the money, buy,
> They sobered poor Augustus who
> Had hoped for Worse-than-Ballyhoo.
> Oppressed by ever-deepening gloom,

He peered into the sitting-room
Where Members, dressed in neat attire
Were gathered round a blazing fire
Discussing with a grave restraint
The best and purest way to paint
Or, less exalted, Test Match news
And daily paper crossword clues,
In short the scene was really nice –
Except to those in search of vice.[17]

Yet in the 1920s and 1930s the Bluecoat building welcomed distinguished international radicals from the worlds of literature, music and dance, including George Bernard Shaw, Stravinsky, Bartók and George Balanchine.[18] And Liverpool's turn-of-the-century global connectedness was reflected in the cosmopolitan nature of artists who settled in the city. One Sandon member, and an exhibitor in both Bluecoat Post-Impressionist shows, was Polish émigré Albert Lipczinski, a radical politically if not artistically, who perhaps more than any other artist in the city at this time exemplified the convergence of the local and the international, of art and politics, of bohemia and academia. As David Bingham has argued, 'Lippi' is 'an artist who is lost in time' who nonetheless provides us with a lens through which to understand the extraordinariness of this period in Liverpool's history, tumultuous years before the artist was interned as an enemy alien at the outbreak of the First World War and eventually deported. Lipczinski's home, the 'Schloss' off Roscoe Street, was frequented by his friends – artists like Augustus John, professors like Charles Reilly and trade union leaders like Jim Larkin and Thomas Mann – a stimulating cultural milieu, which dissolved class divisions and statuses, all gathering in a run-down location, perplexing the police who observed this strange mix.[19] It has been observed that the Sandon 'accepted the idea of the artist as gypsy, as gentleman or as scholar. It was more than doubtful about his role in civic life',[20] but in Lipczinski one can detect an advocate for a more socially engaged art, though his left-wing leanings and later his 'alien' status would have denied him civic approval. His portrait of Larkin was reputedly held aloft by strikers prior to the Easter Uprising in Dublin and shot down by the Black and Tans.[21]

Although the Sandon never recaptured the heady times around the Post-Impressionist exhibitions it remained an important cultural society, and not just a dining club with some voluntary arts activities thrown in, as it has sometimes been caricatured. Epstein's controversial sculpture of a pregnant woman, *Genesis*, was brought to Liverpool to raise funds for the

Bluecoat, but Picasso's *Guernica*, shown in Manchester in 1939, sadly did not travel to the city.[22] If insular at times, concerned more with parties than the latest advances in art, during the 1930s the Sandon did produce one artist of particular significance with an international perspective, Roderick Bisson, who was to chronicle the Society's history.[23] Self taught, he joined the Sandon in 1931. His enthusiasm for Cubism's analytical approach, and his early adoption of Surrealism (before it reached London), in particular the metaphysical paintings of Giorgio de Chirico, garnered through frequent visits to Paris and voracious reading of advanced art magazines like *Blast*, *Minotaure* and *Verve*, contributed to the creation of a highly distinctive style that was at odds with the Sandon orthodoxy. Bisson's reputation as the Society's lone modernist painter is captured in a 1936 painting by Donald Lynch, *So you won't talk, eh?* (a pastiche of William Frederick Yeames's *And when did you last see your father?* of 1878 in the Walker Art Gallery, it is also known as *And when did you last see your oculist?*), in which the young rebel is being interrogated by members of the Sandon's Painters' and Sculptors' Group, one of whom brandishes Bisson's offending geometric painting as evidence. Ann Compton has argued that had Bisson 'moved to London and taken a more actively commercial approach to his art ... He would surely have earned national recognition for his extended dialogue with international modernism and the vivid imagination, wit and sensuous treatment of form which typifies his paintings'.[24] Nicholas Horsfield also claims this 'remarkable innovator' could have been successful in the London marketplace.[25] Indeed, in the 1960s, a painting by Bisson dating from 1925 was mistakenly attributed to the French Cubist Albert Gleizes when shown at the Redfern Gallery in London. The gallery's director Rex Nan Kivell admitted 'He would be considered another Wyndham Lewis ... an undiscovered genius if you like'.[26] Bisson, however, had given up painting after he became art critic for the *Liverpool Daily Post*, which he continued to do until his death in 1987.

Radical Reawakening

In the period following the Sandon's pioneering years, with the interruption of the Second World War and the downturn in the port's fortunes with catastrophic economic consequences, contemporary art struggled to have a presence in Liverpool. It was not until after the formal establishment of the Arts Council in 1946 that grants would start to become available for regional arts venues to develop their programmes, which the Bluecoat did particularly from the late-1960s onwards, securing annual revenue funding and eventually grants for a major capital development. It was largely *private* rather than public patronage that had maintained the Sandon, and it was another patron, John Moores, the founder of the Little-woods business empire and himself a keen amateur painter, who in the 1950s reinvigorated William Roscoe's legacy in Liverpool. Roscoe's idea that regard for progressive art in the city was an expression of its sophistication and enlightenment informed Moores' decision to set up a biennial art prize (initially including sculpture as well as painting) in his name in 1957 at the Walker Art Gallery, six years after it reopened following the end of the war. The John Moores exhibition quickly became the most important painting competition in the country, 'an essential reason to visit Liverpool at least every other year'.[27] Moores was concerned that the over-concentration of art and art criticism in London was having a stultifying effect on provincial museums and galleries, which instead of offering second-rate imitations of developments in the capital should become a focus for the cultural life of the cities they serve.[28] And his enterprise to show – and in the process to build up a collection of – the best UK painting in Liverpool, and to encourage progressive, and particularly young, artists certainly put the city on the map as a significant contemporary art destination. (In 2010 the John Moores Painting Prize went international, with a version opening in Liverpool's twin city of Shanghai, using the same model of selection.) Open to any artist, the Liverpool competition established itself, especially during the 1960s and 1970s, as a barometer of painting in the UK, its prize winners an impressive roll call, including Jack Smith, Roger Hilton, Patrick Heron, David Hockney, John Walker, Euan Uglow, Richard Hamilton, John Hoyland, Bruce McLean, Tim Head, Peter Doig and Michael Raedecker. However, with Mary Martin and Lisa Milroy the only two women to have won the prize in over half a century (and with the balance of the overall selection predominantly male), the competition has not necessarily reflected the full breadth of studio practice, particularly that informed by discourses beyond purely aesthetic or formal considerations. Admittedly, the competition's strict guidelines as to what constitutes a painting has limited it from reflecting vital developments in art, making it appear during the emergence of conceptualism, minimalism, video, installation or performance art, for instance, somewhat anachronistic. However, in the face of repeated declarations of the death of painting, the John Moores has reflected the medium's remarkable resilience. Moreover, the exhibition's popular appeal (a contrast to Shaw's gloomy prognosis of the masses' intolerance to progressive art quoted above) and the ownership the city feels for it remain strong, despite the relative dearth of Merseyside artists included in the shows.

One local artist who did enjoy John Moores' success in 1959 was Stuart Sutcliffe, whose canvas was purchased by the patron himself, enabling the promising Liverpool Art College-trained painter to obtain a bass guitar with the proceeds, and entry into the Beatles. Art schools had a major influence on the development of popular music in the UK, exemplified in the late 1950s and early 1960s in Liverpool by Sutcliffe and John Lennon,[29] and where this area of interdisciplinary practice developed further – bringing together the worlds of visual art, pop culture, poetry and performance – the city witnessed a new creative energy, small in scale but distinctly radical. The existence of a concentrated, lively bohemia, Liverpool 8, close to the art school and pubs, clubs and other hangouts on the fringes of the city centre, helped to facilitate creative cross-fertilisation. Its 'high priest' was Adrian Henri. Henri's influences, like Sutcliffe's, were wide-ranging: the vigorous New York painting scene, American Beat writing, the European avant-garde, jazz, pop culture and cinema, while Richard Hamilton – Henri's tutor when studying art in Newcastle – provided an important catalyst. From these diverse interests Henri developed parallel careers as poet (for which he is best known), painter, performer, musician and later critic. The early 1960s Liverpool 8 scene was stimulated by its poets and their interaction with visiting UK Beats. Spike Hawkins and Johnny Byrne, part of this itinerant band, helped kick-start Liverpool's poetry scene in 1961, while another, Pete Brown, hitchhiking from London around the country with Widnes-born, Liverpool Art College-trained and future jazz illustrator for *Melody Maker*, Mal Dean, found the city conducive to his brand of jazz-meets-poetry.[30] What developed was wholly unique. The Mersey poets (notably Henri, Roger McGough and Brian Patten) drew heavily on and became synonymous with the city, referencing in their work streets and buildings, stories and histories, everyday life, the fabric and culture of Liverpool. Critic Edward Lucie-Smith discerned a 'lack of cultural hierarchies' in Liverpool poetry, claiming that it 'differs from other contemporary verse because it has made its impact by being spoken and listened to, rather than being read', and he noted the similarities between a poetry event and a pop gig, taking poetry out of its elitist, high art environment: 'the audience is hardly conscious that there is a distinction'.[31] The poetry circuit attracted the same young people who followed the Beatles and other bands at the Cavern, rather than just a traditionally 'arty' crowd. Ringo Starr and George Harrison turned up in the audience at one poetry reading in the basement of an old chapel-turned-cinema, Hope Hall, now the Everyman Theatre.

More so than in London, a fresh new regional arts scene in centres far from the capital, like Newcastle, Bradford and Edinburgh, was being created based on live reading. The US Beat poets provided inspiration, especially the charismatic Allen Ginsberg, who befriended Henri and, following Black Mountain College poet Robert Creeley, who came to Liverpool in 1964, visited the city in 1965 and made his famous pronouncement that 'Liverpool is at the present moment the centre of the consciousness of the human universe'. Henri felt more attuned to the experimentation taking place across the Atlantic than the stratified cultural offer to be found in London. He picked up on the first stirrings of American performance art, the 'happenings' of Allan Kaprow, in particular, and Claes Oldenberg, with his environments made from cheap materials like cardboard. Inspired by the dissolution of categories between fine art, theatre, dance and music that artists like Kaprow, Merce Cunningham, John Cage and Robert Rauschenberg were effecting in the United States, Henri's early mixed-media 'happenings' at Hope Hall combined poetry, painting and pop. These performances between 1962 and 1964 were arguably the first 'happenings' in the UK, and their significance was recognised as such by Kaprow in a letter to Henri: 'I've been hearing that London's so-called vitality was a figment of our *Time Magazine*'s publicity staff. The signals have been pointing instead to Liverpool and your letter, full of hints, confirms them.'[32] Henri's performances also took place in pubs like Ye Cracke and at the Cavern (an anti-bomb piece in 1964). The equipment for *City Event* (1962) included: two tape recorders with sound effects of the city, a gramophone, a moveable spotlight with an on/off switch, a portable radio tuned to Radio Luxembourg for most of the action, a staple gun and scent spray. John Gorman (a Dadaist-leaning Post Office engineer) and Roger McGough – who both went on to form pop outfit the Scaffold with Paul McCartney's brother Mike McGear – participated, together with dancers, while Henri painted a backdrop live. 'Daffodil Story – An Experiment in Communication' (1963) starts with the Coasters' novelty R&B record 'Along Came Jones' and the Beatles' 'I Want to Hold Your Hand', and ends with dancing to the overture to Alfred Jarry's absurdist play *Ubu Roi*.[33] Henri's sixth 'happening', *Nightblues*, included live music from Merseybeat group the Roadrunners, the use of pop music a significant move away from the poetry-meets-jazz performances or from the prevalence for avant-garde music in New York 'happenings' (and several years before Andy Warhol's collaboration with the Velvet Underground). Although Liverpool at this time was not exactly a mini-version of Greenwich Village, Henri's performances echoed its subversion of the literary, artistic and theatrical establishments while seeking to enrich the old, fixed art forms, and he was well placed to write one of the first critical accounts of environments, 'happenings' and performance art, published in 1974.[34]

Success would come to Henri through his poetry and painting – and briefly with poetry/rock band the Liverpool Scene, which performed in front of 250,000 people at 'Britain's Woodstock', the 1969 Isle of Wight festival, supporting Bob Dylan (to whom, with Henri in full throttle, they apparently proved a highly entertaining and irreverent warm-up). But, in the context of the *radical*, Henri's enduring legacy is in imbuing the local with a melancholic sense of its connected cultural past – a psychogeographical continuum in which the ghosts of Mikhail Bakunin, Alfred Jarry, Kurt Schwitters, William Blake, Malcolm Lowry, Allen Ginsberg and the Beatles stalk the streets of Liverpool – and as a fertile site for creative exploration, drawing on the vernacular and the quotidian. Importantly, too, Henri showed that art need not remain in silos – either art form or stylistic – that endorsement from London was not necessary (though the success of his poetry and to a degree his painting also were due to early championing by Lucie-Smith) and that radical art need not be the privilege of an educated few.

The breaking down of barriers – between different types of art and also of access to art by a general audience – was a feature of Liverpool in the 1960s, the city's culture given new self-confidence by the Merseybeat phenomenon, the success of the John Moores competition, the emergence of the Mersey poets and the footballing spectacle of the Kop, much of this disseminated through the increasingly ubiquitous and persuasive medium of television. In 1967, radical Fluxus artist Yoko Ono performed to a full and largely non-art audience at the Bluecoat, which by the end of the decade was becoming a significant gallery outside London for showcasing UK artists such as Mark Boyle and John Latham, who were experimenting with different media, creating 'environments' and process-based, performative work. Not everyone approved of this avant-garde art 'imported' from London – the self-taught Catholic-Communist sculptor Arthur Dooley staging a protest demonstrating that the cost of showing at the Bluecoat was pricing out local artists by hanging work on the railings outside. It led to a 'Railings Union' that promoted the site as an alternative exhibition space, with Dooley declaring 'Art should be a part of everyday people's lives and it isn't. There is no real contact between the artist and the ordinary people'.[35] This theme, and the role of the artist in relation to civic life, had gained new urgency with the publication in 1967 of John Willett's *Art in a City*. Now regarded as the first sociology of the arts to focus on a single city, the study, commissioned by the Bluecoat earlier that decade, analysed Liverpool's arts institutions, its artists and the artistic tastes of its population, relating this to the problems of patronage in the

UK and in comparable foreign cities, and setting it in the context of 150 years of argument about art and society. This new approach was an invitation to artists, architects, planners, social scientists and local politicians to consider a more civic and social role for art, outlined by Willett in specific proposals 'designed to set the arts in a new framework: that of a modern community's interests, plans and needs'.[36]

As I have argued elsewhere,[37] *Art in a City* was prescient: much of what Willett advocated has now come to pass, though not necessarily in the ways he imagined – notably the strength and interconnectedness of Liverpool's current visual arts infrastructure and the way that art has embedded itself in much of the fabric of city life, for instance, through participative initiatives involving communities, education projects, public art and other interventions into the public realm and major festivals like the Biennial. Even if *Art in a City*'s somewhat paternalistic tone, its language and discursive thrust have been superseded by theoretical frameworks not available to Willett at the time, the study remains radical in its challenge both to artists in relation to their social role and to municipal and other authorities responsible for aspects of public life: 'For the real question in the arts in a city like Liverpool is how far the shift of patronage and policy-making into municipal hands can be used to stimulate rather than merely alienate the artist.'[38]

Willett's recommendations, set out in a blueprint for the future in the book's final chapter, were generally ignored by the Corporation and subsequent administrations, for whom culture slipped further down the agenda whenever more pressing social and economic needs came to the fore; art was regarded variously as a luxury or an elitist activity. The vision for much of Liverpool's development as an art city that followed, right up until the council ran with the idea of culture in its successful bid to become European Capital of Culture in 2008, came from elsewhere: from the local grassroots, like the establishment in 1968 of the Blackie in the city's Chinatown district, the UK's first community arts centre (which continues today, renamed the Black-E); from enlightened, passionate and determined individuals; or from national policy decision-making – the opening in 1988 on the banks of the Mersey of the Tate's first regional gallery proving especially significant. Willett cited the main visual arts initiatives in the city, including the Walker and its Roscoe old masters collection, the Art College, the Liverpool Academy, the Sandon, the Bluecoat and art/art history at the university, as phenomena 'founded on a set of ideas which has not necessarily been fulfilled, yet arose from a local situation and the growth of the city and is still somehow hanging in the air'.[39] The story over the past forty-odd years since Willett's assessment has generally, however, been one of fulfilment. The extent to which any of this explosion in the growth of art in the city was 'radical' is the focus of this final section.

Radical Regeneration?

Following republication of Willett's seminal study in 2007, a new collection of essays, *Art in a City Revisited* (2009), used his template as a starting point to look again at visual art in Liverpool, examining the significant developments that had taken place in the intervening four decades and looking at future prospects, post-Capital of Culture.[40] The book paints a positive picture of art in the city, taking in patronage, practice, policy and a framework enhanced by the arrival of the Open Eye Gallery, Tate Liverpool, FACT, the Biennial and James Moores' A Foundation, the Bluecoat's refurbishment, artists' studio groups and much more.[41] Yet the book also sounds a note of caution, Sara Selwood analysing just how dependent this infrastructure is on public subsidy: as the reality of harsh economic times she foresaw starts to be experienced, the sustainability of Liverpool's cultural environment looks more vulnerable.[42] Radical solutions will need to be found, and the city has the recent example of one high-level cultural forum, LARC – the Liverpool Arts Regeneration Consortium – from which to build a collective approach.[43] While practical measures like shared services might help, the real issue of over-reliance on the public purse at a time of stringency will, however, represent the real challenge, amidst fears that the imbalance in funding between London (with its powerful, apparently 'indispensable' flagship arts institutions) and the regions will become more acute, as venues compete for a shrinking pot of resources and are compelled to seek alternative income streams.

The relationship of periphery to centre has long been a bone of contention for the arts, not just in terms of public funding and sponsorship potential, but also to those experiencing a drain of creative talent to the capital, and what is seen as an unhealthy centralisation of media power in London, with the inevitable predominance of coverage of cultural events there at the expense of equally deserving enterprises in the regions. Yet this distance from the metropolis has also allowed regional centres to find their own cultural voice, and with London's pre-eminence as an international art world player, the visual arts outside the capital have prospered most when they have not tried to compete. As Sean Cubitt has observed, 'The anomalous position of London as a world city in a relatively small country, makes it on the one hand the hegemonic power in the construction of taste, but on the other remote from its own hinterland',[44] with the consequence that 'marginal' cities like Liverpool become part of a process of globalisation driven from the bottom up. The *Video Positive* festival, which ran biannually between 1989 and 2000, organised by Merseyside Moviola (later rebranded as FACT – the Foundation for Art and Creative Technology), was an example of this new global connectivity, radical in terms both of its international network that bypassed the old centres of power and its embrace of art exploring video and new digital media. The festival's Collaboration Programme was also pioneering in bringing together contemporary moving image work with local communities. From this relationship sprang Tenantspin, established in 1999 from an initiative by Danish artists' collective Superflex working with high-rise tenants in Liverpool, which went on to have a life of its own as an enduring and endearing community internet television project that continues to explore 'issues around contemporary ways of living and ways of seeing'.[45]

When in the 1980s Thatcherite policies proved especially punitive for Northern cities, art in Liverpool was not slow to respond. As Gabriel Gee has pointed out, the programmes of the Bluecoat – showing local artists while giving 'exposure for oppositional practices such as the Black art movement and engaged feminist practices' – together with those of venues like the Orchard Gallery in Derry, Newcastle's Projects UK, or artist-led initiatives in Glasgow 'reinforced the independence potential of the British regions … it is no coincidence that these developments occurred in the context of acute political tensions'.[46] During this period artists such as Pete Clarke and Sue and David Campbell at the Liverpool Artists Workshop, David Jacques at Kirkby Unemployed Centre, community photography projects like Bootle Arts in Action and the social documentary work commissioned by the Open Eye were part of a network of politically engaged practice in the North – much of it under the radar – that articulated the effects on post-industrial cities of neo-liberal economic policies and central government attacks on local democracy. In the 1980s and 1990s the legacy of Henri's 'happenings' was also invoked, as what was now called 'live art' made this interdisciplinary practice more public and politically attuned, with artists like Visual Stress and Nina Edge taking to the streets with disruptive, processional, participatory interventions interrogating Liverpool's colonial past, its economic malaise and its uncertain future, as well as the new agendas around globalisation and diversity – art events that were radical in form as well as content. Their context informed their oppositional nature, taking place in a city marginalised by political and economic forces and caricatured by a high level of national media prejudice. The impulses for these artists' actions stemmed from an awareness of wider historical and global contexts but were borne essentially out of local experience.

Since its arrival in 1988, Tate Liverpool has undoubtedly had an impact both on the local scene and on how the city is perceived as a serious art player. Its presence, together with that of the Bluecoat, FACT and the John Moores Painting Prize, was instrumental in James Moores' decision to start a contemporary art biennial in Liverpool in 1999. Another example of private patronage (following his grandfather John's example at the Walker), Moores' ambition for the festival – which he also hoped would help to counter Liverpool's propensity for looking inward – was that it would realise the city's potential to host an international art event, the first in the UK of its kind. His belief was based on an abundance of 'found' as well as official art spaces in central Liverpool, the enthusiasm and collaborative working of its arts organisations and, importantly, its edginess and capacity to take risks, to do things differently: 'The Liverpool temperament is well suited to contemporary art. It plays with ideas, flips things over and never takes things at face value. When the Liverpool intelligence is applied to art, it'll do great things.'[47] The status of biennials was becoming increasingly devalued, its format outmoded. However, as part of a new generation of such gatherings, Liverpool's biennial exploited the opportunity to explore new relationships to the local brought about through globalisation. Under the direction of Lewis Biggs[48] the Biennial has sought new ways for art to have a deeper and more meaningful engagement with place, with history and memory and with audience, while emphasising the focus always on the art itself, the majority of this – unlike in most biennials – being new commissions.

One measure of how radical Liverpool Biennial's approach has been is the quality of the art presented, and there are many memorable interventions such as Tatsurou Bashi's *Villa Victoria* (2002), or Rigo 23's caged lions on Lime Street (2006), which remain potent examples of artists contesting the public realm, profoundly reimagining our 'forgotten' memorials. The Biennial has also attempted to create a new, if not necessarily radical, model for its curatorial process, shunning the traditional 'star' curator in favour of a consultative and collaborative approach involving dialogue between local and global expertise. This was criticised when introduced after the first Biennial as lacking a coherent 'authorial' voice, but has since been widely adopted. Embedding the event in the city in the way it has was also seen as a welcome alternative to the more familiar 'off the shelf' or parachuted-in models adopted by other new biennial cities that did not have the advantage of a well-developed arts infrastructure. This local focus,

and the high expectations of public engagement it engenders, has brought
with it attendant dangers of the art becoming too localised, parochial, or
being too wedded to instrumentalist or regeneration agendas, resulting
in compromised or weak work. Critical appraisal of the new biennials
includes scepticism that such large-scale site-specific exhibitions are
not the most appropriate contexts in which to commission art: 'Recent
history has shown that the curatorial emphasis on the city as research
subject, interlocutor, social context and physical site may lead to exhibitions which are too interpretative, too quasianthropological in character.'[49]
There is much to justify this view, yet at the same time the nature of much
'engaged' practice demands greater attention – in order for it to perco-
late or evolve over time – than the critic (particularly the reviewer in a
hurry to catch the train back to London) has time for. Genuinely engaging
community-based projects, such as Eva Kot'átková's *Stories From the Living
Room* at Tate Liverpool in the 2010 Biennial, a compelling intergenera-
tional project involving local people in conversation, which continued to
evolve throughout the exhibition, require time to savour and reflect on,
developing a dynamic with the audience – as well as the participants – that
is quietly radical.

By selecting moments in the early years, in the middle decade and in the
final quarter of the century under discussion, I have tried to show that
a succession of initiatives, from the individual to the institutional, has
impacted on how art has been experienced in Liverpool, in ways that can be
considered radical. Though its members produced little art that we would
now consider groundbreaking, the Sandon's embrace of the modern, and
its vision for the arts concentrated in a single building, laid the foundations for the arts centre that thrives at the Bluecoat today. Through their
patronage of the painting prize at the Walker and the Biennial, the Moores
family's personal passions for contemporary art showed that Liverpool
could command international respect as a serious art player and helped
bring confidence to the city. John Willett's identification of the sizeable gap
between art and everyday life was as pioneering as his study's vision of the
potentialities for art in the city was prescient. This is reflected in the way
that gap has closed in the last forty years and how art has entered public
life: major works like Antony Gormley's *Another Place* on Crosby Beach or
Richard Wilson's ingenious disruption of the facade of an old Yates's Wine
Lodge in Moorfields, *Turning the Place Over*, are thought-provoking interventions into the public realm and not just clever art co-opted into the
service of urban regeneration. Neither of these artists is from Merseyside,

but they illustrate the appetite the city now has for world-class art and the ambition, through institutions like the Biennial, Tate Liverpool, FACT, Open Eye, the Bluecoat, Metal and Ceri Hand Gallery, to realise it by inviting artists, who may come from anywhere, to respond to the Liverpool context. This is not to suggest that in the new global environment the indigenous artistic community is overlooked. On the contrary, in Liverpool as in any other art city this community is its creative lifeblood, and though a few earlier 'radicals' have been discussed – Lipczinski, Bisson, Henri – a list of innovative artists working in the region today would illustrate that it remains a conducive environment to practise in, with its envied contemporary art infrastructure (which can only be enhanced once Liverpool John Moores University's recently opened Art and Design Academy realises its potential). Such a survey of current practice is, however, beyond the scope of this study, other than to highlight artists like Imogen Stidworthy, Paul Rooney, David Jacques, Gina Czarnecki, Pete Clarke, Leo Fitzmaurice, Amrit and Rabindra Kaur Singh and Philip Jeck who prove that it is possible to maintain an international profile from a Liverpool base.[50] An exhibition like *Global Studio* (2010), curated by Sara-Jayne Parsons at the Bluecoat, which presented Liverpool artists collaborating with their counterparts in places such as Berlin, Linz and Karachi, demonstrates the local/global dynamic of contemporary practice. A group like the Royal Standard reflects this globally connected, collectivist approach, their members for example taking a suitcase-sized show on the road to Asia, participating in an artists-led initiative at Tate Modern or putting on critically acclaimed shows at their studios in Liverpool's Vauxhall area. Artists' groups like this are developing different strategies that weave in and out of the traditional white cube space, the type of strategies mentioned at the start of this chapter – and Liverpool provides fertile ground for such exploration. Participation by local people in particular has been at the forefront of much of this new practice, with FACT's aforementioned Tenantspin and the Bluecoat's Blue Room project – a new model for working creatively with adults with learning disabilities as an alternative to day care provision – two among many examples available in the city, of art, often involving international artists, having a tangible social as well as a creative impact. Such programmes run the risk of, and are often criticised for, creating mediocre art, but, as these two examples demonstrate, the results can be as unexpected and innovative as the process is empowering for artists and participants alike.

In the challenging times ahead in a city as heavily dependent on the public purse as Liverpool, with its large voluntary and cultural sectors, participative programmes will come under increasing pressure. It will be interesting to see what form creative responses to the new austerity take, and if they develop in radical directions. We may see an echo of the more politically aligned localised strategies adopted by artists in the 1980s, but now with the advantage of being part of wider networks. As we have seen, Liverpool has at key moments across the past century proved receptive to radical influences in art from outside, using them from time to time to inform and forge an indigenous radicalism. New creative ideas now circulate with increasing speed, are absorbed more readily, and perhaps because of this their radical impact may seem diminished. So, whereas the Post-Impressionists in 1911 or 'happenings' in 1962 either shocked or were seen as the latest strange manifestation from Paris or New York, the very idea of the avant-garde has lost its privileged place amidst the landscape of collapsed modernism and globalisation's rapacious appropriation of the new. Yet, creative innovation and new ways of experiencing art are as likely to emerge in a city like Liverpool as they are in the established vanguard centres.

Notes

1 *Centre of the Creative Universe: Liverpool and the Avant-Garde*, Tate Liverpool exhibition, 2007.

2 George Bernard Shaw, quoted in Roger Fry's 'Art and Socialism', one of his essays in the collection *Vision and Design* (London: Chatto & Windus, 1920), p. 63. Shaw was speaking in Liverpool on 29 December 1911 at the autumn exhibition of the Walker Art Gallery at the invitation of its Director, E. R. Dibden, and, far from endorsing the exhibition, he proceeded to lay into it.

3 Introduction to the Sandon Studios Society's spring exhibition catalogue (n.d.: 1950s), p. 2.

4 'Post-Impressionist Pictures and Others. A Liverpool Exhibition'. Review by B.D.T., *Manchester Guardian* (6 Mar. 1911). I am grateful to Xanthe Brooke, Curator Fine Art (European) at National Museums Liverpool for showing me a copy of this review.

5 Virginia Woolf, *Mr Bennett and Mrs Brown* (London: Hogarth Press, 1924).

6 Frank Rutter, curator of Leeds City Art Gallery, at the opening of a second Post-Impressionist exhibition at the Bluecoat two years later, reported in *Sandon Bulletin*, 5 (June 1913). Rutter was also a leading art critic and activist who used the term 'Post-Impressionist' in print in *Art News* (15 Oct. 1910), three weeks before Fry's exhibition.

7 Quotes from 'Anarchy in the Paint Pot. Liverpool Debate on Post-Impressionism. Amusing Attacks on the New "Art"', *Liverpool Courier* (31 Mar. 1911), p. 9. I am grateful to Jeremy Hawthorn for showing me a copy of this report.

8 'Anarchy in the Paint Pot'. The quote here is from the report, not Legge's words.

9 Introduction to the Sandon Studios Society's spring exhibition catalogue, p. 2.

10 Arnold Bennett in the *Strand Magazine* (Feb. 1913), quoted in the second Post-Impressionist exhibition catalogue at the Bluecoat (15 Feb.–8 Mar. 1913).

11 *Sandon Bulletin*, 5 (June 1913). An anonymous report of the opening of the second Post-Impressionist exhibition is followed by an article entitled 'Post-Impressionism. Second Depressions', credited to A.T.E.

12 Roderick Bisson, *The Sandon Studios and the Arts* (Liverpool: Parry Books, 1965), p.86.

13 William Rothenstein, 'Art and the Municipality', in William Rothenstein, Frank Rutter *et al.*, *The Sport of Civic Life or, Art and the Municipality* (Liverpool: C. W. Sharpe, 1909), pp. 5–9.

14 John Willett, *Art in a City* (London: Methuen, 1967; repr. Liverpool University Press, 2007), p. 65.

15 See Roderick Bisson's colourful history of the Sandon, *The Sandon Studios and the Arts* and W. S. MacCunn's drier account of the transition into the Bluecoat Society of Arts, *Bluecoat Chambers: The Origins and Development of an Art Centre* (Liverpool University Press, 1956).

16 George Melly, *Scouse Mouse, or I Never Got Over It* (London: Weidenfeld & Nicolson, 1984).

17 Maud Budden, 'In Search of Sin: A Cautionary Tale for the Youth of Liverpool', *Liverpolitan* (Jan. 1933): 11.

18 These and many other distinguished visitors to the Bluecoat signed the Sandon Visitors' Book from 1922 to the 1980s, now in the Liverpool Record Office (367 SAN 4/1/5).

19 David Bingham, *1911: Art and Revolution in Liverpool – The Life and Times of Albert Lipczinski* (Bristol: Sansom & Company, 2011). See chapter entitled 'Synthesists'.

20 Willett, *Art in a City*, p. 66.

21 Bingham, *1911: Art and Revolution in Liverpool*. See chapter entitled 'Syndicalists'.

22 The Sandon rejected a request from the Merseyside Foodship for Spain Fund to show the painting on the grounds that 'the interest likely to be shown did not justify the expense. Most people were interested in Spain and many would have been interested in "Guernica"'. Bisson, *The Sandon Studios and the Arts*, p. 195.

23 Ibid.

24 Ann Compton, catalogue to the exhibition, *Roderick Bisson: Telling Lines* (University of Liverpool Art Gallery, 1999), p. 2.

25 Nicholas Horsfield, brochure for the exhibition, *Roderick Bisson: A Survey of his Work, 1930s–1950s* (Liverpool: Walker Art Gallery, 1987).

26 Barrie Sturt-Penrose, '"Undiscovered Genius" Shocks Art Gallery', *Observer* (28 Jan. 1968).

27 Lewis Biggs, 'The Magic Ingredient – What You See is What You Get', catalogue to the exhibition, *John Moores Painting Prize 2010* (Liverpool: Walker Art Gallery, 2010), p. 134.

28 John Moores, letter to the *Sunday Times* (7 Aug. 1957).

29 See Matthew H. Clough and Colin Fallows (eds), *Stuart Sutcliffe: A Retrospective* (Liverpool: Victoria Gallery and Museum/Liverpool University Press, 2008), which includes essays by Bryan Biggs and Jon Savage concerning Sutcliffe's art/pop connection.

30 Pete Brown, *White Rooms & Imaginary Westerns* (London: JR Books, 2010).

31 Edward Lucie-Smith (ed.), *The Liverpool Scene* (London: Rapp & Carroll, 1967; 2nd impression 1971), p. 3.

32 Allan Kaprow, letter to Adrian Henri dated 5 Sept. 1966, in the collection of Catherine Marcangeli. Kaprow's son, Bram Kaprow, was at the 2010 Liverpool Biennial re-enacting some of his father's performances with Tania Bruguera and other artists.

33 These details of Henri's performances are from the artist's notes, in the collection of Catherine Marcangeli.

34 *Adrian Henri, Environments and Happenings* (London: Thames & Hudson, 1974).

35 Arthur Dooley, quoted in *Arthur Dooley Sculpture Trail Guide* (2008). Dooley formed the Railings Union with painter Brian Burgess in 1968.

36 Willett, *Art in a City*, p. 2.

37 In the introduction to the republished *Art in a City* (2007) and in the introduction, co-written with Julie Sheldon, to *Art in a City Revisited* (Liverpool University Press: 2009).

38 Willett, *Art in a City*, p. 66.

39 Ibid., p. 40.

40 Biggs and Sheldon, *Art in a City Revisited*.

41 Lewis Biggs, 'Individuals and Institutions in Dialogue', ibid.

42 Sara Selwood, 'Art City?', ibid.

43 LARC comprises seven of the major arts institutions in the city.

44 Sean Cubitt, 'Liverpool Glocal', in Biggs and Sheldon, *Art in a City Revisited*, pp. 117–20.

45 See <www.tenantspin.org>.

46 Gabriel Gee, 'Artistic Strategies within Glocalisation in the United Kingdom', *One Piece at a Time*, issue 1. <www.geiab.org>. Accessed 4 May 2010.

47 James Collard interview, 'James Moores: The Visionary, Local Boy and Littlewoods Heir James Moores Turns Cultural Impresario to Bring Buzz, Art and Artists to Liverpool', *The Times* (10 Nov. 2007).

48 Tony Bond curated the first Biennial in 1999 and all subsequent festivals were directed by Lewis Biggs.

49 Claire Doherty, Carlos Basualdo, Julie Ault and Lars Bang Larsen, 'Curating Wrong Places ... Or Where Have All the Penguins Gone?', in Paul O'Neill (ed.), *Curating Subjects* (London: Open Editions, 2006).

50 Interestingly, four Turner prize winners (Fiona Banner, Phil Collins, Tony Cragg and Mark Leckey) are from Merseyside, but all left to study art and have few connections with the city's art scene, Cragg being the only one with work permanently sited there.

4

The Revolution Will Not Be Dramatised

Roger Hill

– Meaning what?

– *Give me your proposition again.*

– 'Theatre on Merseyside has acted as a significant conduit for the region's radical impulses.'

– *That's what I mean. No way does theatre radicalise things.*

– Why not?

– *It's become the subsidised pastime of the arts-aware, a commodity amongst many other cultural 'products'.*

– You're saying this about a city whose Playhouse Theatre is the oldest repertory theatre still in existence and a city which has produced plays by Alan Bleasdale, Willy Russell, Jimmy McGovern, and others?

– *I am, and there's a big flaw in an argument which cites those writers, which I will deal with in due course. But I have a better proposition for you.*

– Your alternative then?

– *'The region's radical impulses have often found dramatic form in an era of multiple performative media.'*

– Meaning what, then?

– *Screen-based work, like film and television, live art, spectacle and events.*

– And theatre has no part in that?

– *I'm saying that they have something that theatre lacks.*

– Go on ...

– *Here's another proposition for you – 'There is something we might call a "Radical Moment".'*

– Which is ...?

– *Radicalism is not a quality, and, even as a tendency, does not achieve anything. It's only when it happens, when it produces a moment, that it's effectual as a cultural and political force. And for this to be the case there needs to be an amalgam of a number of elements.*

– And they are?

– *They are: radical content; a broad democratised audience; a dramatic structure which dislocates expectations; a medium or art form which can embrace or develop a relationship with popular forms; a production machinery which is open to experiment (and not economically dependent on commodi-fication). And, social outcomes which are historically irreversible, progressive.*

– Always the generalist, aren't you? I'm making a case for local radicalism and you haven't cited a single piece of evidence yet. Are you saying that there has been no radical performance on Merseyside?

– *No, I'm just saying that the theatres are the least likely places to find it.*

– All right, let's take this 'democratised audience' of yours and let's look back for a moment. I am attempting a historical survey, after all. Wasn't the audience for the Everyman Theatre in the seventies democ-ratised? And what about the Merseyside Unity Theatre which started out in the thirties as the Merseyside Left Theatre? Liverpool has a history of democratic theatre initiatives. And, if you must keep to the present, what about the Royal Court, which is currently drawing in a big popular audience for Scouse plays and Scousified dramas? Doesn't popular equate with radical?

– *It can do, but it doesn't have to. And in the case of the Royal Court nobody has claimed that a lot of local people laughing out loud at the local stereotypes is radical. Populist but not revolutionary, I'd say.*

– I'm not sure Nicky Allt would agree with you.[1] These plays are the descendants of the Everyman repertory productions of the 1970s. Try this for size then – 'Radical theatre requires a Popular Theatre Moment'.

– *Well, some time soon I might agree with you that the most radical thing about theatre on Merseyside is, or has been, the audiences. And, yes, if Liverpool is a city built on the rock of family then local audiences are a kind of family. But family and family life are not universally good, and families don't always hang together. Scouseness needs scrutiny or it collapses in on itself. And it's still consumption of a commodity. In its heyday the Everyman could count on a loyal audience who would go to see plays there because it was the Everyman, in the same way as people would go to Eric's[2] – or the Cavern before that – to see bands just because of where they were playing. But that's all fragmented now, in the same way as people channel hop when they're watching television, even assuming that they watch anything live. Now people go to plays not theatre. A 'Popular Theatre Moment' isn't enough to dignify local theatre with the word radical.*

– So, I'm going to challenge you to say what's missing. But before I do I want to remind you that locality involves uniqueness, and local mythology here makes a big deal of the uniqueness of Scouse. Merseyside has a natural theatre – Orange Lodge marches, river arrivals and departures, football,

Aintree, the crazy *passagietta* of weekend nights – things that are special to here. Isn't, or wasn't, there a certain radicalism in putting these things on stage, in plays like Willy Russell's *Stags And Hens*, for example?

– *Your 'crazy* passagietta' *isn't limited to Merseyside, you know. And how many local plays have featured the rest? Well, now I say it, there's a lot of football theatre about currently, but ... anyway, the 'natural theatre' comes with its stereotypes, and theatre which relies on its appeal is basically conservative. Not that there's anything wrong with self-conservation, especially when you're a city outlawed by central government. But it's not radical – or only radical resistance, not radical transformation – and nowhere near being revolutionary.*

– You introduced the word 'revolutionary'. It's not in my brief. Has theatre ever been revolutionary, by the way?

– *It's been a key element in revolutionary struggle – look at Russia in the 1920s. And it played its part in radical social change in, oh, where do I start? – the Market Theatre of Johannesburg, New York in the sixties and seventies, Berlin or Paris cabaret between the wars. And much of that wasn't theatre as you might define it, which is why, or at least how, it was radical.*

– I'm having Johannesburg and Berlin, the struggles against repressive regimes, but New York?

– *Well, that's another kind of radicalism, about which we might agree in due course, and one which Liverpool has had some part in; but let's concentrate on struggle for a minute. When the city was really outlawed in the seventies and eighties there was a lot of vacancy in the backdraft of the city's decline, and theatre did little enough to mobilise the population. Help it to cry about its wounds, maybe – a response to a perceived right-wing drift which people felt powerless to oppose, I think – but not activate, not mobilise. If you're going to transform you're involved in irreversible social outcomes, ones with progressive results, felt by everybody. Listen, back to my essential elements for radicalism, for a moment. I'll give you another proposition – 'There is something we might call "Radical Content".' Without that, local theatre is just genre painting, which is what I'd argue local theatre has often become.*

– Define 'Radical Content'.

– *It's political, for a start. It has overt agendas. Here it has to do with the Labour Party, with city politics, with women and their rights, with inequalities of income and opportunity. There's a crucial element of non-fiction about it, even if it's not fully documentary. Like a local radio station, a city's drama is as good as the events thrown at it. And this city has had its full share of radical events.*

– You're talking about the Toxteth riots, Militant Tendency, the docks dispute, Hillsborough, the opening of the Roman Catholic Cathedral,

Jamie Bulger?

– *And I'm talking about the slave trade. And any number of labour disputes and protests throughout the twentieth century here.*

– And unemployment.

– *Not an event really. Something like Jim Morris's* Blood On The Dole *did a fair job of it.[3] I suppose I'm talking about anywhere where issues of money and power and accountability are played out in human terms. Have we dealt with any of that sufficiently? Because if we haven't we can't claim radicalism here.*

– Local theatre has touched on all of that.

– *'Touched on' – exactly. As with all content it all depends on what you do with it. It's me doing all the propositioning now. 'Radicalism can only happen when the parameters are challenged or changed.'*

– Is this your 'dramatic structure which dislocates expectations'? I've been taking notes, you see.

– *Part of it, I suppose. Take that thing about audiences. A lot of people went to the Everyman in its populist heyday but, for every theatre-aware individual there were many theatre-unaware, theatre-resistant types, you might say. That particular set of parameters needed challenging. Theatre had to get out of the theatres to reach them.*

– And when the Everyman closed for its 1970s rebuild, it did.

– *Yes, and a classic like Claire Luckham's* Tuebrook Tanzi *was the result.[4] Popular theatre amongst the populace. In pubs and clubs. And, note, it had radical content.*

– Well, the Blackie took theatre into the parks.

– *The Blackie.[5] Ah, yes, back to them in a minute. It's about a change of performance spaces but it's also a change of context. And it all depends on radical content. At its best now local theatre and all that live art, and alternative performance, is more on the nail than anything in the 1960s or seventies. It happens in unconventional spaces, and addresses key issues. But it's often not what I'd call theatre.*

– So, what about, say, the opening event of the Capital of Culture year.[6] That was theatre. And democratic – free, anyway.

– *Theatrical. But not radical theatre. They gave it a good go, I'll say that for them, though. It was a celebration but, as I've said many times before, celebration without criticism is not enough – for radicalism at least.*

– And the spider? La Machine?[7]

– *Spectacle, pure spectacle. They tried to bolt on a bit of localised story but I'm not sure many people cottoned on to it. You've heard the phrase 'bread and circuses'?*

– Now, don't patronise me. I'm just trying to get at what you mean by these 'challenged parameters'. And I'm trying to tie you down to some actual examples.

– *Right. Example 1. You change the way theatre is managed. In the early eighties, four men took over the Playhouse, playwrights all, determined to manage not just the scripts but the running of the theatre, as an artist-led enterprise.*[8]

– It wasn't a particular success, in the end?

– *It was an experiment. It tried to break the mould.*

– And not much in that line has happened since.

– *The Gorbals lot used to finance their productions from donations from the community, though they didn't try that here.*[9] *And now we're all subsidy dependent. But here's another example: to challenge parameters, you put the audience on stage.*

– You're talking about Community Theatre here?

– *Well, broadly, but Merseyside hasn't a particularly distinguished history of community theatre. The Gorbals people came in the early eighties, to Bootle, and put the locals on the stage of the Everyman, but it didn't start a rush. And Ann Jellicoe didn't work in theatres so much as the open air. Welfare State didn't start, or base itself, in Liverpool. And the city never generated Theatre in Education in the same way as Leeds or Coventry, probably due to the backwardness of the education provision here in the sixties and seventies. No, I'm referring to getting local people to create their own theatre. Here's the example. You mentioned the Toxteth riots. More than a year after the events the Everyman, and later the Playhouse, main companies, and since them a few others, had a go at the riots. But the most immediate, most exciting – theatrically exciting – dramatisation of the riots was barely two months after they happened.*

– Produced by whom?

– *By the Everyman Youth Theatre:* Suffer The Children. *And not least because it was current and made by the same people – young people – who had played such a major part in the events.*

– And you had much to do with that, I seem to remember ...

– *Me, or someone quite like me, yes. But, contradict me if you dare, you were involved too. I'd argue that Merseyside in the 1980s was the crucible of a new generation of youth theatre, plays and performers, and that was, at its best, radical in all the ways I'm suggesting.*

– It needs to be good ...

– *And it was. But being good is not enough. It needs to be real. And that will show in the performances. There has been a particular breed of local performer attuned to radical performance, like George Costigan, Pete Postlethwaite, Drew Schofield. Their involvement helped local theatre to avoid stereotypes and create not only genre painting but performance which touches some truth about the way we live together.*

– *Blood Brothers* – that seems to fit the bill.

– *It started out as children's theatre, I'll give you that. But apply my criteria to that, or any production, and draw your own conclusions. And actually Willy Russell may not have been aiming for radicalism, not in the terms I'm using.*

– There has to be an appetite for radicalism in the city. Another proposition, then – 'Liverpool offers a ready home for theatrical experiment'.

– *And that's, by definition, mainly from the outside. It was Yoko Ono, after all, who gave the earliest demonstration of performance art here, in 1967, at the Bluecoat.*[10] *That's where New York comes in, the crucible of performance experiment. Fluxus and stuff. And the Blackie, yes, has opened up to some of that.*

– And, according to you, that's not theatre.

– *Well, most experimental performance is part of a circuit of arts centres and universities. Adrian Henri was your man for all that, from those odd performances with the Liverpool Scene*[11] *to poetry happenings, but it's all associated with the 'art' crowd, and we're lucky here that people are reasonably indulgent towards local artists and their apparent eccentricities. Now the city is awash with live art events and interventions and installations. And the Liverpool Biennial is as much about performance as it is about fine art: much of it is theatrical.*

– I must say, you don't sound so impressed.

– *It's what you said before, it has to be done well, and it should still meet my five criteria. It is in democratic spaces, a lot of it, and challenges parameters. A good proportion of it pays attention to popular forms, even as it criticises them, but it's just that the nature of expectation has changed. The status quo or, if you like, the lay audience who, in places like streets and informal locations, can be very numerous, have got used to interventions and installations. They have their responses ready, which may be routine indifference, or a quickness to take up a photo opportunity and then move on, or they have learned to behave like a live art audience.*

– Which makes it *not* radical?

– *Exactly. What I will give you is that the city has seized upon a number of radicals and radical techniques and made them its own. Now here the Everyman has got a claim. That informal performance style of the Alan Dossor and Chris Bond period,*[12] *a mixture of music hall, poor theatre and cabaret, didn't start here. It came from Brecht, if you want to go that far back, and had already been pioneered in Britain by Joan Littlewood – and Peter Cheeseman in Stoke at the Victoria Theatre. But the theatre here made it its own and, yes, used it, like Cheeseman did, to focus on local issues, like, say, Kirkby and rehousing and corruption in* Love and Kisses From Kirkby,[13] *and to shape classical productions too.*

– And that was the style the Royal Shakespeare Company used in *Nicholas Nickleby.*

– *Yes, it travelled from Liverpool, but with budgets the local theatres would have died for. And the technique effectively died in the travelling. But it was here.*

– And so was Ken Campbell.

– *You could have fired that one at me ages ago. Yes, Ken Campbell has the greatest potential to be considered the creator of radical local theatre. His Science Fiction Theatre work was genuinely challenging and reached a motley audience, small but representative of a wider demographic, and in an unconventional space, on Mathew Street, above a shop.[14] It appealed to the surrealist ethos which lurks in the city's psyche.*

– And then Ken came back and made real theatre.

– *Now I think you're being provocative. Yes, he came back for nearly two seasons to the Everyman.*

– And that was radical – the seats taken out, the *Warp* sequence, newts swimming on stage, a disco pantomime[15] – there's your parameters altered, expectations challenged, popular forms referenced, the element of real fantasy which always strikes a chord with audiences ...

– *Maybe so, but, you know, the audiences didn't go with it, as far as they needed to anyway for good box office. Ken beat a dignified retreat, and the theatre went back to a more conventionally populist style.*

– But lives were changed.

– *Individual lives are always changed by theatre, any kind of performance. For it to be radical whole swathes of the population need to be activated. That's what I mean about immutable change. Our imported geniuses have been influential but not radical in their effects on city life. Robyn Archer brought in the Builders Association from the US in advance of the Capital of Culture year, and again audiences were limited.[16]*

– All right, all right, all right. Everything you say local theatre hasn't been, locally produced television and film has been. I propose this: 'Liverpool's principal contribution to radical drama has been in screen-based work.'

– *A mighty proposition! And that, my friend, is what I was going to tell you – although I'd put a question mark by 'film', and query whether half of the things I think you're referring to were actually 'locally produced'. But, yes, Merseyside has been one of the key centres for radical screenwork for the last forty years.*

– And suddenly a democratic audience, radical content, changed parameters ... *The Boys from the Blackstuff*. Oh and of course *Z Cars* ... *Brookside!*

– *Hold on there! I sense a Road to Damascus moment happening here. But don't get too dewy-eyed yet, mate. There's questions to be asked about some of that screenwork. And, please to note, the pantheon of local writers you cited way back when have achieved their eminence through television and film ...*

– ... but would never have had the chance to work in that if they hadn't had stage success.

– *Not then – now, maybe. Theatre as an incubator for screen talent – is that a good enough recommendation? Is it radical even? Didn't the democratised audience come from television viewers? There's no denying that* Boys from the Blackstuff, *in all its versions, changed perceptions worldwide. Suddenly, the city – its actual material manifestation out there, behind the characters, with them an expression of it – the city becomes the focus. That's the strong suit of television.* Brookside *achieved something of the same effect.*

– But not *Hollyoaks*?

– *No way. A lesbian kiss has its impact in the real world, a localised plague not so much, and beefcake antics, no way.*[17] *And not really – for all their well-intentioned populism – most of the locally produced films. And the backdrop has been co-opted for a thousand other films. That's the slippery nature of location filming. Liverpool will agree to be whatever you want it to be when there's money on offer. But you're missing the chance to have one over on me here.*

– Give me a clue.

– *Remember I said, 'A production machinery which is open to experiment (and not economically dependent on commodification)'.*

– Well, then television is all about commodity. It's not radical.

– *No, it's not, by its nature. It's an industry, and it involves an elaborate and expensive production machinery which dilutes radical impulses through economic strictures.*

– And you're advocating it as Merseyside's radical cutting edge.

– *But, you see, there are loopholes and strategies. A healthy medium ...*

– This from a dedicated anti-capitalist ...

– *Thanks for the character reference. I'll ignore that. A healthy medium relies on failure as well as success. It thrives on the successes and spits out the failures.* Z Cars *was a calculated risk. It was cheap, and it caught on. If it hadn't we wouldn't be talking about it now. And it was on the BBC, during one of its more adventurous periods. It captured audiences. It was shorter than plays in the theatre and suited the attention spans of our time. It was cheap in the way that* Brookside, *with its estate of houses, was a cheap way of doing soap opera. Not for nothing was Phil Redmond a former quantity surveyor. And he set a precedent in television.*

– He set up his own company.

– *And thereby controlled all aspects of that production machinery. And all around him writers like Alan Beasdale and Willy Russell were insisting on a say in production decisions, like casting and choice of director, when their scripts were produced for television and film. And now one of the most successful men in television, and a Scouser through and through, is Jimmy McGovern, who's producing, running a production company. He often works with the BBC. He doesn't get involved in casting but he adopts writers and comes up with ideas and works on them with the writers until they're successful. For radicalism to achieve radical outcomes the whole process of actioning needs to be radicalised. That's the radical strategy – 'control of the means of production'. Remember that one?*

– Pure socialism. Ken Loach is another like that.

– *Ken Loach works here a lot. Like John McGrath in theatre,*[18] *he adopted the city as a favoured location for some of his work. And both of them have dealt with local issues. In McGovern's case, some of the ones you mentioned quite directly – the docks dispute, Hillsborough – and some more indirectly. But film hasn't expressed the local zeitgeist as well as television. A few honourable exceptions, maybe* – Business as Usual, Priest,[19] – *but beyond that ...*

– Listen, this has got to be about the uniqueness of the city.

– *Make performance too unique and localised and it has got nothing to say to the rest of the world. Radical is about roots – but the roots of all our culture, a global culture even. A world city should be able to manage this.*

– Then I'll give you my final proposition – 'Liverpool is a unique context for theatre'.

– *Go easy on that 'theatre' word. You may be talking about all that other stuff as well.*

– Maybe I am. All your screen-based work – like film and television, live art, spectacle and events, as well as theatre – they all need to grow out of, address, if you like, things that are typical and, all together, a unique profile of the city. I'm talking, for example, about Liverpool's constant emphasis on the individual. It's not as co-operative in its culture as, say, Tyneside. It likes protagonists and the consequences of their actions.

– *I'd agree. Go on.*

– Its radicalism is oppositional and its unity comes from having an outside enemy.

– *Yes, again.*

– Catholicism. It's a special kind here. Community Catholicism, but with dark depths.

– *Like most Catholicism, I'd say, but then I'm a free thinker. Maybe Catholicism helped us to a major guilt complex when we fell from grace as the major city of Empire.*

– Strong women. There's nowhere quite like the place for strong, feisty women, and they carry their own dramas with them. And gambling. That's a local culture with its own inflections.

– *Both products of a major port city. I wonder about Glasgow, though …*

– There's a different kind of working-class here. The industry was different – not so much about manufacturing.

– *And therefore a different kind of man. Ever since the city's historical decline, anyway. So now there's a kind of post-masculinism, which often looks, in these 'scally and charlie' times,*[20] *like rank narcissism. But then Mersey men were never the tough guys really.*

– So, on this we agree: 'there is a unique complexion to the city, and the best drama made here reflects it …'

– *Sounds like a proposition to me.*

– Taking into account, of course, your 'radical' criteria.

– *Careful with those quotation marks, you! But I will go with you on all of that, and take it all one step further. Suppose for a moment that there was something particularly unique about the actual location of Merseyside. I'm no advocate of Scouseness – 'In England but not of England', or however it goes – but there are places in the world which are thought to be in some kind of psychic network, Weimar is one, places where, if we were getting poetic, we could say there is a particular ripple in the psychic universe. It may be that the city is one of them. Maybe it has something to do with being a port, where the land meets the sea, fluid meets solid, flux and fixity. And everything that happens here, and everybody who really immerses themselves in the place, whether they're incomers or natives, partakes of that peculiarity.*

– And is that radical?

– *Not of itself, but it is a special kind of space–time location, where innovation and a particular kind of fantasy can flourish and awkward questions can get asked (and even answered), and a unique kind of compact is established between the people and their artists, and statements of some brilliance can be made which will be heard beyond the boundaries. It doesn't make the place pre-eminent. But it's a mark of some distinction, and worth having after all the imperialist brouhaha has died down. Radicalism is an aggregation of eventualities, a complexion, and Liverpool has many of the elements of radicalism, and has a unique profile as a result. It's not necessarily infectious or influential but it has its place in the widest of histories.*

    – So you're not so much the materialist, after all?

    – *I see the bigger picture. The revolution will not be dramatised, but your theatre, and all the rest, can draw upon all that psychic energy, that kink in the ether, and that's not true of everywhere – when it's good, of course, which it hasn't always been. It's a sloppy place – too many compromises, too much kowtowing, despite all the bluster, to other people's agendas, too much buried guilt. But when it taps into the, whatever ...*

    – Oh, you're off on one there. Nobody's going to take psychic ripples seriously.

    – *Well, it's where we've got to start if we're going to produce the radicalism we need now – whatever we have to do to jump-start renewal in an age of recession and oppression.*

    – The renewal has started?

    – *The briefest hint of it.*

    – You know, I think I might not write this thing after all – I'll leave it to someone else.

    – *No, write it. Waste of all this bloody argument otherwise.*

Notes

1 The reference here is to Nicky Allt, the writer and producer of a number of plays on Merseyside themes, including *Brick Up The Mersey Tunnels* and *One Night In Istanbul*.

2 Eric's Club was, like the Cavern, on Mathew Street in Liverpool, and was the focus for the city's punk and post-punk music scene from 1976 until it was closed in 1980.

3 Jim Morris's play, first presented at Liverpool's Unity Theatre in September 1981, is more widely known in its screen version produced in 1995.

4 Tuebrook is a district in Liverpool. The play is better known in its later version, *Trafford Tanzi*. A version was tried out in New York in 1983 as *Teaneck Tanzi* starring Debbie Harry.

5 The Great George's Project based in a former Liverpool church (the Blackie) began in 1968 as one of the UK's earliest community arts projects. It recently rebranded itself as the Black-E.

6 This event on 11 January 2008 was a multimedia and live spectacle staged in front of St George's Hall for an estimated 50,000 spectators.

7 A giant mechanical spider, *La Princesse*, was one of the public spectacles commissioned for Liverpool's Capital of Culture year in 2008. It was produced by François Delarozière for La Machine.

8 The speaker is here referring to Alan Bleasdale, Chris Bond, Bill Morrison and Willy Russell, who took over the Playhouse Theatre in 1981. Ros Merkin, the theatre's current chronicler, points out that Chris Bond was in fact the Artistic Director, and the others Associate Directors.

9 Bill Dolce of Bootle Art In Action suggests that this refers to a one-night performance of a community play by the Bootle Festival Society entitled *Scouse Scrooge* at
   the Everyman Theatre in February 1982. Three members of Artworks, a Glasgow-
   based theatre production company, helped the Bootle Festival Society to produce
   its community play entitled *Forever Bootle* in 1981. This play was not shown at the
   Everyman Theatre.

10 The speaker here is incorrect in his reference. Adrian Henri started his 'happenings'
   in 1962 at Hope Hall (which later became the Everyman Theatre) and elsewhere,
   well in advance of Yoko Ono's visit.

11 'The Liverpool Scene' refers to the celebrated poetry-rock group, which included
   Adrian Henri, Andy Roberts, Mike Evans, Mike Hart and others. It was active from
   1967 to 1970.

12 Alan Dossor was Artistic Director of the Everyman Theatre from 1970 to 1975 and
   Chris Bond from 1976 to early 1979.

13 Kirkby is a 'new town' on the north-eastern edge of the Merseyside conurbation and
   is now part of the Metropolitan Borough of Knowsley.

14 The Science Fiction Theatre of Liverpool was formed in 1976 and its main production, performed in an upstairs space on Liverpool's Mathew Street, was *Illuminatus*,
   adapted by Campbell and Chris Langham from the *Illuminatus!* trilogy of novels by
   Robert Shea and Robert Anton Wilson.

15 *The Warp* was another contemporary-historical epic by Ken Campbell and Neil
   Oram. The newts featured in *War with the Newts* and the 'disco pantomime' was
   Disco Queen.

16 This refers to one of the events produced by the Australian performer and festival
   director during her brief tenure as Artistic Director of Liverpool's Capital of Culture
   programme, from 2004 to 2006.

17 The speaker here is referring to two incidents dramatised in *Brookside* and, more or
   less derogatively, to aspects of *Hollyoaks*.

18 John McGrath became nationally famous for his work with Scottish theatre company
   7.84, but was born in Birkenhead and directed seminal productions at the Everyman
   Theatre and many episodes of *Z Cars*.

19 These films were released for national distribution in 1987 and 1995 respectively.

20 The speaker seems to be referring here to the species of proletarian youth and the
   paranoia-inducing effects of the over-consumption of cocaine.

5

The Heavens Above and the Dirt Below: Liverpool's Radical Music

Paul Du Noyer

The River Mersey is a radical waterway, a troublemaker. Its tides are swift and sudden, its depths are treacherous. And the current is always changing colour. Day and night, the Mersey shifts a colossal quantity of sand, scooping it up from Liverpool Bay, dragging it up to Runcorn then hauling it back out to sea again.

Thanks to this eternal, Sisyphean task the surface may look as brown as ferry-boat tea, when the tides are racing and full of their muddy burden. But later comes a peaceful point of stasis between the ebb and flood, when those particles sink and settle awhile. Given a sunny sky you might then find the Mersey wears an azure shade, almost Mediterranean. This has been the river's job, long before men built their big dock buildings out into the stream, and it is what the river will still be doing when Albert and the Graces have crumbled. The river reflects the heavens while it churns the dirt below.

The River Mersey is like a psychic continuation of the Mississippi, another blue-and-brown highway of musical legend, to which the town of Liverpool once owed much of its merchant fortune. Blues music took shape along those slave-state banks and its legacy found a welcome, famously, in the singing city on the Mersey. Among the most persistent of the African-American blues stories was that of the Travellin' Man, sometimes called Po' Shine: he was a kind of superhuman scamp whose wit and strength could out master anyone. This character crops up in lots of songs – his appeal to a population in bondage is not hard to fathom – but he is forever doing one strange thing. He is escaping to Liverpool. He swims the ocean. He hitches a ride on the Titanic, jumps ship before the iceberg hits, walks on a whale. He is last seen shooting dice in a Liverpool bar.[1]

You have to conclude that Po' Shine would have felt at home there. This is a radical place, of dramatic buildings and unruly people. Where other towns regard entertainment as a luxury, in Liverpool it is a necessity and pursued with sleepless vigour. Authority is mocked and order is subverted; the English language is mangled and refashioned; storytellers hold the room and new songs are written every day. In the race memory of every citizen are the days when immigrants brushed past emigrants in a teeming two-way swarm, when poverty stalked the alleys while wealth took its leisure. Its history is peopled by privateers, slave traders, abolitionists and philanthropists, agitators, fighters and artists of every sort.

We might expect such a city to be rife with radical music – radical in the political sense – and there is certainly a rich catalogue of protest songs by local artists, from John Lennon's neo-sea-shanty, 'Give Peace A Chance' to Elvis Costello and Clive Langer's 'Shipbuilding' (responses to the Vietnam and Falklands wars respectively). We might expect the music to be radical in the artistic sense, too: Liverpool is a place of extremes, with a reckless streak in its nature. And it is true that some of the greatest innovations in popular song can be traced to this city, most obviously in the groundbreaking records of the Beatles' later period, including *Revolver* and the White Album.

And yet, the dominant impression is that Liverpool's popular music is most of all melodic. To generalise, it tends to dreaminess more often than to anger. It shows a great attachment to 'retro' elements. And it is nearly always of the mainstream (though we could make a plausible case to say that Liverpool helped to define that very mainstream in the first place). 'Radical', then, would not be the first word that springs to mind. In late 2010, a Google search for the words 'Liverpool avant-garde' brings up a multitude of links. However, they mostly relate to a popular chain of hairdressing salons.

There is a duality in the city's music, a contrast between the grit of its people, with their workaday concerns, and the romantic escapism inherent in their songs. I am personally put in mind of the huge, overhanging sky, with its psychedelic Celtic sunsets, and the cramped streets and houses underneath. Ian McCulloch, the singer of Echo & the Bunnymen, describes Liverpool as a city of daydreamers. His band has done as much as any act to encourage the 'cosmic' tag that Liverpool musicians attract. Among his most gifted contemporaries is Mick Head, of Shack, who said in 1992: 'I'm into escapism ... I take so many drugs, when I go to bed at night, I don't dream. It's like I do all my dreaming in the day.'[2]

Yet both those bands are inspired by the real city in which they still live. They are doing, through music, the same thing as the River Mersey. They reflect the heavens while they churn the dirt below.

In the eyes of the wider world, Liverpool music is synonymous with the Beatles. Despite the wealth of important music created in the city before and since the group's eight-year reign over pop from 1962, they absolutely shape the narrative. So we can take their pre-eminence as read, and the stunning durability of their success, now manifest in digital technologies undreamt of in the time of Merseybeat. But what of their radical credentials? It is not uncommon to hear voices in the city complain of the Beatles' omnipresent tourist industry, alleging a baleful, inhibiting influence on present-day creativity.

There are many others who embody the musical soul of Liverpool: Billy Fury, the Real Thing, the Zutons, to name a few. But in the scale of their popularity the Beatles outweigh everyone else put together. They are worth examining, as well, because the sheer breadth of their output (especially if we add the subsequent solo music) represents a sort of radical ideal: innovate, dare to dream, take astonishing risks, but above all carry the people with you. Radicalism and popularity are never sure to go hand-in-hand. But, in the artistic sense of radicalism (and the political, in John Lennon's case), here was an act who pushed boundaries while remaining absolutely central.

In this they kept faith with their home town's habitual populism. Entertainment in Liverpool is strongly communal. Whether expressed in Paul McCartney's fun-for-all-the-family numbers, or in John Lennon's calculated collectivism ('We all shine on', 'Power to the People', 'Imagine all the people'), they addressed themselves to the masses. Even George Harrison's adoption of Eastern mysticism kept an eye on accessibility: 'Show me that I'm everywhere,' he sang, 'and get me home for tea.'[3] (He also steered the Radha Krishna Temple into the Top 10.) In the best traditions of Scouse show business, the Beatles liked to reach the farthest corners of the ballroom.

In their different ways, Lennon and McCartney enact the contrasting sides of Liverpool life: the former a freelance provocateur, the latter a champion of neighbourhood and kinship. John's political radicalism became explicit in the Beatles' final years (although, at the point of 1968's 'Revolution 1', he was still ambivalent about his support for the cause). It would certainly dominate his early solo output, numbers such as 'Working Class Hero' and 'Gimme Some Truth' sound-tracking his well-publicised peace campaigning with Yoko Ono. He embraced feminism ('Woman is the Nigger of the World') and condemned British troops in Northern Ireland ('Sunday Bloody Sunday'). He also made some excursions into sonic radicalism, the White Album's extraordinary collage 'Revolution 9' being the supreme example, as well as a series of avant-garde recordings with Ono.

Despite such challenging gestures, Lennon remained at heart a great communicator, whose dearest wish was to see compositions like 'Give Peace a Chance', 'Imagine' and 'Happy Xmas (War is Over)' become new anthems of the masses. McCartney, on the other hand, while he has seldom strayed far in that direction (the proselytising 'Give Ireland Back to the Irish' remains highly atypical of his catalogue), repeatedly reminds us that he, more than John, was the musical pathfinder, a devotee of Berio and Stockhausen. Indeed, McCartney has continued to dabble in surprising musical projects, from formal classical pieces to dance floor electronica. His image as the 'play-it-safe' Beatle severely underestimates the work of Liverpool's most adventurous (and simultaneously most successful) musical son.

What both writers had in common was a thoroughly Liverpudlian notion of solidarity. It is a mystery that the great Fruit Machine of Fate could produce four male Beatles, in the city of Liverpool and Everton football teams, without a single committed fan among them. Nevertheless, the Beatles understood the controlling passions of the place they grew up in. In the 1960s, despite the bubble of Beatlemania, they knew all about the resurgent Kop at Bill Shankly's Anfield and the rival triumphs of Goodison Park. Between 1963 and 1965, national media applied the catch-phrase 'Mersey Sound' to beat groups and football crowds equally. This terrific terrace fellowship, most sublimely caught in Gerry and The Pacemakers' 'You'll Never Walk Alone', was not lost on Lennon and McCartney, who replicated its cadences in 'Yellow Submarine' (a song adapted by Scouse football fans to the present day) and the prolonged coda to 'Hey Jude'.

A glance at the Beatles' career might suggest a transition from showbiz caution to wild artistic daring: as the suits and ties gave way to exotic finery, so the songs progressed from conventional (if effervescent) pop to outright experimentalism, from 'I Want to Hold Your Hand' to 'Tomorrow Never Knows'. But actually the Beatles already had roots in a certain 'arty' scene that most of their Merseybeat peers did not. Where the Searchers, Gerry and the Pacemakers, the Fourmost *et al.*, were generally working-class Scousers with a faith in straightforward entertainment, Lennon and McCartney were denizens of a beatnik clique surrounding the School of Art that John attended. (Paul, two years younger and still at the grammar school next door, was smitten by student chic: the French section of 'Michelle' was an attempt to seem sophisticated when strumming at college parties.)

In their circle, as teenage rockers, were poets and painters; they mooched between the scruffy ateliers of Gambier Terrace and the semi-bohemian alehouses of Hope Street. Even their eventual home base, the Cavern Club, some distance 'downtown', was initially conceived as a quixotic homage to

the Left Bank jazz cellars of Paris. The Beatles' name had multiple conno-
tations, but their bass-player Stuart Sutcliffe, like their friends Bill Harry
and the poet Royston Ellis, would certainly appreciate its echo of US 'Beat'
culture (in his book *The Big Beat Scene*, Ellis actually claims he suggested
the Beatles spelling as a reference to Beat).[4] A few years later, when the
group were world famous, Beat guru Allen Ginsberg would cement that
bond by visiting and declaring Liverpool 'at the present moment the centre
of consciousness of the human universe.'

The Georgian area around Hope Street, on the fringe of Toxteth (often
known by its postal district as Liverpool 8), was the little Montparnasse of
the city, its own Greenwich Village; it was also home to ethnic communities
and the Beatles were certainly exposed to some inspirational figures here,
not least the Trinidadian bandleader Lord Woodbine, who would introduce them to the Hamburg circuit, and the Somali guitarist Vinnie Ismail.
A great deal of the Beatles' musical range, in fact, arose from the diversity
of their Merseyside apprenticeship. The Beatles' musical radicalism was
in their readiness to try anything. Such a sense of music's possibilities was
instilled in the group before they left for London.

By virtue of its seafaring links the city was highly adapted to US styles,
whether it was African-American R&B or white country and western. The
Beatles were steeped in this environment of curiosity, with country being
so prevalent that Liverpool was called the Nashville of the North. (George
Harrison the guitar picker and Ringo Starr the sentimental crooner were
the most influenced.) Yet, while American black music has long had a
radical aura, by virtue of the energy, sexual directness and racial self-affir-
mation it presented to a British audience, country music has a reputation
for social and stylistic conservatism.

It is true that, like the blues, country songs prefer a clear and simple
template, but their celebrations of the working man (or sometimes, his
put-upon wife) have for decades found a sympathetic home in proletarian
Liverpool, where their lack of pretence and their emotional force are
exactly what is wanted. As perfected by Hank Williams and Johnny Cash,
country is underdog music, growling with flinty pride as much as senti-
mental resignation. Today it is still the noise you are apt to hear from the
less-gentrified pubs of the city centre. Some years ago I worked briefly in a
Liverpool factory, whose shop floor had a large portrait of Che Guevara at
one end and a ramshackle hi-fi playing non-stop George Jones at the other.

Between 1968, when Lennon's partnership with Yoko Ono encouraged him
to make much bolder music, and 1973, when his relatively unsuccessful

Some Time in New York City LP induced a certain fatigue with politicised song writing, the senior Beatle had done more than anyone apart from Bob Dylan to legitimise the idea of 'radical' pop music. No doubt a proportion of John's motivation came from his Liverpudlian background: in contemporary interviews he stressed the city's Irish and proletarian heritage as formative influences, despite his own upbringing in genteel suburban circumstances. The Beatles in general had revolutionised rock'n'roll, turning a formulaic youth style into a potent force for creative exploration.

If the city had never produced anything else, its place in musical history would be secure. But the Beatles were neither the beginning nor the end of this story. No sooner had they left the city, obliged to do so by London's centrality in the British music and media industries, than Liverpool soared to renewed prominence. The army of acts that was collectively dubbed Merseybeat helped establish the guitar-led line-up that is standard in rock even now. By 1965, however, the standard Mersey band was simply *not radical enough* for emerging tastes. The Beatles excepted (they, after all, were prime architects of the changes), the rise of psychedelia and explicit social protest bypassed the majority of local acts. Apart from Cilla Back and Gerry Marsden, who would both take homely Scouse personas into mainstream entertainment, the rest were cruelly scattered.

And yet a distinctly radical moment was at hand, back in Liverpool's bohemia. An underground taste for jazz and poetry events at the Hope Hall (soon to become the pioneering Everyman Theatre) had developed in parallel with the more commercial Beat scene found elsewhere in the city. Its leading lights, among them the painter and poet Adrian Henri and the poets Roger McGough and Brian Patten, had witnessed the Beatles' explosive rise from close quarters and made inclusiveness a feature of their own work. By 1967, the triumvirate were published to best-selling acclaim (their joint anthology was entitled *The Mersey Sound*), aspiring to write verse with all the accessibility of a Beatle chorus or a Kop chant.

Their radicalism as poets lay in a willingness to celebrate the everyday: a pop artist, said Henri, 'stands with one foot in the art gallery and the other in the supermarket'. And they saw a ready-made audience among the rock generation. McGough formed a satirical trio, the Scaffold, with Paul McCartney's brother Mike McGear and John Gorman. Assisted briefly by the Beatles' manager Brian Epstein and producer George Martin, the Scaffold became more popular than they had dared imagine, recording universal singalongs 'Thank U Very Much' and 'Lily the Pink'. But if the experimental yearnings of the Scaffold were soon hobbled by the machinery of pop stardom, Adrian Henri's band the Liverpool Scene preserved a more radical edge, to somewhat smaller sales. (The Wirral-born Henri is a reminder that the River Mersey has two banks, and figures from 'over the water' have always played a big part in Liverpool's music scene: John Peel, Jayne Casey, OMD, Half Man Half Biscuit and the Coral are just a few others forever linked with Liverpool despite originating from the Birkenhead side.)

'Ginsberg and the Beat poetry were getting to Liverpool then,' remembered Mike McGear/McCartney. 'We're doing this up in Hope Street, our kid [Paul] and the beat groups were down in the centre of town ... So our thing was different: it was poetry, art, comedy, rhythm and blues.'[5] The Liverpool Scene made LPs that took in free-form jazz, polemical folk songs and a highly localised strand of hippy surrealism. They consciously strove to bridge mass culture and the avant-garde, an ambition made plausible by the Beatles' unstoppable rise. Their beatnik pop has the ambiguity of Bob Dylan, whose disciples could not agree if his name was taken from Dylan Thomas or a character in the television cowboy series *Gunsmoke*.

A few years later came Deaf School, almost the archetypal art school band, whose members were part of the furniture at Hope Street. They shared the Liverpool Scene's fondness for pastiche, and likewise harboured several superb musicians. They enlivened the local live circuit in a fallow period of the 1970s, after the excitements of the heavy rock boom and just before punk. The intensity of the latter, in fact, may have spelt doom for Deaf School's ramshackle cabaret, but Liverpool liked their anarchic whimsy. Indeed, Liverpool was unique among the provincial cities that embraced punk, in that it responded with acts who scorned to copy punk's harsh aesthetic. We would see, repeatedly, over the years ahead, that Liverpool preferred spacious, dreamy and idiosyncratic songs to explicit narratives of anger and alienation. Considering that the city was becoming a national symbol of militant resistance to economic disaster – and in 1981 the epicentre of national rioting – the apparent mismatch was striking.

The nucleus of a scene that emerged after Deaf School was Eric's Club, a Mathew Street cellar right opposite the original Cavern site (full of rubble by now, for Liverpool was yet to nurse a lucrative pride in its Beatle past). From 1976 to 1980 Eric's was the nerve centre of local new wave music, and its core clientele spawned a huge variety of acts. Of this generation, Pete Wylie (and his several Wah line-ups) was the most inclined to marry rock aggression with radical messages, and he has recently prepared a song anticipating the death of Margaret Thatcher, the prime minister whose 1980s reign still triggers much Liverpudlian rancour. Even so, Wylie's best-loved song is surely 'Heart as Big as Liverpool', a rousing anthem of civic solidarity that celebrates 'us', rather than attacking 'them'.

Big in Japan, effectively Eric's in-house band, wonderfully encapsulate that time. Theirs was an untutored art-radicalism, punk in spirit, Dada in execution. Their vocalist Jayne Casey, a prominent local figure to this day, dressed then as an art-statement in herself, akin to Alfred Jarry, Leigh Bowery or (another Eric's regular) Pete Burns of Dead or Alive. Other members of Big in Japan's fluid collective included Holly Johnson: his next band, Frankie Goes to Hollywood, emulated Merseybeat's dominance of the charts, given a dance music makeover that echoed the links between Eric's and Liverpool's equally underground gay scene. Flamboyance can be a tough call in Liverpool. Any aesthetic 'radical' in the city risks censure for challenging common values. Scouse solidarity, laudable in most contexts, presents a grimly conformist face in others.

Big in Japan's guitarist Ian Broudie would make a similar journey from the radical fringes of music (and Big in Japan could be defiantly unlisten-able) to the very heart of commercial acceptance. In subsequent decades his band the Lightning Seeds perfected a Liverpool way with melody and pop uplift. Yet another member, Bill Drummond, took a more wayward path to the Top 20: he managed the two most successful Eric's bands, Echo and the Bunnymen and the Teardrop Explodes, and later made a series of brazenly subversive hits with KLF and others (as well as going on to develop an 'oppositional' art practice through gestures such as burning a million quid, which met with indifference from the art establishment it was meant to attack). All of these stories can be traced back to the musical atmosphere of Eric's and its inspirational co-owner Roger Eagle. The club's eclecticism was an education, its DJs combining dub reggae, vintage rockabilly, New York punk and almost anything else in ways that would profoundly shape local musicians' tastes.

Uphill from the Mersey, the racially diverse area of Liverpool 8 was, as noted, a district familiar to white artists and musicians. From its perma-nent population came the Real Thing, a soul group with a unique place in the city's musical history. Their standing as a black British chart act, and moreover one with serious artistic ambitions, is also without parallel. Evolving from the Chants, one of several black harmony acts operating in the area (and who appeared with the Beatles at the Cavern), the Real Thing found a winning formula in upbeat anthems like 'You to Me are Every-thing' (1976). And they made a concept album called *4 From 8* that explored their Liverpool 8 roots in socially realistic numbers such as 'Children of the Ghetto'.

The Christians, another black harmony act (later joined by the white songwriter Henry Priestman), maintained a Liverpool tradition of charming the public with sweet sounds, while reserving room for pungent commentary in certain lyrics. Their 'Forgotten Town' together with the Lightning Seeds' 'Tales of the Riverbank' and Orchestral Manoeuvres in the Dark's 'Enola Gay' are prime examples of the most accessible pop with a darker subject matter. But, as the decades rolled on, it was Liverpool's romantic and dreamier side that was uppermost, at least to the eyes of the record-buying public: Icicle Works, China Crisis, A Flock of Seagulls, Atomic Kitten, the Coral, Zutons and Wombats are seldom thought of as politically charged (though one finds that Liverpool musicians are usually left-leaning); nor were they greeted as outright musical radicals, for all that they were pleasingly innovative.

The Farm, perhaps, made more explicit statements than most, though their well-known 'All Together Now' suggests Liverpool communality as much as socialist unity. Arriving a little later than the Eric's scene, the Farm stressed their distance from the artier end of student style and preferred to dress in ways reflecting street-and-football culture – the Liverpool 'scally' tribe, especially – fusing indie rock with the rising dance music that culminated in that Liverpool icon, Cream Club. Ever since Cream, in fact, the city's reputation for nightlife has revolved around outright hedonism more than live music.

Irreverence, of course, can be subversive and the Scouse impulse to mock is strong. From their redoubt on the Wirral peninsula, Half Man Half Biscuit have proved as much through a twenty-five-year campaign of wittily scabrous satire. Signed to Liverpool's Probe Plus label, their songs supply an ongoing critique of contemporary junk culture but also of 'hip' pretensions. Titles such as 'Joy Division Oven Gloves', 'Eno Collaboration (Remix)' and Cammell Laird Social Club poke fun at music's most hallowed names. On the artwork of their album Achtung Bono a group member poses, terrorist style, with a guitar inscribed 'This machine kills wasps'; it is a pastiche of Woody Guthrie's 'This guitar kills fascists' that makes subtle fun of rock's vainglorious posturing.

In the lineage of Echo & the Bunnymen and the Teardrop Explodes (whose singer Julian Cope went on to pursue a solo career of notable eccentricity), local music became identified with neo-psychedelia. This was fitting, inasmuch as early English classics of the genre, especially the Beatles' 'Strawberry Fields Forever', 'Penny Lane' and 'I am the Walrus', were born of narcotically hazed childhood memories of the city. But 1967's 'Summer of Love' and hippy culture in general were not much evident in Liverpool at the time. Even the Eric's bands were not literally psychedelic, in the sense of LSD-inspired. But there is a case for saying that Liverpool was psychedelic *avant la lettre*, and that its musicians found the style well suited to their native inclination for abstract reverie and linguistic playfulness.

As long ago as 1808, the Liverpool poet and abolitionist William Roscoe was prefiguring the fantasias of Lewis Carroll and John Lennon with highly wrought works like *The Butterfly Ball and the Grasshopper's Feast*, adopted in 2010 for the title of a Liverpool psychedelic night (where young local bands like El Toro and the Wicked Whispers rubbed reverent shoulders with that grizzled original the Crazy World of Arthur Brown). Twentieth-century Scouse comedians such as Arthur Askey, Tommy Handley and Ken Dodd were beguiling British radio audiences with surrealistic word play long before Liverpool 8 or Cantril Farm had dropped its first tab of acid. It would be wonderful to know more of the songs that the sailors sang, and those that echoed around the local music halls; perhaps they too were rich in mental absurdity.

Whereas post-punk Manchester forged a hard, rhythmic style befitting a true industrial city, Liverpool's style was oceanic, metaphysical. (Historians contrast Liverpool's maritime outlook, ruled by the tides and characterised by the erratic working patterns of deck and dockside, with the disciplined clock-in/clock-out lives of other workers. Here was a city of Celtic and often Catholic mystics, in daily confrontation with Protestant orthodoxy and Anglo-Saxon regularity, frustratingly hard to organise.) New Order had a more mechanical beat and appeared on their city's emblematically named Factory Records. Manchester's best melodist was the Smiths' guitarist Johnny Marr, often viewed as a 'Liverpool'-style musician.

The La's, Shack and the Coral were called 'cosmic scallies' by outside commentators, struck by a drowsily romantic tendency, where tunefulness was matched by mystical obscurity and anachronistic touches. Among the musical community there was a marked attachment to early sonic adventurers, notably Captain Beefheart (from whose guitarist, Zoot Horn Rollo, the Zutons took their name), Arthur Lee of Love, the Doors, early Pink Floyd and Frank Zappa. Significantly, Beefheart's first exhibition of artworks was held at Liverpool's Bluecoat Gallery in 1972; the same institution had hosted Yoko Ono as early as 1967.

An influential stalwart of the local scene is Edgar Jones, formerly Edgar Summertyme, whose work displays encyclopaedic knowledge of arcane blues, sung in a growl recalling another Scouse maverick, the late jazz legend George Melly. Of his early, neo-psychedelic band the Stairs, Jones says, 'We were 30 years behind the game or five years ahead, depending how you look at it'.[6] His comment evokes so much of Liverpool's latter-day music, which can sound eerily detached from its own times. A hard but perceptive comment was made by one visitor to Liverpool in its Capital of Culture year, 2008: 'Meanwhile, like cultural marsupials with no land-bridge to the mainstream, Liverpool bands became a more and more peculiar breed – destined to be peered at, prodded and patronised by onlookers.'[7]

To do the wider Liverpool scene full justice we should recognise that an appetite for musical progression is definitely evident. The Royal Liverpool Philharmonic, through its Ensemble 10/10, presents a tremendous programme of contemporary music, including commissions from local composers like Gary Carpenter, Emily Howard and Kenneth Hesketh. ('Serious' new music, indeed, always did enjoy a following in the city, with receptive crowds for Stravinsky, Bartók, Cage and Reich.) The improvisational band Frakture welcomes fellow adventurers into its ranks; the Hive Collective breaks new ground in electronic sound; the experiments of the playful a.P.A.t.T. simply defy category.

And a lot of Liverpool music is radical in its social content. The Liverpool Scene's Mike Hart had the confrontational pungency of a young Bob Dylan. Singer and songwriter Alun Parry stands explicitly in the heritage of Woody Guthrie and has founded the city's Working Class Music Festival. Ian Prowse and his band Amsterdam present a set that is richly freighted with polemic as well as a heady swell of Mersey romanticism. It is no accident that one of the city's seminal venues, the Picket, has its origins in trade union activism.

In a sense, nearly all Liverpool music is radical, because it is heart felt. Although we commonly take it to mean 'extreme' or 'out-there', radical is simply a word for the root. (Semantically speaking, the radical is related to that blameless vegetable the radish.) The songwriter Ian McNabb called his 1998 album (*A Party Political Broadcast on Behalf of*) *The Emotional Party*, which aptly sums up this classic Liverpool artist, so full of wit and generous spirit, so concerned to hymn the fundamental yearnings of our human nature. If such songs take a traditional structure, they are not therefore conservative. If they soothe and reassure, they are not therefore reactionary. And they are the songs that arise most naturally on the Liverpool shore, where we watch that river reflect the heavens, churning the dirt below.

Notes

1 Alan Lomax, *The Land Where Blues Began* (New York: Minerva, 1993), pp. 53–54, 137.

2 *You'll Never Walk Alone*, dir. JD Beauvallet (Noe Productions, 1992).

3 The Beatles, 'It's All Too Much', written by George Harrison, *Yellow Submarine* (Apple/EMI, 1969).

4 Royston Ellis, *The Big Beat Scene: An Outspoken Exposé of the Teenage World of Rock'n'roll*, 2nd edn (Upper Poppleton: Music Mentor Books, 2010), pp. 170–71.

5 Paul du Noyer, *Liverpool: Wondrous Place – Music from Cavern to Cream* (London: Virgin Books, 2002), pp. 95–96.

6 Interview with author, *The Word* (Oct. 2007).

7 Danny Eccleston, online report for *Mojo* magazine website, 18 Jan. 2008. <www.mojo4music.com/blog/2008/01/liverpool_european_capital_of.html>.

6

Women and Radicalism in Liverpool, c.1890–1930

Krista Cowman

Introduction

When seen from a national perspective, radicalism in Liverpool often appears a masculine preserve. At key moments in the city's radical history – industrial unrest of 1911; the police strike; the interwar unemployed movement; dock strikes; the conflict between the city council and national government in the 1980s – images of male militancy held sway. In a city dominated by male industries, opportunities for women's radicalism appeared few; women such as Eleanor Rathbone and Bessie Braddock who practised their politics on a national scale were rare exceptions. Liverpool women's radicalism, particularly among working-class women, seemed to be restricted to the arena of support, standing by their men folk rather than formulating demands of their own.

There have been times when the view from within the city looked somewhat different. The nineteenth-century Lancashire socialist and suffragette Hannah Mitchell summed up the experience of political activism for many of her women contemporaries, writing that 'no cause can be won between dinner and tea, and most of us who were married had to work with one hand tied behind us'.[1] Female radicalism was much more likely to take place in a local than a national setting where it could be fitted around the labour-intensive demands of running a home and the need for paid labour in the case of working-class activists.[2] Middle-class women were less restricted by domestic labour but often had demanding duties as hostesses at social functions that played an essential part in maintaining a family's commercial status. Yet, despite this, Liverpool women from different classes took part in a number of radical campaigns before the First World War, and continued their tradition of activity into the interwar period and beyond.

Nineteenth-century Precedents

The radicalism practised by Liverpool women before the First World War had its roots in the later decades of the nineteenth century. Women's radicalism in this era was not the unique preserve of the city's working classes. The city had a number of large and thriving branches of the Women's Liberal Federation. The women who set up and led these branches were simultaneously involved in a number of causes that ranged from opposition to the Contagious Diseases Acts and animal cruelty to demanding better educational opportunities for women and girls. The familial and political networks that they established were augmented by the university. Nessie Stewart Brown, Julia Solly and Stella Permewan were all daughters of the first Chancellor, Edmund Muspratt, while Eleanor Rendall, wife of the Principal of the University College, played a critical role in 'moulding public opinion' towards the desirability of mixed-sex classes.[3] Along with Eleanor Rathbone, these women were at the forefront of Liverpool's first women's suffrage society that formed in 1893. Yet at the same time they were careful to distinguish their activities from those of other radical women in the city whose politics leaned more towards socialism. Liberal women such as Edith Bright and Nessie Stewart-Brown were inclined to describe themselves as 'progressive' or 'advanced' rather than radical.[4] They took equal care to distance themselves from the figure of the 'New Woman', who Mrs Bright warned was a 'most dangerous all[y]'.[5] As a consequence, Liverpool's leading women Liberals negotiated a public role for themselves via involvement in a number of progressive causes without losing the respectability that underpinned Victorian middle-class femininity. '[T]he Shrieking Sisterhood does not flourish in the North', noted Vevey Webster, columnist for *Womanhood* magazine, when she visited Liverpool to report on 'the social progress of women' in the city in 1901. The typical 'Lady of Liverpool' (as a series of pen portraits in *Woman at Home* described her) was no more accepting of the gendered norms of Edwardian society than her metropolitan counterparts but sought to achieve her emancipation in ways that 'only strengthened her essentially feminine qualities'.[6]

Other Liverpool women espoused a different form of radicalism that was less concerned with preserving the respectability of its practitioners. Liverpool's first socialist women were as committed to sexual emancipation as Liberal feminists but were equally keen to point out the particular inequities facing working-class women in the city. Many of their energies went into campaigns that aimed to encourage working-class women to take control of their own circumstances. Jeannie Mole, the wife of a local fruit merchant, was one of a small group who founded Liverpool's first socialist society, the Workers' Brotherhood, in 1896, subsequently working in the Fabian Society and the Independent Labour Party.[7] Mole's tireless efforts to unionise Liverpool's lowest-paid women workers resulted in some successes. With her help and encouragement, unions of tailor-esses, ropeworkers and tobacco spinners took industrial action that won higher wages for their members or improved their working conditions by abolishing the draconian fines levied by employers.[8] Radicalism of this sort could be costly for women. When Jeannie Mole moved to Liverpool after her marriage in 1879 her wealth and intelligence brought her to the heart of the city's fashionable progressive circles and she was welcomed into groups such as the Rathbone Literary Club.[9] This changed when her support for socialism led to her vilification in the local press and split her off from former allies. *Porcupine* condemned her efforts as 'middle-class interference', while at the same time Nessie Stewart Brown criticised her and others of the 'advanced wing' of the Women's Industrial Council for what she called their 'misapprehension of what the council was formed for'.[10]

Liverpool's Liberal women, by contrast, developed a feminism that challenged gendered inequalities but had no critique of class. Any work that they undertook on behalf of working-class women was intended to alleviate immediate circumstances rather than bring about dramatic change in their lives. There was much emphasis on encouraging self-improvement through bodies such as the Inquiry and Employment Bureau for Educated Women, which was set up in 1898 'to assist the class who are called ladies in distress' to find suitable work.[11] When Liberal women took over the leader-ship of the Liverpool branch of the Women's Industrial Council in 1896 they reversed its priority of encouraging women to form trade unions but concentrated on carrying out published investigations into the conditions of women's work.[12] The results of these investigations had little impact on the low levels of organisation among working-class women. However, they informed a series of articles in the *Liverpool Review of Literature, Politics and the Arts* in October 1890 that played a critical role in drawing wider public attention to the problems faced by working women and especially those in low-paid or unskilled trades. This pattern reflected the work being under-taken elsewhere by the Fabian women's group and feminist social scientists at the London School of Economics, and influenced the young Margaret Simey in shaping the university's School of Social Science.

Socialist women in Liverpool continued to organise working-class women before the First World War. The unions that formed were often sporadic and short-lived; many women seemed keen to join a union when they had specific grievances against their employers but would quickly drift away when it appeared that their demands had been met. There were some exceptions, however. A union set up among the city's upholstresses kept going into the twentieth century. Women such as Alice Duggan, the tailoress's leader, set a precedent for working-class self-organisation that other women could follow. The comparatively low levels of female employment in Liverpool meant that they remained exceptions, however. Most of the working-class women who involved themselves in radical politics were married, and not economically independent.

The New Woman

The figure of the 'New Woman' mentioned by Mrs Bright above preoccupied social commentators at the start of the last century and in many ways epitomised the radicalism of Liverpool women across classes. Although some have argued that the New Woman was a journalistic construction rather than a reality there was no doubt among contemporary observers as to what she looked like, or what she would do.

> She smokes. She rides a bicycle – not in skirts. She demands a vote. She belongs to a club. She would like a latch key – if she has not already got one. She holds drawing room meetings and crowds to public halls to discuss her place in the world.[13]

This extract from the student magazine of Owens College, Manchester reminds us that the figure of the New Woman was not restricted to London. She was every bit as much at home in the provinces, perhaps more so as cities such as Liverpool defined their own strong civic identities against the prevailing mores of the metropolis. Many radical women in Liverpool became strong defenders of the New Woman. The Liverpool socialist Eleanor Keeling, who briefly edited a woman's column for the *Clarion*, used one of her editorials to remind her readers that the possibilities contained in this new identity were to be celebrated rather than feared: 'A New Woman is one who has high ideals on what life should be and ... Is determined *to think for herself* to use her newly discovered reasoning powers.'[14] Keeling was one of several Liverpool women whose politics involved a radical rethinking of private as well as public lives in ways that prefigured the 1970s Women's Liberation Movement's belief that 'the personal [was] political'. They were less concerned with adhering to prevailing ideas concerning appropriate feminine behaviour, but looked for new ways of living that they believed better represented the broader ideals of socialism. Keeling did marry Joseph Edwards, editor of the *Labour Annual*, rather than live with him, but the couple opted for a register office ceremony, with *Clarion* editor Robert Blatchford acting as their witness, and Keeling did not change her name, despite public criticism of this decision.[15] The couple's first child, Fay, named after a member of the *Clarion*'s editorial board, was not baptised but welcomed into the socialist movement in an open-air ceremony on the beach at Wallasey on May Day 1897, with many socialist friends in attendance.[16] Keeling, Mole and others were keen dress reformers, unafraid of adopting an appearance that was unconventional by the standards of the day. Although the industrial composition of Liverpool offered fewer opportunities for women to take part in work-based action than elsewhere in Lancashire, socialist women joined in street politics when this was possible. One woman, Elizabeth Turner, was among a group of socialists who were prosecuted for holding public meetings in Liverpool in the summer of 1896 and was one of the most vociferous in defending the right to do so when she appeared in court.[17]

Militant Suffrage

It was from this dual background of middle-class progressive feminism and socialist radicalism that the militant suffrage movement emerged in Liverpool. Suffrage was one of many causes supported by local women liberals, and a Women's Suffrage Society was formed in Liverpool in 1871. In 1904, Emmeline Pankhurst set up the Women's Social and Political Union in Manchester to act as a 'ginger group' within the Independent Labour Party and ensure that its commitment to women's suffrage went beyond resolutions on paper.[18] The WSPU initiated a separate propaganda campaign in and around Manchester addressing ILP branches and other socialist groups and speaking in the open air during wakes weeks. In the autumn of 1905 an impending election persuaded the Union to shift its tactics, taking advantage of the proximity of a general election to put pressure on the Liberal Party around the question of votes for women. A systematic disruption of Liberal meetings began that brought the first arrests in the suffrage campaign when Christabel Pankhurst and Annie Kenney were ejected from the Free Trade Hall in Manchester after demanding to know whether a Liberal government would 'give votes to women'. Building on the momentum from the publicity this raised the WSPU continued to disrupt Liberal meetings within reach of Manchester. The Free Trade Hall scenes were replicated at Liverpool's Sun Hall on 9 January 1906, when Henry Campbell-Bannerman's speech was consistently interrupted. This event was carefully choreographed by WSPU members from Manchester and supporters in Liverpool who would have known each other through northern socialist circles.

Liberal women who were present at the meeting were outraged. Most of them were keen suffragists who fought hard to persuade their party to take a more supportive position on the question, but vehemently disagreed with the WSPU's external attacks on Liberal policy. Socialist women felt differently. The famous banner that Christabel Pankhurst and Annie Kenney had unfurled in the Free Trade Hall had simply demanded 'votes for women', but the one which hung from the gallery at the Sun Hall asked the Liberal government to 'give votes to working women'.[19] When women like Josephine Butler first articulated Liverpool women's claim for a parliamentary vote in the 1870s, the mere expression of the demand could be said to be radical. Thirty years later it seemed less so; many women were participating in municipal politics as voters or as elected representatives and the eminently respectable leaders of the city's Women's Liberal Federation were calling for women's suffrage. The WSPU's militancy shifted calls for women's suffrage from the opulent drawing rooms of Liberal ladies out onto the city's streets. The first Liverpool suffragettes had learned their politics in the socialist movement and imported a direct, confrontational style of street politics into their campaign for the vote. One, Alice Morrissey, withdrew from the local women's suffrage society in protest at its lack of engagement with working-class women and was instrumental in setting up a local branch of the WSPU.[20]

The WSPU in Liverpool grew rapidly, and separate branches were soon set up on the Wirral, although the main focus of their activity remained centred on Liverpool. The city employed a paid organiser from March 1909. The WSPU had a number of paid workers throughout the country who received about two pounds per week in return for overseeing the organisation of branches in particular areas. This salary could come from the WSPU's central funds or could be raised locally from a levy among members. Militant suffrage was sufficiently strong in Liverpool for the local branch (along with those on the Wirral) to be able to demand an organiser and to continue to employ one when the post had been lost in most other Northern districts; even Manchester, proud of its status as the 'mother branch' of the Union, was unable to retain an organiser when Jessie Stephenson stepped down in 1911. Organisers enabled branches to undertake higher levels of public activity. Liverpool WSPU was one of a handful of branches nationally to open a shop that sold a number of items to raise funds for the Union while removing room hire costs for business meetings. Liverpool had a relatively low turnover in organisers. Although the first organiser, Mary Phillips, only stayed for a matter of months, the next three, Ada Flatman, Alice Davies and Helen Jollie, were in post for eighteen, fifteen and twenty-three months respectively.

Who were Liverpool's Suffragettes?

Liverpool WSPU managed to retain the services of an organiser through the auspices of a core of dedicated members who remained committed to the Union's militant suffrage campaign from the first days of the branch through to the outbreak of the First World War. Martin Pugh's recent analysis of militant suffrage argued that the WSPU 'made a very deliberate decision to sacrifice' its connection with working-class women and 'move [its] campaign up the social scale' when the Union shifted its headquarters to London in 1906.[21] Elsewhere in Lancashire it has been suggested that working-class radicalism found a more comfortable outlet in constitutional suffrage that was boosted when the National Union of Women's Suffrage Societies established the Election Fighting Fund to support Labour candidates.[22] Liverpool's suffrage activists represented a more eclectic mix. Many of them were working-class women, sometimes independent but often married to working men. The lack of sustained employment activities for working-class women in Liverpool may have played a part in this, giving those with an interest in politics more time to devote to the cause than may have been the case had they lived in cotton towns. Alice Morrissey, the wife of John Wolfe Tone Morrissey, Liverpool's first elected socialist, certainly fitted this category and worked almost full time for suffrage and socialist campaigns between 1905 and 1912. Another identifiable group of suffragettes were involved in Liverpool's progressive artistic circles including the Sandon Studios. These included Ethel Frimstone (née Martin), a sculptress, and the artists Mary Palethorpe, Constance Copeman and Jessica Walker, as well as Patricia Woodlock, the daughter of local artist David Woodlock. There were also women pioneers from other fields, such as Dr Alice Ker, a widowed Birkenhead GP who had been one of the first British women to qualify as a doctor, and Hattie Mahood, a woman deacon in Liverpool's radical Pembroke Chapel. The WSPU has been criticised for its centralised structure and high levels of autocracy but these Liverpool women were evidently happy with what it offered. The Women's Freedom League, the alternative militant suffrage society that Teresa Billington Grieg set up in opposition to the WSPU in 1907, had branches close to the city in Waterloo, Aintree and Anfield but never managed to compete directly with the WSPU or to persuade its membership to move into a new society.

Liverpool suffragettes were at the forefront of some of the Union's earliest acts of militancy nationally. From February 1907, the Union began to arrange 'Women's Parliaments' in London. These were highly symbolic occasions that took place close to Westminster, usually in the Caxton Hall, and were arranged to coincide with events such as the state opening of Parliament or a debate on a private member's suffrage bill. As well as emphasising women's physical exclusion from the floor of the House of Commons, the Women's Parliaments were intended to show the spread and strength of the Union's support. Women were encouraged to attend from branches throughout Britain, and the Union would sometimes pay their travel expenses either centrally or through a series of branch collections. Liverpool sent good numbers of delegates to each of the Women's Parliaments who were often well to the fore in subsequent demonstrations. Although no woman attending the Women's Parliaments was forced to undergo arrest, she was expected to indicate whether or not she would be willing to go to prison. Only those who agreed would be sent out on deputations, but Liverpool suffragettes were numbered among those arrested at the first, second, third, sixth, seventh, eighth, ninth and tenth Women's Parliaments as well as at the mass window-smashing raids of 1911 and 1912. Over twenty Liverpool women went to prison for their actions on the deputations, and some of them went more than once. The most persistent local offender was Patricia Woodlock, who was sent to prison for three months after her fourth arrest in 1909. The sentence, which was intended to act as a deterrent to future delegates, was the most severe one passed on a suffragette to date. Woodlock was not easily intimidated. She consistently located her protests in her Liverpool roots. 'What else could I do,' she asked the magistrate after her first arrest, 'when I come from the North where there is such misery and poverty?'[23] Woodlock later had three more arrests in London and was also imprisoned in Birmingham's Winson Green for her part in a demonstration at the city's Bingley Hall in September 1909.

Women who went away from Liverpool to take part in militant activity may have been spared the embarrassment of arrest in front of friends and neighbours, but this did not necessarily ease their actions. Many were concerned about the effects their imprisonment might have on their families. The presence of a strong WSPU branch in Liverpool made it possible to alleviate some of this and political networks took the place of family for some suffragettes. The widowed GP Dr Alice Ker advised her young daughters to keep in close touch with the other suffragettes during her own imprisonment and to visit the local offices on a regular basis. WSPU visitors were able to reassure her as to the girls' welfare.[24] Another local WSPU member, Mrs Healis, volunteered to look after the child of one of her colleagues so that she could go on a later deputation.[25] There was also suffragette militancy on the streets of Liverpool. The most violent protests coincided with the run up to the general election in December 1909 when protests at the meetings of Winston Churchill and Herbert Asquith led to several arrests. Most of the arrested women were not local, as the WSPU realised that suffragettes who were likely to be recognised by the local police would have less chance of approaching cabinet ministers to make their protest. Militancy by local women tended to be of a lower level. The WSPU carved out a very public presence for itself in the city's streets in the years before the First World War. There were regular paper sales of the WSPU's official newspapers *Votes for Women* and the *Suffragette*. Women transformed themselves into walking billboards, parading the streets in large groups dressed up in sandwich boards promoting their cause. There were other militant acts too. Under the leadership of Helen Jollie, Liverpool suffragettes began a campaign of disrupting performances in the city's theatre and cinema when the subject matter of films and plays was appropriate. James Sexton's play *The Riot Act* was singled out for special attention owing to the fact that it portrayed a suffragette as a less than wholesome character, something Sexton promised to address after the protest.[26] There were also disruptions to services at the newly opened Anglican cathedral (part of a national initiative called 'prayers for prisoners' that the WSPU ran in 1914). None of these protests involved arrests, but the women who undertook them were violently ejected from theatre, church and cinema.

Although the WSPU was officially politically independent it remained close to the ILP in Liverpool. A very few women remained active in both groups; the WSPU forbad its members from working for other political parties, but Alice Morrissey held office in the Union in Liverpool (including a spell as temporary organiser in 1911) and worked directly for the Labour candidate in the Kirkdale by-election of 1907, when the WSPU took no official part. In the year before her death in 1912 she undertook a national speaking tour on behalf of the ILP. On the party side a number of socialist women who expressed their sympathy for the militant movement included trade union organiser Mary Bamber, who sometimes appeared on WSPU platforms. The local constitutional suffrage society, by contrast, remained

1 'Near to revolution': crowds on St. George's Plateau during the 1911 Transport Strike. *Photo: Carbonara, courtesy of Liverpool Record Office.*

2 David Jacques, *The Great Money Trick*. The banner was commissioned for this site on Dale Street by Liverpool City Council to mark the centenary in 2011 of the death of Robert Tressell, author of influential socialist novel *The Ragged Trousered Philanthropists*, who is buried in a pauper's grave in the city. *Photo: Liverpool City Council.*

3 Self-confessed 'whole-hearted feminist' and campaigner Eleanor Rathbone (third from left) and other suffragists outside the Liverpool Women's Suffrage Society Shop supporting the pro-women's campaign in the Kirkdale by-election, 1910. *Photo courtesy of the University of Liverpool Library.*

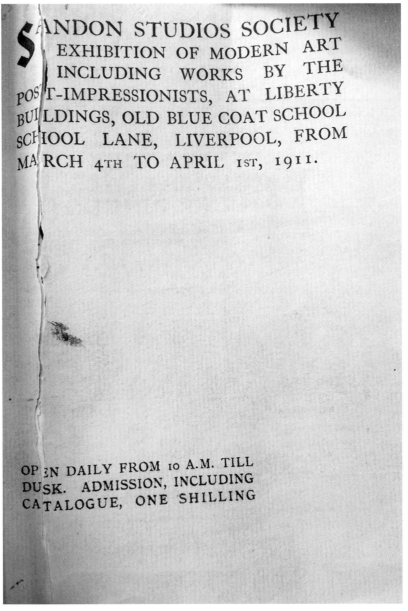

SANDON STUDIOS SOCIETY
EXHIBITION OF MODERN ART
INCLUDING WORKS BY THE
POST-IMPRESSIONISTS, AT LIBERTY
BUILDINGS, OLD BLUE COAT SCHOOL
SCHOOL LANE, LIVERPOOL, FROM
MARCH 4TH TO APRIL 1ST, 1911.

OPEN DAILY FROM 10 A.M. TILL
DUSK. ADMISSION, INCLUDING
CATALOGUE, ONE SHILLING

4 Catalogue for the 1911 Post-Impressionists exhibition held at the Bluecoat at the
invitation of progressive Liverpool artists' group, the Sandon Studios Society, whose
members showed alongside Cézanne, Picasso, Matisse and other 'shocking' artists.
Courtesy of Liverpool Record Office.

5 Charles Reilly, charismatic head of the Liverpool School of Architecture, 1904–1933.
Photo: E. Chambré Hardman, © National Trust/E. Chambré Hardman Collection.

6 Donald Lynch, *So you won't talk, eh?* (1936), showing Sandon Studios Society members interrogating the radical artist Roderick Bisson (standing centre), whose 'offending' painting is being shown as evidence of his embrace of modernism. © *National Museums Liverpool.*

7 After their triumphant 1964 tour of America, the Beatles share a joke at Liverpool Town Hall with local black vocal group the Chants. Left to right: Nat Smeda, John Lennon, Lord Mayor Louis Caplan, Edmund Ankarah, Eddie Amoo, Paul McCartney, Ringo Starr, Joey Ankarah, Alan Harding, Bessie Braddock MP, George Harrison, and (seated) Lady Mayoress Fanny Bodeker. *Photo: with thanks to Joey Ankarah and Jonathan Hitchen.*

8 (*left*) Adrian Henri, 'high priest' of Liverpool bohemia, in an advert for his group the Liverpool Scene's first LP (1968). *The Estate of Adrian Henri.*

9 (*right*) Cult Californian musician Captain Beefheart (Don Van Vliet) in Liverpool in 1972 outside the Bluecoat at the opening of his first exhibition of paintings. *Photo courtesy the Bluecoat.*

10 Programme cover from the Liverpool Everyman production of Chris Bond's *Under New Management* in 1974, which focused on the Fisher-Bendix plant in Kirkby and the occupation by its workers.

11 Alternative community newspaper *Liverpool Free Press*. This edition from May/June 1975 uncovered what became a celebrated local authority corruption case.

12 Staff outside News From Nowhere, Liverpool's radical bookshop, which was established on May Day 1974. Left to right: Mandy, Maria, Sara, Kate, Julie, Sally. *Photo courtesy of News From Nowhere.*

LIVERPOOL 8

JOHN CORNELIUS

LIVERPOOL ON THE BRINK

Michael Parkinson

POLICY JOURNALS

MERSEYSIDE IN CRISIS

Merseyside Socialist Research Group

What Happened at SPEKE?

"A car designed on the basis of major motoring needs for the next twenty years."

BRITISH LEYLAND

BUILDING THE UNION

Studies on the growth of the worker's movement : Merseyside 1756 — 1967

To celebrate the 125th Anniversary of the Liverpool Trades Council.

THERE'S NO OTHER WAY

FRANK DEEGAN

13 Publications reflecting turbulent political times and radical threads across a century.

15 Liverpool FC striker Robbie Fowler celebrated a goal by revealing his support for sacked dockers during their dispute with the Mersey Docks and Harbour Company, 1995–98. The t-shirt image was adapted for a life-size cut-out of Fowler, one of 80 contemporary heroes in a reworked *Sgt Pepper* tableau at a Bluecoat exhibition in 1997 marking 30 years since the Beatles released their album with its iconic sleeve.

14 Comedian Ken Dodd and a Diddyman, on the cover of a Liverpool City Council public relations booklet.

16 Militant on the march: supporters of the Militant-led Liverpool City Council outside the Town Hall, 1985. *Photo: Dave Sinclair.*

17 Liverpool school students strike against enforced youth training schemes, 1985, echoing an earlier school strike in the city in 1911. *Photo: Dave Sinclair.*

18 Protestors in the centre of Liverpool demonstrate against the British National Party's presence on Church Street, 2010. *Photo: Michael Kirkham.*

19 The Royal Liver Building (right) had a radical impact in 1911, with its controversial design by Walter Aubrey Thomas, use of reinforced concrete – the first major structure in Britain, and one of the first in the world, to be constructed this way – and pair of liver birds designed by Carl Bernard Bartels. It is now less prominent in a changing waterfront skyline. *Photo: Andy Dawson.*

dominated by members of Liverpool's Women's Liberal Federation branches, limiting its appeal to socialist women.

The events of August 1911 were centred around male trade unions, offering women little opportunity to participate directly. This did not mean that women were completely absent; as Eric Taplin has observed, illustrations of the strike showed that 'women played an important role in supporting their men' in street violence, while Robert Holton's analysis of those involved found evidence for the persistence of 'popular community involvement with the unrest'.[27] Suffrage protests did not directly link up to the wider events of 1911, but the earlier activities of both socialist and suffragette women had brought women's politics onto the streets of Liverpool, making a female presence there less remarkable. There was also continuity in the work of a small number of socialist women who attempted to organise unskilled women workers against the more overt political background. Mary Bamber attempted to organise café workers and formed a union among women working at Wilson's bobbin works in Garston in August 1911. The women took industrial action, along with some male workers, the following June. This prolonged and bitter dispute closed the works for several weeks. The company reopened them in August by bringing in girls from elsewhere in Liverpool, which prompted violent scenes on the picket lines when striking women and men attacked the tramcars transporting the strike-breakers home at the end of their shift.[28]

The First World War and Beyond

Street politics were interrupted by the First World War but the tradition of female radicalism in Liverpool did not disappear completely. The earlier model of progressive feminism favoured by Liberal women began to reassert itself as some women saw the war as an opportunity to demonstrate their claims to citizenship. A Women's War Service Bureau was organised in Gambier Terrace by the Lady Mayoress, Mrs Herbert Rathbone, along with Jessie Beavan and Drs Mary Davies and Frances Ivens from the local constitutional suffrage society. Much of the War Service Bureau's work reflected traditional feminine work – organising parcels for troops at the front, rolling bandages and practising first aid – but it was underpinned by a philosophy that argued this as a form of national service that proved women were 'worthy of citizenship'.[29] Other women sought a more direct role. Phyllis Lovell, an ex-militant suffragette, set up an organisation called the Home Service Corps (HSC). This placed women into jobs temporarily available owing to the war, but was far more than an employment agency.

HSC members wore a uniform, and spoke of their war work as 'service' even when it comprised something as apparently mundane as operating the lifts in the Liver Building. Uniforms were also adopted by members of the city's first Women's Police Patrols, which were set up in connection with the National Union of Women Workers. As with certain forms of suffragette militancy, the radicalism of this work lay more in the fact that women were undertaking it than in the nature of the work itself. The Patrols mainly concerned themselves with policing the moral behaviour of young girls and women and worked in tandem with the criminal justice system. A small number of ex-WSPU members were drawn to this very public campaign but the majority of the Liverpool Patrols' membership came from constitutional suffragists.[30]

At the end of the First World War, women's politics throughout Britain was characterised by a shift away from gender-based politics and back into the political parties that were now working hard to attract members from newly enfranchised women.[31] Although all three main parties now accepted women as equal members, few were keen to put them forward as electoral candidates. Women were also arguably more adversely affected by the collapse of the Liberal Party. The Women's Liberal Federation had been the largest of all of the party women's organisations before the First World War, and continued to be popular throughout the 1920s.[32] At the same time, however, the party's electoral demise limited the opportunities for its more able women. Liverpool, which had some of the strongest WLF branches, was no exception: Nessie Stewart Brown was selected to represent the party in a parliamentary contest for Waterloo, but was defeated, and the eclipse of liberalism within the city offered few opportunities for party women to move into civic life. Liverpool did not elect its first woman MP until Bessie Braddock was returned as part of the Labour landslide of 1945. The city's most prominent woman politician nationally was Eleanor Rathbone, but having failed to be elected as an independent MP for the East Toxteth constituency she opted to stand for the Combined University's seat in 1929, which arguably loosened her connection with local politics.

Following its wartime resurgence, there was some evidence of a continuation of the older model of progressive feminist radicalism after the First World War. An important location for this was the local branch of the Women Citizen's Association (WCA). This organisation, which had many branches across Britain, had been founded in Liverpool in 1911 by Eleanor Rathbone, partly in response to the National Union of Women's Suffrage Society's moves towards the Labour Party. Rathbone wished to guard the political independence of constitutional suffrage, and saw the

WCA as a place where women could receive political education as well as campaigning for the vote. In the 1920s, the WCA nationally continued to press for equal suffrage as well as offering support and advice for women in local government. In Liverpool its role shifted more towards that of educating women in broader social questions, and its political independence isolated it from other groups. Labour councillor Mary Cumella spoke to the branch in October 1937 at a meeting intended to bring the WCA and women city councillors together, but was only able to inform them that 'non-political organisations had no influence with the city council'.[33] The WCA had more success in its work with similarly non-aligned groups, including the Women's League for Peace and Freedom, with which it worked quite closely in the interwar period.

Working-class women's radicalism continued to an extent. Mary Bamber, a city councillor from 1919 to 1924, was also a founder member of the local branch of the Communist Party and attended the Second Congress of the Third International in Moscow in 1920, although she had left the party to concentrate on trade union organisation by the mid-1920s. Bamber was involved in the 'rushing' of the Walker Art Gallery organised by the local branch of the National Unemployed Workers' Committee Movement in 1921. Her daughter, Bessie Braddock, who was also involved in this event, continued to combine street politics with municipal representation when she and her husband involved themselves in demonstrations against the means test in the 1930s. Organising women workers continued to prove difficult, particularly when unemployment rose, but socialist women found space in new groups such as the Labour Party Women's Sections. These were strong in Liverpool in the 1920s when they took up demands for nurseries and wash houses.[34] Some, including Bessie Braddock and Mary Cumella, were even prepared to fight for birth control, although this remained a controversial issue for many Labour women in the interwar years.

Coda

By 1911 there were two traditions of women's radicalism in Liverpool. Socialist women radicals looked to the city's working women and combined their feminism with a militant socialism that brought them onto the streets in double contravention of Edwardian spatial codes. Socialist leaders were often middle-class women, but set themselves aside from polite society, thus losing many of the privileges of class. Suffragettes drew on the examples of socialist women in the 1890s but went further in their single-sex demonstrations, with less emphasis on class. The radicalism of middle-class Liverpool women inclined itself more towards informing and persuading, although its adherents were equally committed to improving the social position of their sex. In the short term this model enjoyed greater longevity, re-emerging in the interwar years in various women's organisations. It was not until after the Second World War that working-class women militants re-emerged to colonise popular images of local radicalism. Post-war demographic changes brought greater numbers of women into the workplace. Although service, the highest female employer in pre-war Liverpool, had declined since the First World War, moves to lighter manufacturing industries offered new opportunities that were more conducive to organisation than domestic service. Although they were not sweated workers like the tailoresses, ropeworkers or tobacco spinners, the production-line women of the post-war era were just as keen to defend their rights at work. Women at the Ford motor plant at Halewood came out on strike in 1968 demanding equal pay with men. The intervention of Barbara Castle, then Home Secretary, resulted in their jobs being regraded, but it was not until a further strike in 1984 that Ford's women workers finally achieved parity with men. Typists and other women workers at Liverpool city council took high-profile industrial action in 1981 in pursuit of equal pay. Other actions revealed women developing broader political concerns. In 1983, when women working at the fashion store Lady at Lord John were sacked for attempting to unionise the subsequent picket and boycott of the shop resulted in their reinstatement in a victory that inspired the feature film *Business as Usual*.

Women's action in support of their jobs often revealed a broader concern for home and community, especially as growing unemployment rates raised the importance of their wage to household economies. Meccano, Dunlop and Kraft Foods were just some of the factories with a mainly female workforce where closure or threatened closure prompted women to take actions such as occupation. They also spoke out in defence of men's jobs: the dockers' strike of 1995 saw the emergence of Women on the Waterfront (WOW), a group of women supporters (mainly wives or partners of striking men) who took their campaign to raise awareness of the dispute across the globe. Interviewed in 1997, one of the leaders of WOW remarked that 'working class women, especially in Liverpool, have always been involved in disputes. If you look back in history ... this has been the norm in Liverpool'.[35] This may be right. There have been lulls and less radical times, but past examples suggest that different models of women's radicalism have always been an important dimension of Liverpool's radical politics.

Notes

1 Mitchell, quoted in Jill Liddington and Jill Norris, *One Hand Tied Behind Us* (London: Virago, 1978), front cover and p. 16.

2 On this point, see June Hannam, '"Making Areas Strong for Socialism and Peace": Labour Women and Radical Politics in Bristol, 1906–1939', in Krista Cowman and Ian Packer (eds), *Radical Cultures and Local Identities* (Newcastle: Cambridge Scholars, 2010), pp. 71–94.

3 Sarah Tooley, 'The Ladies of Liverpool', *Woman at Home*, 4.1 (1895): 8.

4 See the descriptions in *Woman at Home*, 4.1 (1895): 1–11 and 4.11 (1895): 166–76.

5 *Woman at Home*, 4.11 (1895): 170.

6 Vevey Webster, 'What Women are Doing in the North of England', *Womanhood*, 6.34 (Sept. 1901): 273; Tooley, 'The Ladies of Liverpool'.

7 For Jeannie Mole, see her entries in the *Dictionary of National Biography* and *Dictionary of Labour Biography*.

8 For details, see Krista Cowman, *Mrs Brown is a Man and a Brother: Women in Merseyside's Political Organisations, 1890–1920* (Liverpool University Press, 2004), pp. 27–36.

9 Rathbone Literary Club Minute Book U11/288 6/6/2, Merseyside Record Office.

10 *Porcupine* (15 Sept. 1894); *Liverpool Review of Politics, Society, Literature and the Arts* (13 Mar. 1897).

11 *Liverpool Daily Post* (19 May 1905).

12 For example, *Liverpool Women's Industrial Council Report on Homework in Liverpool* (Liverpool: Liverpool Women's Industrial Council, 1909); *Liverpool Women's Industrial Council Survey into Widows Under the Poor Law* (Liverpool: Liverpool Women's Industrial Council, 1913).

13 H. Roxburghe, 'On the New Woman', quoted in Gifford Lewis, *Eva Gore-Booth and Esther Roper: A Biography* (London: Pandora, 1988), p. 57.

14 *Clarion* (23 Mar. 1895). For Keeling, see Geoffrey Fidler, 'The Work of Joseph Edwards and Eleanor Keeling, Two Liverpool Enthusiasts', *International Review of Social History*, 24 (1979): 293–379; Krista Cowman, 'Reading Between the Lines: Letters to Eleanor Keeling Edwards', in Caroline Bland and Máire Cross (eds), *Gender and Politics in the Age of Letter-Writing, 1750–2000* (Aldershot: Ashgate, 2004), pp. 173–84.

15 See her defence in the *Clarion* (13 Apr. 1895).

16 *Labour Leader* (8 May 1897; 29 May 1897).

17 For details of Turner's case, see Krista Cowman, 'The Battle of the Boulevards: Class, Gender and the Purpose of Public Space in Nineteenth-Century Liverpool', in Simon Gunn and Robert Morris (eds), *Identities in Space: Contested Terrains in the Western City since 1850* (Aldershot: Ashgate, 2001), pp. 152–64.

18 Sandra Stanley Holton, *Suffrage Days: Stories from the Women's Suffrage Movement* (London: Routledge, 1996), p. 108.

19 The banner can be seen in an illustration of the demonstration carried by the *Liverpool Weekly Courier* for January 1906.

20 *Liverpool Daily Post* (13 Apr. 1906).

21 Martin Pugh, *The March of the Women* (Oxford University Press, 2000), p. 214.

22 The depiction of the Lancashire suffrage campaign in Liddington and Norris, *One Hand Tied Behind Us* sketches this model.

23 Cited in Cowman, *Mrs Brown is a Man and a Brother*, pp. 81–82.

24 Dr Alice Ker prison letters, Women's Library.

25 *Votes for Women* (2 July 1909).

26 Grace Wyndham Goldie, *The Liverpool Repertory Theatre, 1911–1934* (Liverpool University Press, 1935), pp. 92–93.

27 Eric Taplin, *Near to Revolution: The Liverpool General Transport Strike of 1911* (Liverpool: Bluecoat Press, 1994), p. 36; Robert J. Holton, *British Syndicalism, 1900–1914: Myths and Realities* (London: Pluto Press, 1976), pp. 100–01.

28 *Liverpool Daily Post* (14, 15, 16 Aug. 1912). For the experiences of individual women strikers, see the series of testimonies contained in the Liverpool Trades Council and Labour Party Papers, Liverpool Record Office.

29 *Common Cause* (14 Aug. 1914).

30 For the patrols, see Angela Woollacott, '"Khaki Fever" and its Control: Gender, Class, Age and Sexual Morality on the British Homefront in the First World War', *Journal of Contemporary History*, 29 (1994): 325–47; Philippa Levine, '"Walking the Streets in a Way No Decent Woman Should": Women Police in World War One', *Journal of Modern History*, 66 (1994): 34–78; also Liverpool Women's Patrols Annual Reports, Liverpool Record Office.

31 On this point, see Krista Cowman, *Women in British Politics* (Basingstoke: Palgrave, 2010), chap. 8.

32 On this point, see Pat Thane, 'Women, Liberalism and Citizenship', in E. Biagini (ed.), *Citizenship and Community: Liberals and Collective Identities in the British Isles, 1865–1931* (Cambridge University Press, 1996), p. 68.

33 Liverpool Women Citizen's Association minutes, 7 Oct. 1937, Liverpool Record Office.

34 Sam Davies, 'Class, Religion and Gender: Liverpool Labour Party and Women, 1918–39', in John Belchem (ed.), *Popular Politics, Riot and Labour: Essays in Liverpool History, 1790–1940* (Liverpool University Press, 1992), pp. 217–46,

35 Peter Kennedy, 'Working up a Storm in a Port'. <www.labournet.net>. Accessed 10 Dec. 2010.

7

The Liverpool Way, the Matchless Kop and the Anny Road Boys: Notes on the Contradictions in Liverpool Football Supporter Radicalism

John Williams

Introduction: No Football Radicals Here?

To see ranks of Liverpool football supporters, organised and angry, in collective public protest aimed for a period of two years, between 2008 and 2010, at George Gillett and Tom Hicks, the absentee, dishonoured American owners of the club, might have struck the casual viewer outside the city as being merely a case of 'business as usual'. Is this not, after all, the typical way of managing employment and other civil relationships on Merseyside? Liverpool is a city best noted perhaps, especially by outsiders, for its urgent separateness and aspects of its cultural creativity, but also for its urban disturbances and 'political' revolts. And for its sectarianism, army gunboats and bread riots; for strikers at Halewood, as well as Militant under Derek Hatton; and for its periodic 'race' uprisings, marked out most emphatically in 1919, 1948 and again, in spectacular fashion, in 1981. Orderly and pacified is not typically deemed to be the 'Liverpool Way'.

So with association football as one of the driving cultural motors of the city – Merseyside started as a rugby stronghold, but hosted the FA Cup final as far back as 1894, and the city of Liverpool was already established as the 'football capital' of England by 1906 when its two major clubs completed the League and FA Cup double – then surely radicalism, and especially organised football *activism*, among Merseyside spectators must also be deeply etched into the consciousness and history of its people. But, perhaps the surprise here is that some of the dominant narratives that flow around and through local football support on Merseyside are rather different from that which the wider public reputation of the city of Liverpool might imply.

123

In part this is because, in a national sense, football in England has always been less well known for its supporter protest and radicalism than for its firmly embedded working-class cultural conservatism. That is, as a symbol of the way in which English traditions of amateurism have idealised sport as a means of overriding social and cultural divisions rather than being an accessible and appropriate route for dramatising them. In short, the entrenched (if fatuous) dictum of 'keeping politics out of sport' is indeed a well-rooted feature of the English cultural condition. And this is even true in Liverpool, where Englishness itself is such a deeply contested trope. As the sports historian Brian Stoddart has recently put it, historically football in England 'was the bastion of traditional social and political attitudes, far more than it was the harbinger of radicalism'.[1]

Ironically, however, the nineteenth-century *origins* of the major Merseyside clubs had actually bucked the dominant apolitical English trend in football by being positively steeped in local political intrigue. Tory politician, Protestant, Orangeman and Freemason brewer John Houlding, for example, was eventually ejected from his role of club president on the Everton board in 1892 because of irreconcilable commercial and political differences with the dominant Liberal Methodists. When Houlding eventually lost his grip on power at Everton he simply created a new hub at Liverpool FC – and at Everton's old Anfield base. At his new club Houlding used football as an electoral and business vantage point in a city dominated by the ethnicised civic elite he represented.[2] Significantly, no Irish Catholics were invited onto either club board or as major shareholders, and although a number of Irish football clubs were formed in the city, none of them was able to survive the sporting competition from Liverpool and Everton for very long.[3]

Yet despite these early ethnic and political tensions – and even in an 'exceptional' Celtic locale such as Liverpool – there was actually relatively little difference in the way football supporters responded to those who controlled the local clubs that would easily distinguish Merseyside followers from the national picture of sporting conservatism. To the extent that 'radicalism' has existed historically at all inside these elite clubs, or among football supporters in the city, it has typically taken a rather different, more subtle, and more *cultural* direction than the recent collective fan unrest and the wider public perceptions of the historic turbulence of Merseyside public life might suggest.

Managing Football Discontent

Historically, and in part because of its Liberal traditions, the modern Everton had a more democratic structure, and the Goodison club was more amenable to supporter input and was more responsive to fan disquiet than Liverpool.[4] Certainly, followers of Liverpool had plenty of good cause to express their collective displeasure. The club's followers of a certain generation might understandably best remember the Reds' glory years under Bill Shankly and then Bob Paisley in the 1960s, 1970s and 1980s, and also the Anfield club's record four European Cup wins spanning the period from 1977 to 1984. There was little cause for public complaint under these stewardships. Indeed, even today's supposed trophy 'drought' over twelve years under the recent continental technocrats, Gérard Houllier and Rafa Benítez, has actually produced League Cup, FA Cup and major European triumphs (including another European Cup in 2005), if not, of course, the expected, elusive league titles.[5]

In contrast to these supposedly lean, but nevertheless productive, years there were forty-one mainly barren seasons experienced at Liverpool FC between 1923 and 1964, with just one major trophy won (a scrambled first post-war League title in 1947 under manager George Kay) to balance a humiliating Reds relegation to the Second Division in 1954. There may have been wider football disgruntlement in the city, too, had neighbours Everton not passed Liverpool in the opposite direction on their way *out* of the second tier in 1954, thus just avoiding a double calamity for Merseyside football. At the time, the Liverpool board (as it would be for ninety years) was still full of prominent local Conservatives and was made up of an interlocking network of north-west businessmen and magistrates. The club was already nationally renowned for its penny-pinching ways, with its board running the club for decades on tight transfer budgets and an administrative shoestring.

The club's minute books confirm that Liverpool had long perfected a transfer 'policy' of establishing the lowest possible fee that a selling club might accept for a transfer target – and then offering considerably *less* for the player concerned. Moreover, this was no opening gambit, but a final offer.[6] The club's directors, strait-laced to the last, also resolutely resisted the pervasive culture of illegal payments to players, which was popularly supposed to be rife in the English game in the 1950s under the existing primitive maximum wage restrictions.[7] As a result, no established footballer of any real note (or price) supplemented the Liverpool title-winning team of 1947 for at least a dozen years after the war.

Relegation to the less competitive waters of the Second Division offered no respite to Liverpool's downward spiral, or to its supporters' apparent acquiescence in it; it merely seemed to accentuate both. On 11 December in that same difficult year (1954), Liverpool suffered its still record Football League defeat, a 1–9 leathering at St Andrews by Birmingham City. The club's directors blamed the result on the Liverpool players wearing inappropriate footwear for the icy Midlands weather and selected the *same* eleven players for the next fixture, against Doncaster Rovers. Their faith was partly repaid because there was some measurable improvement in the Reds' performance: this time they only lost 1–4.

Today, in the sort of twenty-four-hour sports news cycle that is increasingly focused on the triumphs and perhaps more frequently the failings, in full media glare of managerial gurus,[8] and that is shaped by a culture of accelerated desires conceived of as rights,[9] no major football manager (or, in this case, club board) could possibly survive defeats on this scale. But these were very different times. At Liverpool after the Second World War there was no major outcry from the terraces about these sorts of capitulations; in fact, there was barely audible public discord of any kind. Times were hard: books were burnt for warmth in Bootle in the terrible winter of 1947 and in the same year some Liverpool supporters stoically *cycled* to Blackburn for an FA Cup semi-final because of transport shortages. Football in northern England in this period offered a collective masculinist respite for working people from the recent privations of war – an 'escape from the dark of despondency into the light of combat'[10] – and a powerful local focus for male community solidarity in a world with few other viable leisure options.[11] Winning brought fleeting pleasure, a temporary escape, but defeat invited no great despair. The social and cultural changes that would very soon semi-dislocate ties of identity, locality and belonging around English professional football clubs, thus promoting more success-driven patterns of non-local support and consumption around a cadre of elite clubs, were still only on the English sporting horizon.[12]

Liverpool's autocratic board in the early 1950s also kept a very tight rein on the club's shares and on the re-election of favoured directors, so its AGMs passed with little disharmony or critical press comment. By comparison, the more open management culture at neighbours Everton invited rather more open supporter unrest.[13] Instead, there was only dark Merseyside humour to offer up some welcome Anfield relief. During an amateur boxing contest held between the Liverpool and Birmingham ABAs at Byrne Avenue Baths in the city soon after the St Andrews debacle in 1954, a count of nine was reached against a stricken Birmingham fighter.

A local wag in the audience shouted immediately: 'That's nine back for Liverpool!'[14] But humour alone could not heal local wounds. Later, a glum and resigned Reds supporter told the *Liverpool Football Echo* on 18 December 1954: 'They are going from bad to worse. Don't ask us to keep on cheering, we don't have the heart.' Nor, it seems, the wherewithal to offer any sort of concerted opposition or critique.

But after defeat to non-league Worcester City in January 1959, in the third round of the FA Cup, even Liverpool's inert and parsimonious boardroom regime at last realised things had to change; though they still needed convincing on the matter by *Everton*'s main benefactor, the Littlewoods pools magnate and club chairman John Moores. As the effects of the lifting of the maximum wage in football in 1961 kicked in, the ambitious Moores spent heavily at the 'School of Science' and would be rewarded with the League title for Goodison Park in 1963, Everton's first in forty-four years. But, for good, solid business reasons, the pragmatic Moores also wanted much better competition between the two major local football clubs in the city – the dual sporting interests that his family fortune had done so much to sustain.[15] Moores leant heavily on the Anfield board to spend more money on players and he eventually inserted his own man, Eric Sawyer, as financial director at Liverpool in 1961 to facilitate the process. Pressed into unavoidable action at last, the club's directors under T. V. (Tom) Williams discarded some of their principles and a succession of young puppet 'managers' and in December 1959 brought in a tough, ambitious, fast-talking independent Scot, Bill Shankly, to manage the team. Here was a proselytiser who had unspectacularly toured lesser northern clubs espousing his football philosophy of 'continuous movement' before making some bricks without straw as a young manager at Huddersfield Town.[16] In truth, the Anfield board probably little bargained for what they had done.

For one thing, the Liverpool directors had effectively finally given up the right to select the Reds first team, which they had exercised for good or ill for over seventy years. For another, they had brought into their English Conservative (and conservative) stronghold a native socialist and a Scottish charismatic. This was a major departure, one that could not easily be reversed. As the 1960s swept away some of the aged conservatism and the deference and austerity of previous decades – not least in the new youthful 'Beat city' of Liverpool, then 'a fertile cradle of exceptional creativity and initiative'[17] – the club's ebullient new man would now continuously challenge his own directors, charm the emerging new television partners for the game, loosen the Anfield purse strings, and mobilise the club's young followers in ways that would eventually change the modern profile of Liverpool FC almost beyond recognition.[18]

Despite its radical departure from Anfield traditions, Bill Shankly's brand of West of Scotland collectivism would not easily embrace *all* the communities in the south end of the city – though he later offered his support and advice to a young Howard Gayle from Toxteth, the club's first black player in its eighty-nine years' existence.[19] But Shankly's arrival found a synergy in the response of the club's previously downtrodden supporters. At the 1961 AGM, some members of the nascent Liverpool Supporters Association were even emboldened enough to express publicly for the first time their 'underlying annoyance' about how the club was being run. A supporter, a Mr Adler, called from the floor for an insurrectionary vote of no confidence in the club chairman, Tom Williams.[20] This was extraordinary, the most challenging and single most radical supporter action in the entire history of the Liverpool club. There was no seconder for the resolution, of course, and Williams soon re-established good order: the same old Liverpool directors were re-elected as usual. But this was a sign that something had shifted, perhaps irreconcilably, inside Anfield. In his future disputes with the Liverpool directors – and there would be plenty – Shankly now knew that he would have a potentially decisive court of appeal in reserve, in the shape of at least one-half of the Liverpool football public.

The Birth of Modern Supporter Culture

These conservative and autocratic barriers to necessary change at Anfield, which were defended throughout the 1950s, would later become mythologised among the club's supporters over the next successful thirty years as the 'Liverpool Way': a positive bulwark against the dangers of convulsive change as the game marketised and also a necessary stay on the risks of public exposure of the club's core business.[21] Only the recent Spirit of Shankly protests defy these trends. So where are we to look for other signs of the radical in Liverpool's history if the search for collective supporter action, or local campaigning and resistance during some of the Anfield club's darkest hours on the pitch, offer no real promise? The answer lies in part, of course, in the unique character and the sedimented cultural identity of Anfield's Spion Kop, and the local men and women who made it.

Just two years after the split from Everton, Liverpool's goal end supporters were already showing early signs of a deceptively late-modern knowing and reflexive humour, even in their very early supporting styles.

Against Northwich Victoria on 3 February 1894, for example, the *Liverpool Review* reported that 'So one-sided was the game that it was taken quite humorously by the spectators, and the visitors had to undergo a lot of ironical comments in the way of shouts of "Play up!"'. Many others would endure the same ridicule later at Anfield as Kopites tried to keep themselves amused in the face of vapid resistance on the field. So, from the very start, the Liverpool Kop courted drama and mythology in near equal measure.

It was the *Liverpool Echo*'s sports editor Ernest Edwards who, reportedly, decided in 1906, when the new Anfield sprouted up within a walled-in 'fancy brick setting' offering a towering new 'elevated terrace consisting of 132 tiers of steps, which will afford space for something like 20,000 spectators',[22] that this grand, dark vision of the modern era of British sport actually recalled the fateful camaraderie and the ribbed heights of the killing fields of South Africa. In January 1900, more than 300 Lancashire Fusiliers, some Scousers among them, had died in battle on Spioenkop Hill during the Boer War as British forces attempted to lift a 118-day siege of nearby Ladysmith. The toughness of English professional football made sport a form of symbolic war and it was thought that this great bank filled with supporters might be a fitting and organically *living* memorial for the Liverpool dead. The name stuck and was embraced by the Liverpool crowd as well as by journalists. The melancholic, Irish-inflected oral traditions of the city had found an appropriate public setting for their expression among the Spion Kop's mainly working-class male members.

Accounts of the genealogy of football songs at Anfield often identity 1962 as the year it *really* began for the Liverpool Kop when a band called the Routers established in their song 'Let's Go' the rhythmic drumming that would transform into clapping for a terrace song/chant about Liverpool's young tyro Scot centre-forward, Ian St John.[23] But at an FA Cup replay at Barnsley as far back as 1914 the *Liverpool Echo* had reported that travelling Reds supporters were already at work and had 'transposed the song of 1906 and made it "Aye, Aye, Lacey scores the goals"'.[24] The Wexford-born winger Bill Lacey had transferred from Everton to Liverpool in 1912 and would win consecutive League titles at Anfield in 1922 and 1923, so the forward deserved his own ballad for this future glorious treachery alone. But what exactly had been the original version of his song referred to here? On 31 August 1907, a Mr Seddon from Tuebrook had written to the *Echo* with the words of a self-penned anthem for the Kop, 'Hurrah for the Reds', which extolled the virtues of the club's first great team under manager Tom Watson, and which included the key lines:

There's Hewitt and Mac to lead the attack
With Hardy to hold the fort, boys.
There's Goddard and Cox and Raisbeck the fox
And more to the good old sort, boys.

Joe Hewitt would go on to serve the club in various capacities for sixty years, though fellow forward Bill McPherson (Mac) would last only two. Handsome Sam Hardy was the first in a long line of great Liverpool goalkeepers, and 'Graceful Arti' Goddard and Jack Cox would play tricky bookends down the title winning Anfield flanks in the early 1900s. But it was the shock-blond Alex Raisbeck who excelled in the pivotal centre-half role, a footballer of boundless energy and considerable bravery and skill; a man 'beyond comparison ... in the football firmament', reasoned the *Liverpool Daily Post* on 29 April 1907: 'Without Alex Raisbeck Liverpool would have to be born again, so to speak'. One of seven brothers, the Stirlingshire-born pivot would go on to father fourteen children. Remarkable surviving footage from the Mitchell and Kenyon film collection at the British Film Institute briefly shows Raisbeck in electrifying action during Liverpool's 0–1 loss at Newcastle United on 23 November 1901. The Scot's non-stop running and brutal tackling consumes the screen, even in defeat.[25] Against considerable post-war competition, he is still arguably Liverpool's greatest ever player.

We cannot tell whether Mr Seddon's song was in fact ever performed on the Kop – 'Hurrah to the Reds' sounds more Merchant Taylors' posh than working-class Walton Vale – but we do know that by comparison most early local English football subcultures produced, at best, rather wooden terrace chants or else they imported and then rendered one standard song – and did so endlessly. But for periods during the next one hundred years and more it would be Liverpool supporters who, invariably, produced some of the most original hymns to their football heroes, songs often composed in pubs outside the Kop before being carefully trialled on supporters.[26] Accordingly – and probably uniquely – a substantial volume has recently been published of Anfield terrace songs.[27] But, more than this, Liverpool supporters also developed quite extraordinary relationships with a number of those men in red who crossed the white lines.

Elisha Scott and the Mythologising of the 'Matchless' Kop

On 3 February 1923, a *Liverpool Echo* reporter at Wolverhampton commented that travelling Liverpool fans were 'loyal to the core and their vocal efforts would put some army camp to shame. There was a vocalian company behind me at Molyneux', wrote the scribe, 'and their chants were stunning the natives.' These sorts of supporters had already shaped the football terraces in the city, in Ray Oldenburg's words, as an authentic and native 'third place':²⁸ one constructed out of 'the many little episodes of personal interaction between guests, mediated by dialogue as well as visual contact, by bar-room slogans as well as sophisticated conversation – they are symbolic and signifying forms and worlds of socialization'.²⁹ But it was especially the Kop's unique relationship established in the 1920s with the long-serving Ulster-born Reds goalkeeper Elisha Scott that marked off the great terrace as a very special public site – as a truly radical space – for cultural expression and exchange among working-class people in the city.

When Liverpool first scouted Scott as a teenager, the report came back that the Ulsterman was 'raw as meat': he fitted the city well. Scott was soon an iconic hero for Liverpool followers, especially for his exchanges on and off the pitch with Everton's centre forward Bill 'Dixie' Dean.³⁰ Scott was certainly as publicly brutal in his judgment of his fellow defenders and opponents on the pitch as he was emollient in his relationships with the fans on the Kop. Scott's high-pitched expletives and calls of 'rate' (right) routinely boomed across the pitch and settled on the Anfield terraces. Unlike any player on Merseyside before or since, Scott actively *communed* with the men and women standing behind him: 'They have heard him, he holds conferences with them,' the *Echo* reported. 'He chats and back-chats; they hear his opinion about positions and positional play. He was built in with the Kop.'³¹ This notion was pervasive. A story circulated in the city (one among many about the Irishman) that the keeper was once talking on the street to a perfect stranger who was so at ease with the situation and his football 'friend' that Scott eventually asked: 'Do I know you?' Affronted, the man replied 'I should hope so. I threw the ball back to you from the Kop last Saturday!'³² In the eyes of the Kop, 'Lisha' had 28,000 close comrades stacked behind his home goal.

Even during matches the irascible Scott would rather discuss football matters with Kopites to his rear than his own team mates in front. Enthralled and intrigued in equal measure by these sorts of highly public exchanges, and keen to uncover the Kop's secrets, in 1932 the *Liverpool Echo* sent its football correspondent *Bee* onto the great terrace, thus claiming one of the very first pieces of journalistic anthropology to explore 'inside' the world of British working-class football-supporter culture. This direct encounter with the local press marked out the Kop as highly atypical in cultural terms, a radical departure among British football fans. There were no similar press excursions elsewhere, and certainly not into the Gwladys Street enclaves at nearby Goodison Park.

The view of the typical Kopite that emerges from these remarkable press accounts – idealised no doubt – is one of unbending loyalty to the club (if not to its directors), and also one of considerable sporting knowledge, as well as some rather exotic cultural diversity. All these themes would be revisited over time. Liverpool had just subsided to Chelsea in the FA Cup, so there was some soreness conveyed in these notes on a tumultuous and engaged football crowd. 'Here was loyalty, here was a trusting nature, here was belief,' began *Bee* rather grandly in his dispatches from Liverpool football's front line. He went on:

> They cursed the directors for having missed the [FA] Cup boat; they had commentaries on all phases of play, players, press and from their unequalled view they reckoned they saw things that the people in other parts of the ground could not hope to see. Yes, the Kop is the home of the loyalists.

> Two women were there, one in chocolate brown and another daring to wear a blue hat, a tricky thing of beret design, but the colour scheme did not seem to be quite inviting, as she was in the Anfield ground. Two swarthy sons of Ireland came beside me. They had come to see the MA of goalkeepers, Elisha Scott. One wore a black velvet beret and a film face that suggested a Valentino. He was plainly of Basque extraction and was silent as the grave ...

> Where I had expected slashing attacks on players, I found praise and kindness. The kind way they talked of the players astonished me. True, Liverpool were playing better, but these were embittered partisans who could hardly forgive a Cup defeat. They were an object lesson to me ... Their sportsmanship was a great feature; their language was fit and proper, and they treated the players encouragingly and in a sporting manner. Anfield's all right if they can keep this man at their back. They have tantalised him, he says, by some of their movements, but he's loyal to the core and he goes on talking his matches, debating his matches. This spectator is matchless.[33]

The specific mention here of *female* fans and of Irish Kopites is perhaps especially significant. The former are often excluded from discussions about the history and traditions of the Kop[34] and the latter have their own special place in Liverpool football lore and in recent public record.[35] Sadly, there would be no more press excursions into the Anfield crowd, but after the Second World War the Kop continued in its vocal and irreverent ways, though it never quite found another acolyte on the pitch to match Elisha Scott. Instead, the great terrace sang popular tunes to accompany the half-time bands at Anfield,[36] and when Mr Philpott arrived at Anfield to conduct the Liverpool choir in 'community singing' before an FA Cup tie in 1950 the Kop's massed ranks wilfully (and predictably) sang their own preferred repertoire.[37]

It was in 1964, as Liverpool was about to win only its second League title in forty-one years in a period of relative plenty for the people of a city boasting the Beatles as global music kings, that the British media again returned to its early anthropological analysis of the Anfield crowd and the men and women who made it. This time the focus was national: the BBC's flagship *Panorama* programme invited television viewers to gawp at the Kop's wildly swaying ranks in all its respectable working-class, full-throated Merseybeat roar, with songs from the Beatles and Cilla Black to the fore. Presenter John Morgan, in a clipped BBC delivery and reflecting the social chasm that then existed between 'official' culture and its many variants in the north of England, proclaimed the Kop 'as rich and mystifying a popular culture as any South Sea Island'.[38] Writing perceptively about Liverpool and the Kop in the late 1960s, the author and playwright Arthur Hopcraft compared the game there to a form of art that working men in the city knew intuitively, 'as they know their families'.[39] He described the terrace as 'an incomparable entanglement of bodies and emotions' and argued that 'It is the physical interaction which makes the monster the figure of unavoid-able dreams it becomes. To kill off this animal, this monstrous, odorous national pet would be a cruel act of denial to us.'[40]

Hopcraft was correct on both counts: the Kop was, by now, both a hideously uncomfortable and slightly troubling purple mass of belching working-class creativity and obscenity, but it was also, increasingly, a benign sporting treasure – a 'national pet' – one faithfully booming out its 'You'll Never Walk Alone' laments. In short, the Liverpool Kop had already become semi-institutionalised and something of an 'official' public performer, perhaps past its true organic and irreverent peak – though it would take another thirty years completely to emasculate the great beast, with seats finally replacing its standing terraces in 1994.[41] In fact, the mantle of football 'radicalism' at Anfield was about to be claimed in the 1970s by some of the Kop's frustrated departing young sons.

The New Young 'Radicals': The Rise (and Re-rise) of the Anny Road Boys

Hooliganism had been a subterranean feature of post-war Liverpool supporter culture even as the Kop was busily projecting very different messages for the popular media about Merseyside football support. After the all-Merseyside FA Cup semi-final of 1950 staged in Manchester, for example, letter writers to the *Liverpool Echo* reported on numerous fights between rival fans, the sighting of a beaten Manchester bus conductor, and of youths from the city who were 'bragging about what they had pinched'.[42] It was a story that seemed ill-fitting for the supposed harmonious early 1950s, but could easily have featured in any decade since. On 4 April 1956, after an equally turbulent trip to Doncaster, another Liverpool fan warned the *Echo* of 'the element of sheer, savage hooliganism among some of our supporters', and in Blackburn in March 1958 police used truncheons to deal with rioting Liverpool supporters who had smashed shop windows, stolen goods and fought with the police.[43]

And trouble at football would get steadily worse as, over the following three decades, the city of Liverpool's economic problems escalated. First, large multinational companies rationalised and restructured production processes, resulting in the closure of many small local businesses in the 1960s. Secondly, neoliberal policies and the collapse of the Fordist regime of accumulation in the 1970s and 1980s exacerbated the city's increasing disconnection from the networks that had previously maintained its position of global trading significance.[44] At the same time, football hooligan rivalries in England intensified, though supporters in Liverpool generally eschewed the media-orchestrated national gang culture around the sport that would produce 'end' leaders, named mobs, calling cards and the embryonic memorabilia emerging from organised hooligan 'firms'.[45]

Typically, too, Merseyside hooliganism was peculiarly creative and *instrumental* rather than overtly destructive or collectively violent, a pattern built cumulatively on well-established local traditions. In the late-1950s and early 1960s, for example, unwary football visitors to the city would often be directed or transported by locals from around Lime Street to run-down housing estates where they were stripped of valuables and sometimes their clothes and shoes.[46] The necessities, in a city raised on traditions of unemployment, low wages and trading and exchange cultures around the docks, for 'robbin'' and for 'bunking in' to matches, were also widely recognised and largely sanctioned, especially later, on European football trips.[47] Fighting was more selective, and disorder inside the stadium was strongly abhorred in Liverpool – though fans visiting the city were well versed in the perceived dangers of becoming isolated targets for the much-feared and mythologised Merseyside Stanley knife.[48]

By the late 1970s, the Kop enclosure was being deserted by those 'lads' who found the old terrace's contemporary 'family' reputation too dull, its stylistic gestures and 'woollyback' demeanour too wholesome, and its location just too distant from visiting rival hooligans: relocating to the opposite Anfield Road end of the ground, the Anny Road Boys were born.[49] The new 'Kopites are Gobshites' shtick that this division produced symbolised locally not just a disillusion with tradition and the increasing wider public simpering for the Liverpool Kop, but also a 'conflict of lifestyle aspirations'.[50] It offered a form of distinction for an emerging new Liverpool working-class cultural elite, one that was reinforced by the new cultural economies growing up around the interconnected casual clothing contestations and the English terrace rivalries of the late 1970s and early 1980s.[51] Young Liverpool supporters were better placed than most to wage these domestic, Thatcherised, symbolic 'style wars', not least because of the city's historic cosmopolitanism but also because of their frequent sojourns for European club football abroad. As a result, foreign sports gear – liberated from Italy, German, France and Spain – and also fey 'continental' wedge haircuts, circulated freely in the city in the late 1970s; they were worn to exemplify the club's international success and its loyal and sophisticated support, as well as to goad domestic rivals for their supposed gauche lack of European *savoir faire*.

But what was also important here, in addition to this radical brand of local creativity, was the overtly political gesturing involved in some of these developments, at least as they occurred in Liverpool. Orchestrating these increasingly vituperative debates in the city in the early 1980s, for example, was *The End* fanzine, an acute music/football hybrid, edited by Peter Hooton (later of the band the Farm), which ruled ruthlessly on the essence of terrace style while trashing both gnomic hooligans elsewhere, as well as Kop 'out-of-towners' and Liverpool FC 'anoraks'.[52] Some way ahead of the national fanzine opposition, Hooton was a key member of a small but influential group of emerging cultural intermediaries in the city, which also included novelist Kev Sampson, writer Nicky Allt, poets Jeggsy Dodd and Dave Kirby, musician and songwriter Pete Wylie and journalist Tony Barrett. Young men like these brilliantly articulated the uniquely strong links that had been established in Liverpool – initially, of course, by the historic Kop – between working-class masculinist cultures, football and other creative forms, including art, music and literature.

For such talented and resourceful young white Scousers, following a rampant Liverpool football club around Europe in the 1980s expressed personal and collective aspiration in the face of Thatcherised pessimism and repression – as much a political act as the social formations that then existed around Derek Hatton's flawed Merseyside Militant politics adventure and the street uprisings in Toxteth in 1981. Nicky Allt, for example, testifies to the rebelliousness of foreign tours with the Anny Road boys and Liverpool FC:

> I don't need any shrink to tell me that it [rabble-rousing with Liverpool FC abroad] was about wanting to see a bit of social life and not wanting to be held down or held back by your social background; being absolutely determined not to let a lack of cash tie you to a job centre lifestyle that successive Tory governments were trying to impose on you. Some of those prominent Tories of the past had said ordinary people should never have been given the vote and labelled them cannon fodder and then factory fodder. Well, the factories were all closing down as I left school and I didn't fancy getting left behind on the scrapheap with the rest of the factory fodder, nah that wasn't for me. So there you have it; it's rebellion, or it was for me anyway.[53]

The Beginning of the End – Or the End of the Beginning?

The tragedy that resulted from Union of European Football Associations (UEFA) bungling, the inadequacy of the Belgian authorities and especially the atypical behaviour of some Liverpool followers at the Heysel Stadium in Brussels in 1985, and the ban on English fans that followed, stemmed such foreign excursions. Liverpool has never dominated European football since. But the mass, ticketless Liverpool fan stadium invasion at the Champions' League final in Athens in 2007 in response to UEFA ticketing policies shows some continuities with older traditions. So, too, do publications such as Nicky Allt's recent collection of fans' stories about the Liverpool club in Europe[54] and Jeggsy Dodd's co-authored, drink-soaked account of the 2008/09 Liverpool season, complete with asides about the Spirit of Shankly campaign opposing the club's then American owners and accounts of the authors' organisation of supporter mosaics on the Kop for the 'Free Michael Shields' campaign.[55]

These instances demonstrate, above all, the continuing relevance of the cultural politics of radical working-class support around the club. So, too, of course, in a more formal sense, does the continued impassioned insistence among Liverpool supporters that the *Sun* newspaper be shunned in the city because of its Hillsborough lies, and that the dead from the 1989 disaster should finally be granted 'justice'.[56]

From the early oral traditions of the club, via Elisha Scott's intimate relationship with the flowering Kop and the autocratic rule of the club's directors in the 1950s, through to Bill Shankly's critical intervention at Anfield in the 1960s, followed by the new creative neo-hooligan Anfield supporter cultures from the late 1970s onwards, Merseyside football fans have readily displayed both their intense, often conservative, loyalty but also their innovative, radical edge – and frequently in difficult times. It should come as no surprise therefore that it was a Liverpool supporter's banner at the 2007 Champions' League final in Athens – one among many hundreds that included rhymes drawn from popular songs, clever Scouse in-jokes, and the inevitable extracts from the script of the movie *Gladiator* – that quoted instead the words of Plato: 'This city is what it is because our citizens are what they are.' Enough said, perhaps?

Notes

1 Brian Stoddart, 'Sport, Cultural Politics and International Relations: England versus Germany, 1935', *Soccer and Society*, 7.1 (2006): 34.

2 David Kennedy, 'Class, Ethnicity and Civic Governance: A Social Profile of Football Club Directors on Merseyside in the Late-Nineteenth Century', *International Journal of the History of Sport*, 22.5 (2005): 840–66.

3 David Kennedy and Peter Kennedy, 'Ambiguity, Complexity and Convergence: The Evolution of Liverpool's Irish Football Clubs', *International Journal of the History of Sport*, Annual Review, 24.7 (2007): 894–920.

4 David Kennedy and Michael Collins, 'Community Politics in Liverpool and the Governance of Professional Football in the Late Nineteenth Century', *Historical Journal*, 49 (2006): 761–88.

5 John Williams, *The Miracle of Istanbul: Liverpool FC, from Paisley to Benítez* (Edinburgh: Mainstream, 2005).

6 John Williams, *Red Men: Liverpool Football Club – The Biography* (Edinburgh: Mainstream, 2010), pp. 271–72.

7 Matthew Taylor, *The Association Game: A History of British Football* (London: Longman, 2007).

8 Neil Carter, *The Football Manager: A History* (London: Routledge, 2006).

9 Keith Hayward, *City Limits: Crime, Consumer Culture and the Urban Experience* (London: Routledge, 2004).

10 Arthur Hopcraft, *The Football Man: People and Passions in Soccer* (London: Collins, 1968), p. 197.

11 N. A. Phelps, 'Professional Football and Local Identity in the "Golden Age": Portsmouth in the Mid-Twentieth Century', *Urban History*, 32.3 (2005): 459–80.

12 Gavin Mellor, 'The Genesis of Manchester United as a National and International "Super-Club", 1958–1968', *Soccer and Society*, 1.3 (2000): 151–66.

13 James Corbett, *Everton: The School of Science* (London: Macmillan, 2003).

14 Williams, *Red Men*, p. 281.

15 Carter, *The Football Manager*, p. 88.

16 Dave Bowler, *Shanks: The Authorised Biography of Bill Shankly* (London: Orion, 1996).

17 Alan Edge, 'How the Kop Became a Stage of its Own', in C. McLoughlin (ed.), *Oh ... I am a Liverpudlian and I Come from the Spion Kop* (Liverpool: Trinity Mirror Sport Media, 2010), pp. 108–12.

18 Andrew Ward and John Williams, 'Bill Shankly and Liverpool', in John Williams, Stephen Hopkins and Cathy Long, *Passing Rhythms: Liverpool FC and the Transformation of Football* (Oxford: Berg, 2001).

19 Raymond Henry Costello, *Liverpool Black Pioneers* (Liverpool: Bluecoat Press, 2007), p. 71.

20 Williams, *Red Men*, p. 310.

21 John Williams, *The Liverpool Way: Houllier, Anfield and the New Global Game* (Edinburgh: Mainstream, 2003).

22 *Liverpool Echo* (25 Aug. 1906).

23 Stephen Kelly, 'An Oral History of Footballing Communities at Liverpool and Manchester United Football Clubs', University of Huddersfield PhD thesis (2009), p. 35.

24 Williams, *Red Men*, p. 105.

25 Film extracts of the match can be watched on YouTube at <www.youtube.com/watch?v=DhjTX39xKB4>.

26 Stephen Kelly, *The Kop: The End of an Era* (London: Mandarin, 1993), pp. 67–68.

27 Sport Media, *The Anfield Songbook* (Liverpool: Trinity Mirror Sport Media, 2010).

28 Ray Oldenburg, *The Great Good Place: Cafés, Coffee Shops, Bookstores, Bars, Hair Salons, and Other Hangouts at the Heart of a Community*, 3rd edn (New York: Da Capo Press, 1999), p. xvii.

29 Christoph Jacke, 'Locating Intermediality: Socialization by Communication and Consumption in the Popular-Cultural Third Places of the Music Club and Football Stadium', *Culture Unbound: Journal of Current Cultural Research*, 1 (2009): 332.

30 John Keith, *Dixie Dean: The Inside Story of a Football Icon* (Liverpool: Trinity Mirror Sport Media, 2005).

31 Williams *Red Men*, p. 196.

32 Ibid., p. 206.

33 Ibid., p. 202.

34 Liz Crolley and Cathy Long, 'Sitting Pretty? Women and Football in Liverpool', in Williams, Hopkins and Long, *Passing Rhythms*, pp. 195–214.

35 John Hynes, *The Irish Kop: Stories Round the Fields of Anfield Road* (Liverpool: Trinity Mirror Sport Media, 2009).

36 Kelly, *The Kop*, p. 17.

37 Williams, *Red Men*, p. 258.

38 The Panorama report can be watched on YouTube at <www.youtube.com/watch?v=XNboU_PbZMY>.

39 Hopcraft, *The Football Man*, pp. 9–10.

40 Ibid., p. 162.

41 Hopcraft seemed to suggest this might be the final outcome. See Dave Russell, 'A Reporter Trying to Reach the Heart of What Football is: Arthur Hopcraft's *The Football Man*', *Soccer and Society*, 11.5 (2010): 682.

42 Williams, *Red Men*, p. 261.

43 Ibid., p. 284.

44 Sara Cohen, *Decline, Renewal and the City in Popular Music* (Aldershot: Ashgate, 2007), p. 43.

45 Nicholas Allt, *The Boys From the Mersey: The Story of the Annie Road Crew, Football's First Clobbered-up Mob* (Preston: Milo Books, 2004), p. 83.

46 James McClure, *Spike Island: Portrait of a Police Division* (London: Arrow, 1980), p. 269.

47 Allt, *The Boys From the Mersey*, pp. 107–19.

48 John Williams, 'Kopites, Scallies and Liverpool Fan Cultures: Tales of Triumph and Disasters', in Williams, Hopkins and Long, *Passing Rhythms*.

49 Allt, *The Boys From the Mersey*.

50 Dave Hewitson, *The Liverpool Boys Are in Town: The Birth of Terrace Culture* (Liverpool: Bluecoat Press, 2008), p. 21.

51 John Williams, 'Having an Away Day: English Football Spectators and the Hooliganism Debate', in John Williams and Stephen Wagg (eds), *British Football and Social Change: Getting into Europe* (Leicester University Press, 1999), pp. 160–84.

52 Williams, 'Kopites, Scallies and Liverpool Fan Cultures'.

53 Allt, *The Boys From the Mersey*, p. 114.

54 Nicholas Allt (ed.), *Here We Go Gathering Cups in May: Liverpool in Europe, the Fans' Story* (Edinburgh: Cannongate, 2007).

55 Jegsy Dodd and John Mackin, *Redmen: A Season on the Drink* (Leicester: Matador, 2010).

56 On the twentieth anniversary of the disaster, almost 30,000 supporters turned up for the memorial service at Anfield and barracked Labour Minister (and Everton supporter) Andy Burnham concerning government inaction over Hillsborough.

8

Liverpool 1911 and its Era: Foundational Myth or Authentic Tradition?

Mark O'Brien

Myths and traditions have something in common. They are constructed representations that draw upon the past. They differ, however, in the claims they command for their veracity or, more correctly, their authenticity. A measure of their authenticity, however, will naturally be the degree to which the stories that sustain them stand up to historical scrutiny.

The notion of 'myth' has been used before with respect to our period. In his definitive treatment of British syndicalism in the years before the First World War, Robert Holton made his target the mythology that syndicalism was 'immature', 'amorphous' and 'transitory'.[1] In this present collection, John Belchem, in a beautifully detailed and compelling geo-cultural survey of radical Liverpool in 1911, describes the transport strike of that year as having been since imbued with a 'mythic force', projected as the defining moment of Liverpool's radical identity: in short, a foundational myth.[2] Belchem concludes this point by averring that the 'progressive potential' of Liverpool Labour was not realised in 1911 'at least in the short term'. Reflecting finally upon the modest and pedestrian response of the University of Liverpool by way of a commitment to 'sympathetic' social investigation, his chapter ends on a note of melancholic disappointment: 'Here was an outcome far short of the social and cultural revolution that 1911 seemed to have promised.'[3] It is with this assessment of the strike wave in Liverpool in 1911, tempered by cautious respect for the formidable scholarship that supports it, that I take issue.

Traditions of any kind must by definition last and develop over time – really, generations – to deserve the name. They are structured and defined by images, symbols and rituals. They are also remembered through episodes and transmitted by the stories that these have generated. As much to do with orientations towards the future as with interpretations of the past, a tradition acquires a kind of cultural 'mass' as historical episodes are claimed as 'belonging' to it. Sometimes this means that new events are seen as the latest expressions of that tradition. Sometimes it involves reaching far back into the past. However, an episode in and of itself, say an assemblage, a confrontation or a strike, does not create a tradition. Another necessary element is the work and activity of the conscious bearers and participants of that tradition: of people who say 'this is how we look back, this is where we stand today and this is how we move towards our future'. In other words, they do not spring spontaneously from events in some immediate and simple manner. Rather, there is always a historical lag that separates events from their interpretation and incorporation into the newly embroidered tradition.[4]

Considering the city of Liverpool from the vantage point of 2011, it seems safe to conjecture that its national reputation as a place of left-leaning political activism remains. Key political movements and social struggles have created that reputation: the high levels of mobilisation in 2003 against Britain's involvement in the Iraq war; the huge numbers involved in the campaign against the Poll Tax in the late 1980s; the stand of the Militant-led Labour council in the earlier part of that decade in continuing with a programme of council house construction in defiance of Margaret Thatcher's government; the Toxteth riots of 1981 triggered by police harassment; the confident shop-steward-led trade unionism associated with the automotive, maritime and transport industries that stretched back into the 1960s at least.

The relationship of this post-Second World War cultural–industrial profile to the 1911 transport strike seems tenuous when considered in terms of historical 'cause and effect'.[5] Such a mechanical approach, however, misses the real significance of 1911. The strike of that year is important for trade union and socialist activists today for what it represents as the beginning of a tradition of industrial organisation in which they stand. It is the question of how well the workers' struggles of 1911 and those of the years that followed stand up for this claim that needs to be assessed. We need to decide whether 1911 was indeed a crucial moment in the creation of a tradition of working-class solidarity and collectivism in Liverpool: or whether it better deserves the epithet of 'myth', with its insinuation of historical fantasy.

Sectarianism, Racism and the Breakthrough of 1911

In the opening years of the twentieth century, the cultural soil in Liverpool for traditions of working-class political consciousness, let alone socialist consciousness, was poor. The religious rivalries and conflicts of Protestant Orangeism and Irish Catholicism blighted the working-class districts of the city. There had been no real independent working-class political tradition. Indeed, there had been little in the way of a *dependent* political tradition in the form of working-class Liberalism.[6] Rather, the political complexion of working-class Liverpool in this era was very contradictory. While episodes of solidarity and collectivism occurred throughout the period, so too did episodes of racism, nationalism and sectarian conflict. In this respect Liverpool was unlike Glasgow where, despite the presence of the Orange and Green sectarian divide, socialist traditions were also putting down strong and enduring roots that would create the 'Red Clydeside' of legend. We will consider events over the years either side of the First World War to provide a fuller picture of this 'dark side' of Liverpool's past.

Before 1911, conditions were not at all propitious for the labour revolt that occurred during June and August of 1911. Work on the docks was highly casualised, with only pockets of effective industrial organisation, for example, among certain kinds of machine operators.[7] Indeed, these levels of casualisation were high even by national standards. Through the 'welt' system that characterised worker organisation long after our period, labour gangs would regulate the work between them with half the gang working while the others took their leisure as it suited them, until their 'shift' time arrived. This system, while frustrating the employers who saw it as a chosen culture of easy work practices and absenteeism, did not in fact serve the dockers and their families well. Linked in part to the highs and lows of labour demand associated with Liverpool's extreme tides, as well as to the structure of the unemployment support for unskilled day labourers, earnings on the docks on Merseyside by the 1960s were still three pounds a week below the national average.[8]

The weakness of trade unionism among the Liverpool dock workers was compounded by the ever-present problem of the religious divide between Catholics and Protestants. By the 1890s one-fifth of the national Roman Catholic population was concentrated in Liverpool.[9] Irish Catholic workers were also found disproportionately among the poorest sections of the Liverpool working class. In these circumstances, competition for day-labouring work between Catholic workers and unskilled Protestant workers was intense and pervaded all areas of life.[10] The overall result of these work and religious divides was a culture of acquiescence and a long-standing inability to resist the intensification of the labour process demanded by increasing trade as well as maritime competition with Britain's rivals abroad: principally the USA and Germany.[11] On the occasions when dock workers did take strike action the employers were stunned.[12]

In the period immediately before the transport strike, Liverpool had seen bloody sectarian violence. The night of 20 June 1909 had seen especially sharp confrontations between Protestants and Catholics after Orangemen armed with swords and other weapons attacked a Catholic procession upon a rumour that a consecrated host would be carried. That night, churches, priests and nuns were attacked as were children leaving Catholic schools. By February 1910, in the parishes of Our Lady's, St Anthony's and All Souls in Everton, 3,200 Catholics had been forced out of their homes in order to find safer areas to dwell.[13] Long after the First World War these divisions continued to play a role in the working-class life of the city and its surrounding area, as the 1932 means test riots in Birkenhead were to show when Orange Order police from Liverpool were brought over the Mersey to terrorise Catholic communities.[14]

During the War also, 'street nationalism' of an especially ugly form occurred on the occasion of the sinking of the *Lusitania* on 8 May 1915. Starting in the North End of the city, attacks on German shops, business premises and homes spread through Liverpool, out as far as Bootle and over the Mersey to Birkenhead and Seacombe in Wallasey.[15] Indeed, the anti-alien fury that the riots unleashed began to generalise into a wider xenophobia as Scandinavian, Russian, Italian and Chinese establishments also came under attack.[16]

After the War, race riots occurred. The 'race' (we should say 'racist') riots of June 1919 began with a brawl in a pub between Scandinavian and West Indian seamen. This fight (that began over a cigarette and ended with a knife attack) was the kind of skirmish that would have been all too familiar in and around the docks and harbour parts of the city.[17] But on the night of 8 June, against a background of tensions resulting from demobilisation and unemployment, this became a spark to riots that engulfed the city. That night, a twenty-nine-year-old Bermudan ex-ship's fireman, Charles Wootton, was chased from a sailor's home in Upper Pitt Street by a large crowd. He was thrown into a dock and pelted with stones as he tried to swim away, struggling in the water for some time before sinking.[18] His body was dragged from the Mersey two hours later. Over the next three nights, and with the covert encouragement of the police,[19] thousands of men walked the streets of Toxteth terrorising Ethiopian and Yemeni homes in the area and hostels housing Black seamen. Three West Africans were stabbed.

In this period, then, working-class political outlooks in Liverpool had been shaped by ethnic and religious conflict. In 1919, as we have seen, violent mobs carried out racist attacks. Indeed, this was typical of many of the maritime cities in Britain at the time. Dock work and seafaring, although characterised by the mixing of nationalities and cultures that is intrinsic to maritime industries, were also associated with dawn fights between men for the attention of the harbour master for a day's paid labour. Desperate competition for work following the war sharpened the already existing divisions of religion, ethnicity and even neighbourhood rivalry. This was the background to the racist riots of other port cities in this period, such as those at Cardiff, at Newport on the Usk, around the West India docks in East London, and in South Shields on the Tyne.[20] Seen in this light, the working-class strikes and solidarity actions that did occur are all the more remarkable. Indeed, it is only by seeing the 1911 strike against this uninspiring landscape – rather from the vantage point of a kind of cultural panopticon – that its true importance can really be seen. It is also only in this way that the claim for it as being the start of a *tradition* can be properly appreciated – and acknowledged.

Perhaps 70,000 workers were involved in the actions over the summer months of 1911. This was itself an extraordinary thing. Trade union organisation had strengthened enormously as a result of the strike. Membership of the National Union of Dock Labourers, for example, quadrupled by the end of 1911.[21] Considering the roles of the key leaders of the strike, principally Tom Mann and the syndicalist activists such as Joe Cotter of the Ships Stewards, Frank Pearce of the International Club, James Murphy of the Trades Council (all of the Strike Committee), Peter Larkin (brother of Jim Larkin) and Fred Bower (Liverpool stonemason and syndicalist agitator),[22] it was also an enormous achievement. The fact that syndicalist leaders, though a minority on the Strike Committee, were able to wield such a disproportionate influence, with their message of class unity and the taking of direct action outside of official trade union structures, is itself remarkable. Yet the real achievement was that of the thousands of mostly casual and previously unorganised labourers, who bore the brunt of the dangers and hardships of dock work and haulage and the poverty of below-national-average exploitation wages, in raising themselves to action. Indeed, we can go further. The strike wave of that year can be regarded as a classic example of syndicalist strike action.

> [I]t was in considerable measure a spontaneous, unofficial upsurge that encapsulated everything that syndicalists or anyone else could conceivably have meant by 'direct action'. This was perhaps no accident in view of the not inconsiderable syndicalist influence among the railwaymen, in Liverpool and elsewhere in the country ... the strike witnessed a great deal of violence and bloodshed as the government stationed a gunboat in the River

Mersey with the guns pointing at the city centre and the police instigating a major riot.[23]

The Strike Committee even rose to a level of control in the city that has been described as approaching 'dual power' as it issued permits for the carrying of goods through the streets of Liverpool.[24] Permitted goods were 'milk, "the child's staple diet", and bread, "the staff of life"'.[25] Importantly, also, the influence of the syndicalists was not only something that belonged to the 'heat of the struggle'. The following year, for instance, 60,000 turned out to hear Tom Mann speak at Shiel Park.[26]

Although the syndicalist influence limited the radicalism of the 1911 strike to that of primarily industrial significance, in one important sense it represented a political step forward for Liverpool workers. In 1911, the sectarianism that in so many ways held back Liverpool labour was pushed to the margins. The economic upswing of that year is one explanatory factor here.[27] So too is the fact that the government, in a state of panic over the Agadir crisis of that year, ordered troops into the city.[28] This resulted in the shootings of two workers – and two funerals attended by mourners of both denominations.[29] Nonetheless, it is also clear that the unifying message of the syndicalists had been important. In 1907, during the Belfast transport strike, Jim Larkin's influence had played a similar role in significantly reducing sectarianism.[30] The flavour of this unity is captured wonderfully by Fred Bower in his remembrances of 13 August of that year, the day that was to end as 'Bloody Sunday':

> From Orange Garston, Everton and Toxteth Park, from Roman Catholic Bootle, and the Scotland Road area, they came. Forgotten were their religious feuds, disregarded the dictum of some of their clerics on both sides who affirmed the strike was an atheist stunt. The Garston band had walked five miles and their drum-major proudly whirled his sceptre twined with orange and green ribbons as he led his contingent band, half out of the local Roman Catholic band, half out of the local Orange band. Now, no longer were they the playthings of 'big business'. This day they were MEN.[31]

Against the background of terrible attacks upon Catholic working-class communities by Orange gangs just two years previously and the history of deep religious enmity that had stunted the development of Liverpool trade unionism for so long, this was a remarkable moment. It is not that the religious divide simply disappeared.[32] Indeed, Labour politics retained a religious character in the city long after the strike.[33] Still, the fact remains that the marginalising of the Green and Orange divide in 1911 created a point of reference for the syndicalist and socialist street agitators of that time and of the generation that followed.

After 1911: Strikes, Agitations and
the Growth of a New Tradition

Reports of strikes pepper the local archives over the next year or so after 1911. Prominent in the records are strikes involving women workers. In 1912, nearly 2,000 women workers struck at Wilson's bobbin and shuttle factory in Garston over working conditions. The 'bobbin' strike, staged in the face of serious police aggression, won significant support from factories, pubs and shops across Garston and the city.[34]

Across the Irish Sea in Dublin, Liverpool's own Jim Larkin, also working under the influence of syndicalism and drawing upon the experience of the Liverpool transport strike, between 1911 and 1913 organised and led industrial battles using the tactic of the sympathy strike.[35] In early 1913, tram-workers, under Larkin's leadership, took action to force their employers to recognise the Irish Transport and General Workers' Union (ITGWU). Dublin employers responded with their own sympathetic industrial boycott across all sections of industry. The 1913 Dublin lockout, lasting eight months, was the most significant labour struggle in Irish labour history, only ending with the refusal of the British Trades Union Congress (TUC) to organise national solidarity action.

The 1913 lockout meant months of hardship for Dublin workers and significant financial support had come from the British TUC. More than this, groups of workers in Liverpool, along with those in Birmingham, Crewe and Derby came out in support of the Dublin workers. On 16 October, 3,500 Liverpool rail-workers blocked trade with Dublin in support of the locked-out workers.[36] However, despite the campaign to push the British TUC into calling a solidarity strike, no *national* action transpired. This spelled the end of strike action and these half-starved workers returned to their factories and yards early in 1914. The ITGWU was to recover, however, and the movement did establish the principle of local solidarity action by one group of workers for another. Liverpool workers had played their part in the creation of that tradition.

The onset of war brought the strike wave of 1910–14 to an end. Despite the presence of small pacifist groups and individual anti-militarist campaigners, this was as true of Liverpool as of any city in England at the time. It was in the period shortly following the war that Liverpool was once more at the centre of social and industrial strife. The city again concentrated the minds of the custodians of order. In the aftershock of the War Britain was in turmoil. Malnourishment and a violent flu epidemic struck down the poorest in their hundreds of thousands. Soldiers and non-commissioned officers mutinied, demanding to be demobilised. Sailors refused to embark to Russian waters. Workers came out on strike in industry after industry: on the railways; in engineering factories; in the mines; in the shipyards; and more besides. Six million working days were lost in 1918, nearly 35 million in 1919.[37] At a meeting with the leaders of the Triple Alliance of miners, railwaymen and transport trade unions in the early part of 1919, Lloyd George acknowledged that his government was paralysed.[38]

Against this background of rising industrial militancy across England during 1918, police in Liverpool and London went on strike. In October 1913, police had formed their first union. This was the Metropolitan Police Union that became the National Union of Police and Prison Officers (NUPPO). During the war this union enjoyed no official status and was forced to operate on a semi-clandestine footing. In August 1918, a London organiser, Police Constable Tommy Thiel, was arrested for trade union activity. The strike that ensued for his release and reinstatement (and over pay) forced Lloyd George's hand and the government conceded to the strikers' demands within days. Although the union was still not officially recognised its membership swelled to 55,000 by the following year.

In the summer of 1919, a national police strike was triggered by the introduction of the Police Bill that banned trade union organisation in the police force. During the August 1919 police strike half of the Liverpool force was out. The local Watch Committee was known for its draconian style of command and this, combined with the especially poor conditions of service and pay,[39] had created a well of resentment that now spilled over into the Liverpool movement. The strikers marched from station to station to call out those still at work. Reports of rioting, looting and a general breakdown of law and order caused great concern within the establishment.[40] It was well known in government circles that it had been the breakdown of the state in Russia that had made the Bolshevik revolution of 1917 possible. A fear of revolution was one element in the tactical calculations of the government as Liverpool was put under military control. Two battleships and a destroyer were sent in readiness to the Mersey while tanks were strategically stationed on the streets of the city.[41] Troops took key buildings by force with baton-charges and the threat of deadly force. One looter was shot dead by soldiers. As the grip of the state tightened strikers were dismissed and quickly replaced from the ranks of unemployed ex-soldiers. The Police Bill became law and the NUPPO largely collapsed.

The events in Liverpool in 1911 and in 1919 had been distinctive in their intensity and scale and had marked out the city (along with Glasgow, its cultural sister) for special attention by the state. In the years that followed, Liverpool took its place alongside other cities and regions in the national struggles, campaigns and disturbances that occurred around the country. In 1921, as unemployment in the country rose to 2.5 million, and against the background of the jailing of the Poplar councillors in East London, marches and rallies of the unemployed took place in Liverpool. In 1922, the National Unemployed Workers Movement, influenced by the newly formed Communist Party, organised its first unemployed workers' march to London. This march had its Liverpool contingent.[42]

It was not until 1926 that gunboats were to be seen on the Mersey again. During the General Strike of that year, with memories of the Liverpool transport strike and the police strikes still a factor in the government's calculations, HMS *Ramilies* and HMS *Barnham* as well as troops were sent to control the city. This decision was not made for purely historical reasons, however. It was the case, for instance, that workers on Merseyside were well prepared for the confrontation, having established their 'Council of Action' in 1925. The strike in the city and wider region was especially solid, with over 100,000 workers refusing to work. The engineers and shipyard workers were out in force and the levels of organisation these workers had achieved were to establish local traditions of collective strength that would last for decades. In places where work was continuing, confrontations occurred. In Wallasey and Birkenhead, the tramways that were still running were attacked.

The calling off of the General Strike by the TUC after just ten days, and the wholesale demoralisation it created in the British trade union movement, is well known. Liverpool and Merseyside were no different from any other part of the country in this respect and the years that followed were just as bleak for workers there as anywhere else. Still, against the backdrop of economic depression, soaring unemployment and hunger Merseyside workers played their part in the economic and political class struggles of the era: against the means test in Birkenhead in 1932; in the struggle against fascism in Spain through material aid and volunteers; in the unemployment marches from 1929 onwards.

When the episodes highlighted here are considered together a picture begins to emerge. Increasingly in this era working-class actions are defined by solidarity, sympathy strikes and conflict with the state. Increasingly, also, we see the establishment of general unionism and the emergence of a politics of class over religious denomination. Of course, the process was uneven and for each of the above-mentioned aspects exceptions can be found. The xenophobia and racism of the years during and immediately following the First World War are sobering illustrations of this. Nonetheless, a new mentality among working people in Liverpool did begin to emerge and develop following 1911. It is only when we consider these developments against their historical backdrop before the 1911 transport strike that we begin to appreciate this transformation. The working-class movement in Liverpool before the 1911 strike was wretched: divided by religious bigotry, dominated by clericalism and known for the highest levels of casualism and the lowest rates of pay by national standards.[43] Cowed, immiserated and politically backward working-class Liverpool had been regarded by the national trade union leaders of Edwardian England as a backwater that offered little prospect for organisation. That is what the 1911 strike changed.

Individuals and Families: Socialists who Made a Difference

Looking at the 1911 transport strike as the beginning of a tradition and culture of trade union solidarity, we do need to include some words of appreciation of the people who created it. These were the individuals who during the 1920s and 1930s drew the lessons of that momentous year and conveyed them in their street oratory, theoretical discussions and agitations.

Figures such as Tom Mann and James Larkin can overshadow more local and otherwise less conspicuous figures. Still, it was those less well known activists, in turning out the major rallies, organising the publicity flyers for walls and handcarts and turning their hand to whatever organising and oratorical task was required, who shaped the movement that was to come after them. These individuals varied in political affiliations. Some were revolutionary syndicalists; some had been linked to the Marxist Social Democratic Federation (SDF) or the Independent Labour Party; some were to become members of the Labour Party, some of the British Communist Party, while others would become followers of Leon Trotsky and members of the Revolutionary Socialist League of the 1930s.[44] All, however, were socialist and all preached a doctrine of class over faith, solidarity over competition and opposition to the capitalist system.

On 13 August 1911, police baton-charged demonstrating strikers at St George's Plateau. Among the faces of the demonstrators at that 'Bloody Sunday' was one Mary Bamber. Bamber (or 'Ma' Bamber, as she was to become known) had come to Liverpool from her native Edinburgh as a young women when her previously relatively well-heeled family fell on hard times. As a teenager she began to help out on the soup wagons that provided a basic hot meal for the poorest of the city. These wagons, organised by SDF activists, also carried a political message that was not lost on the young Bamber.

Bamber was appalled at the poverty of the people who came to the wagons and especially of the bag women who came by on their early morning walks to their work mending ropes and sacks for the ships in dock. Bamber was to mature into one of the most talented political figures of her time. She was central to the union organising that led to the bobbin strike of 1912 and the organising of café workers in the city.[45] A radical socialist, a suffragist and a labour organiser, she was to become, in the opinion of Sylvia Pankhurst, the 'finest, fighting platform speaker in the country'.[46] She was central also to the organisation of solidarity with the locked-out Dublin workers in 1913 and to Jim Larkin's speaking tour in the Liverpool region.

Bamber became a popular speaker, addressing working-class audiences at rallies, demonstrations and strike meetings. In 1918, she won the Everton ward on a socialist ticket. In 1920, Bamber was present as a founder member at the Manchester launch of the British Communist Party. Also present at the Manchester launch was Bamber's daughter, Elizabeth ('Bessie') Bamber, and Bessie's future husband, Jack Braddock.[47] Shifting sharply right-wards in later years, Jack and Bessie Braddock were to become a dominating force in the professionalised Labour Party that emerged in a later generation of British machine-style town politics. Although they were to leave the Communist Party in 1922, in this era – as young communists – they did help to shape a nascent local socialism through which those workers who had been radicalised by the class confrontations that had shaken the city were making sense of the world.

Another figure who helped to tilt the political conclusions being reached by the working-class people they influenced was George Garrett. Garrett was an unemployed docker who had been influenced by syndicalism and the organising model of the Industrial Workers of the World, which he had joined while working as a ship's stoker in the USA in 1918. He was also a highly learned man and publisher of ten short stories. George Orwell, who met Garrett, said of him:

> I was very greatly impressed by Garrett. Had I known before that it is he who writes under the pseudonym of Matt Low in the Adelphi and one or two other places, I would have taken steps to meet him earlier ... Apart from the enormous unemployment in Liverpool it is almost impossible for him to get work because he is blacklisted everywhere as a Communist.[48]

More importantly for our theme, he was an agitator, orator and political songster in the style of Joe Hill.[49] He was present, for instance, along with Mary Bamber, at the 'Storming of the Walker Art Gallery' on 12 September 1921.[50] This event had occurred during the 'Work or Maintenance' agitations of the National Unemployed Workers' Committee Movement (organised in Liverpool by Robert Tisseyman, who had led the Liverpool police strike two years earlier). Around 200 protesters who had occupied the gallery were severely beaten by the police that day. There was a real sense in which Garrett's involvement in the rough politics of the Liverpool street agitations of the era helped to challenge anti-alien feeling fostered by street demagogues. A speech he gave at an unemployed workers' demonstration in 1921 illustrates this well. This is what he said:

> Fellow workers, it is all very well criticising the alien as one of your speakers has been doing, and telling you that he is the cause of your unemployment. It is not so. The present rotten system is the cause ... All workers are slaves to the capitalists no matter what their race, colour or creed is, and there is more slavery under British Imperialism and the Union Jack than under any other flag. You Britishers, you sometimes give me a pain. I don't tell people I'm a Britisher. I had no choice in being where I was when I was born. How many of you have the guts of the Indians who are following Gandhi in India today, or following Michael Collins in Ireland? There people are only trying what we should be doing, breaking the bonds of their serfdom.[51]

At a demonstration of the unemployed, with the nationalist frenzy of 1915 and the murder of Charles Wootton in the not too distant past, and intense competition for work at the docks a daily reality, these were important words.

In an era of colourful figures one of the most colourful was Fred Bower. Bower was above all an internationalist. He had travelled widely and developed his syndicalist belief in a unity of interests of workers the world over in the workers' movements of the USA and England. A friend of Jim Larkin, he played an important role in 1911 as an agitator. He was the author of the appeal to troops not to fire upon workers that was published in the *Syndicalist*. Written in a style that was by turns lyrical, historical, biblical and passionate, it ended with the words:

> Out of OUR loins, OUR lives, OUR homes, YOU came.

> Don't disgrace YOUR PARENTS, YOUR CLASS, by being the willing tools any longer of the MASTER CLASS.

> YOU, like US, are of the SLAVE CLASS. When WE rise, YOU rise; when WE fall, even by your bullets, YE fall also.[52]

Five men (including Tom Mann) who were involved in the publishing of this appeal were jailed for up to six months for incitement to mutiny.[53]

At the time of the 1911 strike another of the figures who was to shape Merseyside working-class politics was himself eleven years old: old enough for the strike to leave an impression on a young and developing working-class mind. By the early 1930s Leo McGree was addressing audiences of hundreds at indoor rallies and open-air gatherings. Loved for his oratory, combining heartfelt hatred of capitalists and a razor-like wit, he could entertain as well as fascinate his audiences. A member of the Liverpool Communist Party he would travel across the Mersey to speak regularly on Sunday mornings at the gates of Birkenhead Park to crowds of up to 300 who stopped to listen on their ways to and from church. Stories from the time tell of how people would be moved by his rhetoric. They also tell of the small group of women who would regularly stand somewhere towards the back of the crowd listening and clucking with Catholic disapproval: 'And you wouldn't believe it, his brother's a *priest!*'[54] Indeed, the stories about McGree combined political affection with an admiring fascination at his daringness in organising under the noses of the police and his dodging of arrest for months at a time.[55] McGree was eventually jailed in 1932 for his 'role' in the Birkenhead riots of that year against the means test despite the fact that he had been in Sheffield at the time.

Another name that comes into historical focus in the 1930s, though coming into prominence after the Second World War, is that of Jimmy Deane. Deane became a recruit to the Trotskyist 'Militant Group' (that would become the Workers' International League the following year) in 1937 at the age of sixteen. Family connections here appear as a factor in the emergence of a tradition. Deane's mother Gertie joined the Militant Group the same year, then two brothers, Arthur and Brian, who went on to be significant figures in the Liverpool socialist movement. Gertie Deane's father, Charles Carrick, had been an important early figure in Liverpool Marxism as a prominent SDF organiser. The group that formed around the Deanes in the late 1930s were to become influential in Liverpool and Birkenhead left-wing trade union circles in the post-Second World War era. Deane himself became the convenor of the Amalgamated Engineering Union at the Cammell Laird shipyards in Birkenhead after the war.[56]

We are now a long way from the 1911 strike. But the strike still stands as the backdrop to the class-based politics that developed through the interwar period. The names that have been featured here are only the most prominent local activists and leaders from the records. They have been highlighted to emphasise a point. This is simply that traditions do not arise from events alone. They are created by individuals who interpret those events and make them relevant to their own times. These individuals are also only the most notable figures from many kinds of networks and organisations – as well as families[57] – through which such traditions are promulgated from one place to the next and from one generation to the next.

Conclusion

In his introduction to this volume John Belchem characterises the solidarity of 1911 as that of the consolidation of a 'white working class' settlement and cites the racist rhetoric of James Sexton, the official leader of the dockers' union in 1911. The statements of trade union officials such as Sexton are, however, one element of a more complicated picture. Many of the key moments in the transport strike of 1911 were largely spontaneous. This significantly reduced Sexton's political influence at the high points of the strike movement. Far more important were the syndicalists who wielded a non-sectarian and anti-racist influence that was hugely disproportionate to their numbers. Moreover, religious sectarianism was largely dormant during one of the most volatile and violent strikes in British history.[58]

In reality, Liverpool in the second two decades of the twentieth century was a city in the balance politically. On the one hand there was little sense in which objective conditions had seemed likely to give rise to a left-wing rebel city. There was no spontaneous eruption of socialism, for instance. Political violence, ethnic division and bigotry were very real aspects of working-class Liverpool. Joan Smith puts it well:

> In Liverpool from 1909 to 1922, the pattern of politics was one of alter-
> nating riot: anti-Catholic riot, strike riot, anti-German riot, post-war riots,
> anti-black riot, unemployed riot. Evolutionary socialism was not a 'natural'
> belief in Liverpool.[59]

While collective action, sympathy strikes and solidarity were one part of the story of working-class Liverpool in this era, as we have seen, the other was the club, the brick and the boot. Indeed, the xenophobic outbursts that did occur in the city might have made fertile ground for the British Fascisti launched just a few years later, taking the reputation of the city into quite a different historical trajectory.[60]

On the other hand there was desperation in the struggle to survive from day to day for many thousands of working people and consequently a deep sense of accumulated resentment that comes with always being pushed around. In itself again this does not lead inevitably to socialist conclusions. However, there was also the knowledge of these workers that in 1911 they had moved in their thousands in an act of dramatic resistance to capital and the state. There was something else also, something that this chapter has tried to capture. There were outspoken socialists who were rooted in the working-class communities of the city. There were also socialist families who, at many different levels, across different age groups and from within different brands of leftist politics, transmitted a socialist view of things. It is interesting to note also that in 1911, along with the dockers, transport and haulage workers, school pupils went on strike. The kinds of conversation, discussion and argument that these created around the kitchen table we can only imagine.

The political traditions of modern Liverpool were in formation in the era following 1911. They would not have been obvious to a casual view. The 'episodes' of the era were, as we have seen, of wildly fluctuating political types. And yet in the years shortly after the First World War in workplaces, on the streets, at the rallies, in the skirmishes and on the larger mobilisations there were the Mary Bambers and the George Garretts shaping how working people interpreted their experiences and their actions. In the later interwar years there were the Leo McGrees and the Jimmy Deanes whose influence helped to direct working-class anger away from the pulpit, the Orange club and the dawn fights on the dock gate, towards conclusions that suggested to the poorest of the city than class rather than religion or race provided the best basis for survival. For that we are indebted to the few whose names have been mentioned here, to many more whose names have not been mentioned and to the families that carried their messages of hope and working-class unity from one generation to the next. We are also indebted to the strikers of 1911 and the tradition of non-sectarian industrial organisation that they made possible.

Notes

1 Robert J. Holton, *British Syndicalism, 1900–1914: Myths and Realities* (London: Pluto Press, 1976), p. viii.

2 John Belchem, 'Radical Prelude: 1911', in this volume, p. 25.

3 Ibid., p. 36.

4 Structural factors alone do not usually provide a full explanation of the emergence and continuation of working-class traditions. Occupational composition, class fractions and sub-fractions, industrial upturn and downturn, migration inflows and outflows etc. are all important explanatory variables to consider. Real history, however, can sometimes confound an exclusive use of structural factors. A study

that was important in demonstrating this intuitive point empirically (as well as being directly relevant to the Merseyside area) looked in detail at strikes in the UK between 1968 and 1973 (C. T. B. Smith, R. Clifton, P. Makeham, S. W. Creigh and R. W. Burn, 'Strikes in Britain', Department of Employment, Manpower Paper No. 15 (1978)). Its analysis revealed that Merseyside in this period was the most strike-prone area of the UK, with 2.43 times the national average of workdays lost. It also revealed, however, that national variability in strike statistics could not be explained using structural factors alone. The tradition of Merseyside working-class militancy, long associated with the docks (at least as far back as the 1911 strike), that in the 1970s shifted to the car plants and in the 1980s to local government and other parts of the public sector, has been characterised by radical political outlooks and the militant attitudes that accompanied them. These more subjective (though no less material) factors are not captured by industry-sector and industrial-relations statistics. Yet they do need to be incorporated to complete the story of the transmission of working-class traditions. Political organisation would be one example of subjective factors that need to be factored into a fuller and more adequate analysis of the rise and fall of working-class traditions. Religious affiliations would be another. The national traditions of immigrant groups would be a third. For all of these factors, and more, the working-class family would also serve as a vehicle of transmission of traditions between the generations.

5 In fact, scant research has been done on the threads of working-class radicalism that connect these two historical eras in Liverpool. This is work that is largely waiting to be done. I am grateful to Sam Davis for this insight.

6 Joan Smith, 'Labour Tradition in Glasgow and Liverpool', *History Workshop Journal*, 17 (Spring 1984): 32–56.

7 R. Price, 'The New Unionism and the Labour Process', in W. J. Mommsen and H.-G. Husung (eds), *The Development of Trade Unionism in Great Britain and Germany, 1880–1914* (London: HarperCollins, 1985), p. 140.

8 Francis Kenny, '"Good Men": The History and Culture of Liverpool Dockworkers', *North West Labour History Journal*, 29 (2004): 14.

9 Ibid., 12.

10 Eric Taplin, *Dockers and Seamen, 1870–1890* (University of Hull, 1974), p. 3.

11 George Dangerfield traces the effects of the rapid industrial developments of the USA and Germany, and the inflationary effects of cheap gold, upon the cost of living for British workers from the 1890s through to the Great Unrest period of 1910 to 1914. George Dangerfield, *The Strange Death of Liberal England* (London: Serif, 1997), pp. 180–83.

12 Price, 'The New Unionism and the Labour Process', p. 138.

13 Frank Neal, *Sectarian Violence: The Liverpool Experience, 1819-1914. An Aspect of Anglo-Irish History* (Manchester University Press, 1987), p. 234.

14 This story was recounted to me by my paternal grandmother, Eileen McMahon, who witnessed and experienced first-hand the atrocious behaviour of these policemen towards Birkenhead Catholic communities during the days (and particularly nights) of the disturbances.

15 Gregory Dawson, *Wirral Gleanings* (Irby: Dawson Publishing, 1998), p. 27.

16 John Belchem, *Irish, Catholic and Scouse: The History of the Liverpool-Irish, 1800–1940* (Liverpool University Press, 2007), pp. 255–57.

17 Jacqueline Nassy Brown, *Dropping Anchor, Setting Sail: Geographies of Race in Black Liverpool* (Princeton University Press, 2005), p. 21.

18 Joshua Harris, Tina Wallace and Heather Booth, *To Ride the Storm: The Bristol 'Riot' and the State* (London: Heinemann, 1983), p. 221.

19 Brown, *Dropping Anchor, Setting Sail*, p. 21.

20 Jacqueline Jenkinson, *Black 1919: Riots, Racism and Resistance in Imperial Britain* (Liverpool University Press, 2008).

21 Taplin, *Dockers and Seamen*, p. 17.

22 Robert J. Holton, 'Syndicalism and Labour on Merseyside, 1906–14', in Harold Hikins (ed.), *Building the Union: Studies on the Growth of the Workers' Movement* (Liverpool: Toulouse Press, 1973), p. 138.

23 J. White, 'Syndicalism in a Mature Industrial Setting: The Case of Britain', in M. van der Linden and W. Thorpe (eds), *Revolutionary Syndicalism: An International Perspective* (Aldershot: Scolar Press, 1990), p. 108.

24 Ibid., p. 108.

25 Eric Taplin, *Near to Revolution: The Liverpool General Transport Strike of 1911* (Liverpool: Bluecoat Press, 1994), p. 66.

26 Holton, 'Syndicalism and Labour on Merseyside', p. 142.

27 Robert J. Holton, 'Revolutionary Syndicalism and the British Labour Movement', in Mommsen and Husung, *The Development of Trade Unionism*, p. 272.

28 In July 1911, German gunboat *Panther* moored provocatively off the coast of Morocco precipitating a diplomatic crisis that portended the onset of war.

29 Belchem, 'Radical Prelude: 1911', in this volume, p. 29.

30 Holton, 'Syndicalism and Labour on Merseyside', pp. 139–40.

31 Fred Bower, *Rolling Stonemason: An Autobiography* (London: Jonathan Cape, 1936), p. 195.

32 Holton, 'Syndicalism and Labour on Merseyside', p. 147.

33 Sam Davies, *Liverpool Labour Party and Trades Council: A Brief Introduction to the Microfilm Edition of Liverpool Labour Party and Trades Council Records, 1862–1986* (Wakefield: Microform Academic Publishers, 1999), p. 11.

34 Garston and District Local History Society, *Trouble at the Bobbin Works* (Liverpool: Garston and District Local History Society, 2006).

35 John Newsinger, *Rebel City: Larkin, Connolly and the Dublin Labour Movement* (London: Merlin, 2004), pp. 16–18.

36 Ibid., p. 56.

37 Chanie Rosenberg, *1919: Britain on the Brink of Revolution* (London: Bookmarks, 1987), p. 7.

38 Aneurin Bevan, *In Place of Fear* (London: Heinemann, 1952), pp. 20–21.

39 Anthony Judge and Gerald William Reynolds, *The Night the Police Went on Strike* (London: Weidenfeld & Nicolson 1961), p. 153.

40 Ibid., p. 167.

41 Raymond Challinor, *The Origins of British Bolshevism* (London: Croom Helm, 1977), p. 64.

42 For a fascinating account of the activity and development of the National Unemployed Workers' Movement on Merseyside, see Tony Lane, 'Some Merseyside Militants of the 1930s', in Hikins, *Building the Union*, pp. 154–60.

43 For an account of the social squalor that characterised the lives of the Irish poor of Liverpool, see Pat O'Mara, *The Autobiography of a Liverpool Irish Slummy* (London: Martin Hopkinson, 1934).

44 Each of these political parties and traditions, of course, has significantly different histories that are tied to international and national developments as well as local circumstances. There is no space in this chapter to explore the ways in which these differences played out in Liverpool. The point here is that of the general significance of social agitation in the city.

45 Krista Cowman, 'Women and Radicalism in Liverpool c.1890–1930', in this volume, and Cowman, 'Voices, Votes and Mock Turtle Soup: Liverpool's Socialist Women, 1893–1914', *North West Labour History Journal*, 29 (2004): 9.

46 Quoted in 'Mary Bamber – Free Radical', *Nerve*, 9.

47 The importance of this family link (and radical family links more generally) is highlighted by Thomas Linehan, *Communism in Britain, 1920–39: From the Cradle to the Grave* (Manchester University Press, 2007), p. 80.

48 'The Road to Wigan Pier Diary', in Ian Angus and Sonia Orwell (eds), George Orwell, *The Collected Essays, Journalism and Letters*, vol. 1, *An Age Like This, 1920–1940* (London: Secker and Warburg, 1968), p. 187.

49 Joe Hill was the Swedish-born member of the Industrial Workers of the World who became legendary as a writer and singer of rebel worker songs in the US labour movement of the early twentieth century.

50 Suzanne MacLeod, 'Civil Disobedience and Political Agitation: The Art Museum as a Site of Protest in the Early Twentieth Century', *Museum and Society*, 5.1 (2006): 44–57.

51 Joseph Pridmore, 'George Garrett, Merseyside Labour and the Influence of the United States', in Michael Murphy and Deryn Rees-Jones (eds), *Writing Liverpool: Essays and Interviews* (Liverpool University Press, 2007), p. 34.

52 Bower, *Rolling Stonemason*, p. 181.

53 In his autobiography Bower explains that upon hearing of the arrests he offered to turn himself in but that Tom Mann would have none of it, objecting that one more victim would not help the workers' movement. Ibid., p. 182.

54 This story again comes from Eileen McMahon, who as a young woman would go to the gates of Birkenhead Park to listen to Leo McGree.

55 Marvellous personal remembrances of Leo McGree's activities by three 'Merseyside militants' (Bert Pinguey, Jack Fitzgerald and Joe Byrne) are available in Lane, 'Some Merseyside Militants of the 1930s', pp. 160–76.

56 Jimmy Deane was to go on to become a central figure in the launching of the second Revolutionary Socialist League in 1957 and as such is frequently referred to as one of the originators (if not *the originator*) of what was eventually to become the Militant Tendency in the Liverpool Labour Party.

57 The role of political families is important in the story of 1911 and the creation of class-based politics in Merseyside. For example, the members of Jim Larkin's family

(brother Peter and sister Delia) played significant roles in the 1911 strike. There are also the examples of mother and daughter Mary Bamber and Bessie Braddock, as well as the Deane family who we have considered. One more example would be father and son John Hamilton (elder) and John Hamilton (junior), who have not been discussed here.

58 Taplin does note an increase in sectarian tensions that had previously lain dormant following the deployment of extra police and army regiments. Taplin, *Near to Revolution*, p. 18.

59 Smith, 'Labour Tradition in Glasgow and Liverpool', p. 43.

60 The British Fascisti were founded in 1923, one year after Mussolini's march on Rome. This became the National Fascisti the following year. The emergence of the politically ambiguous, populist New Party in 1931 represented the forerunner of what would become Moseley's British Union of Fascists in 1932. An excellent account of the New Party in the north west is provided in Matthew Worley, 'Who Makes the Nazis? North West Experiences of the New Party, 1931–32', *North West Labour History*, 32 (2007): 7–16.

9
From the Ground Up:
Radical Liverpool Now

Kenn Taylor

This book tells the story of a century in the life of a radical city. One hundred years of turmoil, extreme change, alternative ideas and independent action. Different radical currents have flown through Liverpool over the years but underneath it all the city's inhabitants seem to have developed a fiercely independent nature that defies any attempt to pin it down – a nature that mistrusts external authority, frequently defies conventional logic and seeks practical solutions to seemingly intractable problems.

If you talk about radical politics and activism in Liverpool, there is an inevitable harking back to the radical socialism that was a key component of the city's identity after 1911 – especially during the 1980s, when a local authority dominated by the Militant Tendency infamously refused to set a legal budget as an act of resistance against a hostile Conservative government.[1] This, along with the radical trade union activity throughout the city and the Toxteth riots of 1981, helped cast a view of Liverpool as a hotbed of revolutionary socialism that still persists today.

Yet, as documented elsewhere by John Belchem, this was far from representative of Liverpool's grassroots politics throughout its history. If 1911 was the year that marked Liverpool's shift towards a form of socialism, then the 1980s were perhaps its peak. And almost as soon as this aspect of the city's character entered into the national consciousness it had begun to decline.

Contributing to this, no doubt, was the failure of the Militant council to bring down the Conservative central government and fund the municipal socialism they promised – not to mention distaste within the city for some of their methods. This, along with a decline in trade union membership and disappointment in thirteen years of New Labour government, has considerably reduced the influence of the labour movement in Liverpool at a grassroots level. It has been suggested in light of this that the city has lost its radical nature and become overwhelmed by apathy. Indeed,

Liverpool has some of the lowest voter turnouts in the UK.[2] However, this chapter will argue that this decline has seen an emergence, or perhaps a re-emergence, of a different type of radicalism in the city.

In recent years, large sections of Liverpool have been transformed, mostly in a positive way. But beneath this brave new regenerated city there are still many problems and, with them, a vast undercurrent of grassroots activism that is fighting to rebuild the city from the ground up. The radical spirit that has over the years fuelled protests, riots, strikes, occupations and takeovers, remains. As do the skills, in organising, protesting, publicising and delivering action. Though much of this is still organised and influenced by those who were part of the labour movement, the landscape has changed. This spirit perhaps harks back to something older and deeper in the psyche of Liverpool's citizens: to the culture forged in the dire poverty of Victorian Liverpool, when the character that came to be known as 'Scouse' was being formed and the gulf between rich and poor was so vast.

Perhaps the best-known example of grassroots community activism in Liverpool during the last thirty years has been that surrounding the development of the Eldonian Village. Here, in deprived Vauxhall, a celebrated, self-organised community grew up on wasteland, against the odds and in the face of an actively hostile local authority. In Liverpool it has frequently been individuals rather than movements that have defined the city's activism. This is exemplified by Tony McGann, who led the residents of the Eldon Street and Burlington Street tenements to develop the Eldonian Village. His actions were driven by a desire to prevent their community being broken up and dispersed to estates on the fringes of the city – the fate of so many other working-class communities in Liverpool due to successive slum clearance programmes from the 1930s onwards.[3]

Encouraged by the then Liberal-dominated city council in the early 1980s to form a housing co-operative, the residents that were to become known as the Eldonians had their plans undermined when Labour gained control of the city in 1983. Coming up against a local Labour party keen that it alone should control housing and community development, the residents nevertheless battled on. Determined that they knew what was best for the community, they had come to mistrust the council, of whichever political stripe, for having failed to deliver the services they had promised.

In order to bring their plans to fruition, McGann and his fellow community association members worked not only with the labour movement but also formed alliances with everyone from Conservative 'Minister for

Merseyside' Michael Heseltine to major construction companies, architects, social landlords and even royalty, developing the new 'urban village'
over a number of years and many hurdles.

From a humble start the Eldonian Village has grown into a development
renowned around the world, even winning the UK's first United Nations
World Habitat Award in 2004 for creating 'an internationally recognised model of community-led sustainable regeneration'.[4] The Eldonian
Community Trust and its various subsidiaries have since expanded into
many other areas beyond housing, establishing a local leisure centre,
nursery and village hall. They have also worked with private developers and
other partners on expanding the area and encouraging younger families to
move in. The result is a 'self-regenerating community'.[5]

The Eldonian Village was a radical project at the time, but it was not
Liverpool's first attempt to create better lives through buildings. Poverty
has meant that problems with housing have dominated the city for much of
its existence, as have attempts to find solutions to them. Liverpool Corporation is noted as having built the first local-authority-owned housing in
the UK in 1869,[6] thus bringing new standards into the housing of the poor.
Later, between the wars, the city pioneered continental-style tenement
blocks and developed out-of-town housing estates. As such initiatives
moved from being radical to the norm in the post-war era, Liverpool also
became home to some of the largest housing associations in the UK,[7] these
largely focused on regenerating older, abandoned city-centre properties
that had been left to rot by the council. However, the well meaning that had
seen the city pioneer the first municipal housing eventually became lost
among council bureaucracy and limited funds. Even the housing associations morphed to become huge public corporations, now often perceived
as being as remote as local authorities themselves.

With the emergence of the Eldonian Village, Liverpool also became
a test bed for large-scale co-operative urban development. For many
years the city had searched for solutions to its housing problems and
come up with groundbreaking ideas that were later adopted nationally;
the Eldonian solution, however, was developed from within the community itself, not imposed by outside 'experts'. The Eldonians realised that
rebuilding housing was not on its own enough to tackle deprivation and
create a sustainable community. Control by local people over their own
environment and long-term, multifaceted thinking were key. This was in
contrast to the zealousness with which Liverpool city council had pursued
its flawed modernist-influenced housing developments in the 1950s and
1960s. Whist acknowledging that the dire post-war housing shortage

contributed to this, these schemes, developed by outsiders with utopian ideals and often rigid beliefs, were frequently ill thought out and badly built. Such estates were imposed onto people with little thought for the fragile ecosystems that provided support in poor communities, creating untold damage, the effects of which remain today.

The failure time and again of such grand plans and ideologies dreamt up by outsiders to improve the lives of the poor in Liverpool, be they from politician, academic, architect or otherwise, has helped create a mistrust of such ideas in the city, fostering instead a do-it-yourself mentality where disenfranchised communities have taken matters into their own hands. The work of Tony McGann and the Eldonians prompted Prince Charles to remark, 'Men and women, through the power of their own personalities, can achieve more than millions spent through committees'[8] – a comment no doubt with which many citizens of Liverpool would agree.

It took the prospect of their community being broken up and dispersed to galvanise the residents of Eldon Street and Burlington Street into creating the Eldonian Village. A similar crisis in the Croxteth area of the city was to prompt equally radical action at around about the same time. In 1980, Liverpool city council stated its intention to close Croxteth Comprehensive School, doing so without consulting the local community or even informing the school's head teacher.[9] Croxteth was one of Liverpool's rapidly built, post-war peripheral housing estates and the school was one of the few facilities the deprived community had. Numerous intense protests against closure were quickly organised,[10] but when these came to nothing, parents and local residents took the decision forcibly to occupy the school on the day before its planned closure in 1982. This radical action sent shockwaves through both the community and the authorities, as recalled by local resident Irene Madden: 'I've never known an atmosphere like it ... I think the Council and the government got the shock of their lives, you know when we stood up to them.'[11] Unlike the Eldonians, those involved in the Croxteth occupation were fighting the then Liberal-dominated council and had the support of the Labour group, but once again they were defying the power of a local authority they perceived as remote to try to protect the interests of the local community.

Soon after the occupation, the Croxteth Community Action Committee took the decision to open their own community school in the building, despite overwhelming odds and no real funding. The committee was led largely by Phil Knibb, like Tony McGann, another tough individual who commanded the respect of the local community.[12] It organised and operated all aspects of the school and its round the clock occupation in partnership with parents and pupils. Volunteer teachers came from across the country, donations were successfully sought and supplies given by local factories. They received widespread media coverage and even won celebrity backing from Vanessa Redgrave and UB40 – all this in the face of legal threats from the council and the electricity being cut off.[13] The current UK coalition government are keen on 'free schools' and communities setting up and running their own educational establishments, but in 1982 Liverpool was once again pushing a radical idea that was attacked by many in politics and the media. The *Daily Mail* even suggested that 'the strange Indian cult Anada Marga' was at work in the 'school of chaos'.[14]

After Labour won control of the city council, Croxteth Comprehensive was taken back fully into local authority control in 1985. However, the occupation had helped create a new sense of community activism and empowerment in the area. Early in the occupation the Action Committee formed several subcommittees to work on wider local issues, including providing activities for young people, tackling the area's heroin problem and providing support for older members of the community – work that was to continue long after the school campaign had ended.[15]

In 1999, an old people's residential home in the centre of Croxteth became available for purchase and a number of Committee members pooled their savings and redundancy monies to buy it and turn it into a community-based education centre. Since then, the now Alt Valley Community Trust, still led by Phil Knibb, has grown beyond all recognition. The old people's home has been turned into 'The Communiversity' and is the main base for the organisation's work. Social businesses have been set up in local shopping units purchased by the trust and a vocational skills training centre for young people has opened in the former St Swithin's Church – a project that is now entirely self-financed through contracts.[16] Even the local leisure centre has been taken over by the trust through asset transfer.[17]

Croxteth Comprehensive School was once more threatened with closure by the city council at the end of 2008. The decision again sparked outcry in the local community, which refused to accept the verdict. This time there was no occupation, but they became among only a handful nationally who managed to take their case to the High Court in an unsuccessful bid to challenge the ruling. However, having lost that battle, members of the community are attempting to turn something negative into something positive. At the time of writing, the Alt Valley Community Trust is in discussions with Liverpool city council to take ownership of the modern technology and sports blocks of the school to expand its own education provision.[18] Croxteth is another example of a community being pushed into taking control of its own situation, no longer allowing itself to be at the mercy of external forces. This recurrent theme of recent activism has arguably filled the vacuum left by the decline and failure of the overarching ideologies and systems that such communities had come to rely on.

The mistrust of grand schemes within Liverpool has manifested itself most recently perhaps in campaigns around the city's European Capital of Culture 2008 designation. Winning the status in 2003 was one of, if not *the*, biggest things to happen to the city in the last twenty years. Property values rose overnight[19] and there was nothing short of euphoria in some quarters that Liverpool's importance finally seemed to be officially acknowledged after so much decline and derision. In particular the city's cultural community, which had struggled to survive through years of austerity, felt that its role was finally being recognised.

But it all soon began to slip. The Culture Company running the year was perceived as remote, the programme for 2008 was accused of not acknowledging 'local' culture and links between the title and wider development plans began to emerge. Rightly or wrongly, building developments such as Grosvenor's Liverpool One[20] and the Housing Market Renewal Pathfinder programme instigated by the government were lumped together with the award as the city went through an intense period of growth it had not experienced in years. This development was fuelled not only by the culture title but by increased inward investment and the global easy-credit boom.

As rapid development continued in the build-up to 2008, the city's artistic fringe found itself being pushed out of its studios and venues by the rapidly developing legions of bars and flats. Ironically, however, the Capital of Culture title also provided a hook for the city's artistic grassroots to resist these developments, which, with the credit boom and the like, would probably have happened anyway, as it did in other cities across the UK. A loose anti-2008 movement emerged, questioning not only how plans for the year were being handled but the whole notion of regeneration and the Capital of Culture status in and of itself.

The big spark for all of this appears to have been the fight against the proposed closure of the Quiggins 'alternative' shopping centre to make way for the Liverpool One development.[21] Ultimately, the campaign did not succeed, though the shopping centre has since been moved elsewhere in the city, but it became a powerful symbol and rallying point of the 'independent' and 'local' against the 'corporate' and 'global', even if the Liverpool One development has subsequently proved very popular in the city. Similar campaigns were mounted around the Picket music venue[22] and the Parr Street Studios recording complex, both threatened with conversion into apartments. Angry words were raised in independent local publications such as *Mercy* and *Nerve* and pretty soon even the mainstream media began questioning what was happening in Liverpool.

The city then became a test case for contemporary urban regeneration ideas that had developed over the intervening thirty years. In the aftermath of the 1981 Toxteth riots, the Conservative-backed, quango-led regeneration initiatives around the Garden Festival, the Albert Dock and the Southern Docks meant that Liverpool was among the first cities to experience the sort of leisure- and private-housing-led regeneration later adopted by former industrial areas around the country. And, in the build-up to 2008, what was happening in the city was to highlight the flaws in these ideas.

Liverpool subsequently began to attract considerable criticism from both academia and the broadsheets for its regeneration plans, with commentators questioning just how much of the city's renaissance was trickling down positively to affect poor local communities. That many of the same people had previously talked up the triumphs of similar schemes in London, Manchester, Birmingham *et al.*, despite the fact that these areas all retained similar levels of deprivation masked by redeveloped central areas, seemed lost. Liverpool was blamed for telling a wider truth about the UK's situation that was soon to be exposed by the credit crunch. Many commentators who had previously backed such forms of regeneration subsequently washed their hands of these ideas in the same way as did zealous supporters of post-war modernist development when communities themselves highlighted the flaws of their new towns and high-rises.

The city again showed the rest of the country 'the error of its ways' and demonstrated the power of grassroots action. This perhaps is Liverpool's greatest contribution to the wider world for having been awarded European Capital of Culture: to have been the place that questioned, even deconstructed, the whole concept, in the process changing the way many people think globally about concepts of culture, cities and regeneration.

The other big issue that has provoked intense community activism in Liverpool in recent years is the Housing Market Renewal Initiative (HMRI) Pathfinder programme. Instigated in the early 2000s by the Labour government, its intention was to regenerate areas where housing demand was seen to have failed and that were suffering from dereliction and the inherent problems it creates.[23] Based on a report by academics from the University of Birmingham, the plan advocated wholesale demolition and reconstruction of many deprived areas of the UK.[24]

Liverpool city council adopted the policy enthusiastically and began buying up properties, often through compulsory purchase orders,[25] and instigating a demolition programme. This was perhaps understandable as after years of government underfunding the city was being offered a large amount of money for housing development. But the plans were fiercely resisted in parts of the city as once again the council was seen to be imposing its will unthinkingly on local communities. Some even accused the plans as amounting to 'social cleansing' and an attempt to drive poorer people out of the city.[26]

As with previous demolition schemes, HMRI galvanised local residents into taking control of their own surroundings. In Toxteth, one of several areas where there was a reaction against the programme, committees and residents' groups were created to fight the plans. Alliances were developed with politicians, heritage groups and even Beatles fans, since one house up for demolition in the 'Welsh Streets' area had once been the home of Ringo Starr. Partnerships were also formed with housing co-operatives and private developers who stated their intention to renovate rather than demolish the area's empty properties.[27] There have also been symbolic and imaginative responses against the plans. Poetry and art was daubed on the doors and windows of threatened houses in the Welsh Streets. Meanwhile, in the nearby 'Four Streets' area of Granby, residents have undertaken 'guerrilla gardening',[28] planting flowers and vegetables among the empty buildings to create a veritable oasis of green in an area now blighted by urban decay. Local street markets and parties have also been organised to highlight the strength of feeling and community spirit, again powerful symbols against the might of a massive national government initiative and the council's plans.

Campaigns against HMRI have had mixed successes across the city, and it must also be pointed out that a proportion of the residents involved did back demolition and reconstruction.[29] Nevertheless, at the time of writing, the council had recently announced plans to refurbish rather than demolish some of the houses in the Four Streets area,[30] while the Granby Residents Association hopes the demise of HMRI funding might now allow for more community-led refurbishment schemes to takes its place.[31] However, a question mark continues to remain over whether the high-profile campaign to save the Welsh Streets will be successful.[32]

Communities taking over and reusing spaces left abandoned by Liverpool's economic problems can be seen time and again across the city. Another example is in the Dingle area of Liverpool 8, where a high-profile campaign was instigated to take over, refurbish and bring back into use

a prominent local building that had been left to rot. The Florence Institute was originally gifted to the area by Sir Bernard Hall, a merchant,
Alderman and former Mayor of Liverpool. Named after his daughter, who
died tragically at the age of twenty-two, 'the Florrie' was officially opened
in Mill Street in 1890 and became a focal point for the local youth and
community for many years. With funding running dry, the Florrie was
eventually sold in 1987 with the intention that its charitable work should
be continued by another body. Unfortunately, this never happened and the
building became neglected, a target for vandals and the elements.[33]

As the building decayed, the local community formed a pressure group,
'The Friends of the Florrie', to bring it back into use. A community-led
trust was set up at the end of 2004 and completed a consultation on the
building's future. Denise Devine, chair of the trust and also managing
director of the nearby Toxteth Town Hall, says the needs of local people
were paramount: 'There has been door to door and group consultation
throughout and that will continue ... It really means a lot in the hearts and
minds of local people, the Florrie bettered people, it made them better,
honest, hardworking people ... It will fulfil that function again – from
cradle to grave, Sunday to Sunday.'[34]

The Florence Institute Trust has worked hard over the last few years to
develop a regeneration plan for the building and to raise funds to restore
it into a multi-ethnic community centre for all ages and abilities. The plan
for the new Florrie includes exhibition and performance space, activities
for young people and the elderly, an indoor/outdoor sport area, childcare
facilities, workspaces for local business and a heritage resource centre.
Having raised over £6.4 million from a variety of sources including the
Heritage Lottery Fund and the city council, in June 2010 it was reported
that work was due to start on the new Florrie with a planned completion
at the end of 2011.[35] The trust has also formed an agreement with the main
building contractor that wherever possible jobs on the project should be
sourced from the local community.[36] As Denise Devine documents, once
again this initiative was led by the community itself: 'The Friends of the
Florrie is a home-grown grassroots organisation that has had to take the
lead when no-one else wanted to touch it with a barge pole. Now people
are inspired and have had their faith restored.'[37]

This chapter has attempted to show that grassroots radicalism is still a
key component of Liverpool's culture, and also to draw together some of
the factors that link these different actions and initiatives. Rather than
Liverpool adhering to an overarching radical ideology, there are instead

many instances of the city's deprived communities refusing to be crushed or to have their destiny controlled by external forces. If anything, that is the underlying radical undercurrent in Liverpool now, and possibly always has been.

Community activists in the city have always had general mistrust of external authority or anyone trying to impose anything on them, be it government, institution, trade union, political party or local authority. There is also an equal distrust of grand plans and ideas, usually because time and again they have been shown to fail the people they are most meant to help. The dreams of 1911 and of other attempts at rapid radical change in Liverpool – be they the slum clearances, Militant Tendency or leisure-led regeneration – have rarely brought the transformative benefits they promised.

Although disparate, all the actions I have described – everything from short-term campaigns to full-blown community takeovers – seem to have similar motivations: wresting control of the local environment from distant, unaccountable figures and working towards practical, long-term goals that reflect the needs of the city's people. Such activism has filled the vacuum created by successive local and national government indifference or incompetence and the decline in trade union and Labour party support.

If deprived communities are to survive and prosper, it can only happen with local control and action that comes from the ground up. Some may find the city's and its communities' ruck for independence and self-determination exasperating, while it is also true that it can be hard to strike to strike a balance between this and Liverpool's need to develop its economy and infrastructure; but when this spirit is directed to solid agency it can be magnificent and can transform the lives of those involved with it. Such communities have also time and again pioneered solutions to seemingly intractable problems and highlighted to the rest of the UK where it is going wrong. For doing so, Liverpool often gets the blame for spoiling the party. But, for that the country owes the city a debt, as it is frequently ideas formed in the turmoil of this radical city that become tomorrow's 'common-sense' solutions.

Indeed, many of the campaigns and initiatives mentioned in this chapter that were once considered radical, even dangerous, ideas – self-organised housing co-operatives, community school takeovers and local control over facilities and services – are now in vogue, favoured by the current UK coalition government as part of its 'Big Society' agenda, suggesting that communities will be able to take over from the role of the state services for which it is withdrawing funding. In fact, just before the 2010 general election, Conservative leader David Cameron visited a Liverpool social enterprise called MerseySTRIDE on Great Homer Street in Everton – a furniture workshop that provides work for local unemployed, homeless and otherwise disadvantaged people – saying that it demonstrated his ideas for the 'Big Society' in action: 'The biggest thing is to build a stronger society – we've got to help people who are unemployed for a long time and social enterprises like this help. It demonstrates where giving more power and control to projects like these works.'[37]

Most people in Liverpool would agree that communities themselves know what is best for them. Is the city then not only leading the way in radical new ideas, but for once not going against the grain of the rest of the country? Yet, what promoters of the 'Big Society' do not acknowledge is that many of the most successful initiatives discussed here, from the development of the Eldonian Village to the Florence Institute restoration in Dingle, despite being community-led, have required a complex mesh of external funding and support. In a city that relies heavily on national government funding that is now being withdrawn, this is something that in future will be in short supply. And, despite the grassroots activism of the past thirty years often operating against the grain and with limited support, it was the withdrawal of such funding and support in the past that helped create so much damage in these communities and fostered the need for such radical action in the first place. It is also why it has taken so much work and extra money over the years to build things back up. If all that disappears once again, it can only undo so much of what has been achieved. With the government refusing to admit that the voluntary and the community-led also requires financial support, it has to be asked how many of these projects will be able to continue their current good work, let alone replace the role of local and national government provision. Indeed, despite Cameron's pre-election support for MerseySTRIDE, once in power, the coalition government quickly axed the Future Jobs Fund programme that had provided much of the funding for placements at this social enterprise.[38] It seems the 'Big Society' might end up just being another flawed, top-down ideology that Liverpool's communities will have to resist, counteract and find solutions to.

What then is the future of grassroots activism in Liverpool? Much has changed since 1911, but much remains the same: the interconnected problems associated with poverty, housing, unemployment, crime, ill-health, education and opportunity. As the last hundred years have taught us, there are no easy answers to any of these. Yet something else we have learned over the last century is that Liverpool and its active citizens are resilient: they will not give up and will do whatever they can to look after their communities. In many respects, the city should long ago have ceased to exist, let alone have managed to achieve what it has. And not only that, but also remain a place of radical action that is still influencing thinking globally.

Radical Liverpool today is perhaps the same as it has always been: a collection of tough, bolshie individuals and groups who share a passion for their beliefs and their community and will not be told what to do. There are radical grassroots activities being undertaken across many different communities and over many different issues, but what unites them seems to be what has united radical Liverpool since 1911 and before: a gritty self-determination to succeed against the odds – something that will stand the city in good stead for the inevitable challenges of the next hundred years.

Notes

1 *Workers' Liberty* (5 Jan. 2011). <www.workersliberty.org/node/6876>.

2 BBC (30 Dec. 2010). <http://news.bbc.co.uk/1/hi/uk_politics/election_2010/england/8659596.stm>.

3 Delia Cullen (4 Jan. 2011). <www.catalystmedia.org.uk/issues/nerve16/letters_page.php>.

4 Jack McBane, *The Rebirth of Liverpool: The Eldonian Way* (Liverpool University Press, 2008), p. 28.

5 Ibid., 13.

6 Ibid., 48.

7 Ibid., 78.

8 Ibid., 144.

9 Christine Gibbons, *Effecting Change: Historical Memory, Community Activism and the Legacy of the Occupation of Croxteth Comprehensive School, 1982–1985* (Liverpool, 2010), p. 5.

10 Ritchie Hunter (5 Jan. 2011). <www.catalystmedia.org.uk/issues/nerve4/21_years.htm>.

11 Gibbons, *Effecting Change*, p. 8.

12 Phil Francis Carspecken, *Community Schooling and the Nature of Power: The Battle for Croxteth Comprehensive* (London: Routledge, 1991), p. 80.

13 Gibbons, *Effecting Change*, p. 10.

14 Ritchie Hunter (30 Dec. 2010). <www.catalystmedia.org.uk/issues/nerve4/21_years.htm>.

15 Gibbons, *Effecting Change*, p. 14.

16 David Ward (14 Jan. 2011). <www.guardian.co.uk/education/2006/apr/11/further-education.uk2>.

17 Gibbons, *Effecting Change*, p. 15.

18 Ben Turner (30 Dec. 2010). <www.liverpoolecho.co.uk/liverpool-news/local-news/

2010/07/16/croxteth-comprehensive-closure-plan-could-see-new-lease-of-life-for-school-100252-26863788/>.

19 Stephen Little and Arja Lemmetyninen, *Regional Identity and Regional Development: The Role of Narratives in the European Capital of Culture Programme*, Third Central European Conference in Regional Science, 6–9 October 2009, Kosice, Slovakia, p. 5 (electronic version).

20 *Liverpool One* (10 Jan. 2011). <www.liverpool-one.com/website/home.aspx>.

21 Ibid. <www.liverpoolecho.co.uk/liverpool-news/local-news/2004/06/11/jim-joins-quiggins-campaign-100252-14324699/>.

22 *Picket* (14 Jan. 2011). <www.savethepicket.com/>.

23 *Homes and Communities Agency* (4 Jan. 2011). <www.homesandcommunities.co.uk/housing_market_renewal>.

24 Charles Clover, *The Times* (6 Jan. 2011). <www.timesonline.co.uk/tol/comment/columnists/guest_contributors/article7035090.ece>.

25 Chris Allen, *Housing Market Renewal and Social Class* (London: Routledge, 2008), p. 128.

26 Ibid., 155.

27 Patrick Sawyer, *Telegraph* (4 Jan. 2011). <www.telegraph.co.uk/culture/music/the-beatles/8235146/Let-It-Be-Ringo-Starrs-birthplace-could-be-saved-from-demolition.html>.

28 Wikipedia (10 Jan. 2011). <http://en.wikipedia.org/wiki/Guerrilla_gardening>.

29 Ciara Leeming (4 Jan. 2011). <www.ciaraleeming.co.uk/blog/tag/liverpool/>.

30 BBC (4 Jan. 2011). <www.bbc.co.uk/news/uk-england-merseyside-12006404>.

31 *The Jangler* (newsletter published by Granby Residents Association), issue 36, April 2011.

32 *Daily Mail*, 1 May 2011, ,www.dailymail.co.uk/tvshowbiz/article-1378759/Ringo-Starrs-home-saved bulldozers-Government-blocks-demolition-11th-hour.html? ITO =1490>.

33 The Florence Institute Trust (4 Jan. 2011). <www.theflorrie.org>.

34 Richard Moss (4 Jan. 2011). <www.culture24.org.uk/places+to+go/north+west/liverpool/art40646>.

35 Catharine Jones, *Liverpool Echo* (30 Dec. 2010). <www.liverpoolecho.co.uk/liverpool-news/local-news/2010/01/22/liverpool-s-florence-institute-gets-3-7m-restoration-money-100252-25658600/>.

36 Catharine Jones (10 Jan. 2011). <www.thefreelibrary.com/Work+to+start+on+Florrie%27s+pounds+6.4m+revamp.-a0229656057>.

37 Richard Moss (4 Jan. 2010).

38 Social Enterprise Network (30 Dec. 2010). <www.sen.org.uk/news/david-cameron-visits-liverpool-promote-social-enterprise-campaign>.

39 *Liverpool Daily Post* (30 Dec. 2010). <www.liverpooldailypost.co.uk/liverpool-news/regional-news/2010/04/02/david-cameron-accused-of-hypocrisy-over-mersey-jobs-scheme-92534-26161083/>.

10

Scouse and the City: Radicalism and Identity in Contemporary Liverpool

Clare Devaney

All right ... all right ... but apart from better sanitation and medicine and education and irrigation and public health and roads and a freshwater system and baths and public order ... what have the Romans done for us?
Monty Python's Life of Brian, dir. Terry Jones (Handmade Films, 1979)

Present-day commentators often use 'post-2008' as an affix to Liverpool, with the inference that that year – in which Liverpool was officially designated as European Capital of Culture (with Norway's Stavanger as its non-EU counterpart) – represents a hugely significant moment in the city's recent history, qualifying almost as its own archaeological period. Here is a Liverpool where thirty-somethings go misty-eyed at the thought of simpler times before years had cultural themes while their children gaze in awestruck wonder at legends of gargantuan mechanical spiders and the merciless invasion of a mythological race of half-sheep, half-bananas.[1]

But was it really 'all that'?

Of course, we know about the 27.7 million tourists, and certainly appreciate their spending an extra £753.8 million,[2] but, to paraphrase the much-paraphrased *Life of Brian* ('So funny it was banned in Norway!' – sorry, Stavanger): 'What did Capital of Culture ever do for us?'

As we who survived attempt to navigate these post-apocalyptic, post-feminist, postmodernist, 'post-2008' times, picking our way through the still-smouldering detritus of discarded enamel '08 brooches, street-party bunting and assorted fragments of ceramic lambananas, are we in danger of losing the present? And worse: of losing any sense of the 'pre-', the 'what happens next', the 'where do we go from here'?

Where are our progressive thinkers when we need them? Where are the forward-looking, innovative, avant-garde? And, as the nation balances ever more precariously on the precipice of double-dip recession, 'swingeing' public-funding cuts and mass social unrest, where are Liverpool's famously bolshie, anarchic revolutionaries?

In *Tatler*'s 'Livercool',[3] where the only promise of 'Revolution' is cocktail pitchers for £6, and where our Scouse comes, naturally, with red cabbage jus and beetroot crisps, does the Scouse radical even exist?

Has the newly regenerated, newly polished, newly *sanitised* Liverpool One caused radicalism to retreat uphill and seek out its only available sanctuary in a bookshop on Bold Street?[4]

Or is it condemned to history, sentenced for eternity with historical figures like Jim Larkin, Kitty Wilkinson and the rest of the 'bolshies' to cast a resolute, if disdainful, eye over Cosmo-quaffing revellers from the glossy confines of the Newz Bar ceiling?[5]

What does it even mean to be radical, and indeed to be Scouse in 2011?

'Who are Yer?' – The Great Scouse Identity Crisis

'Curiously disorientating from a distance, downright spectacular up-close'
– Liverpool Biennial commentary for Richard Wilson's 'Turning the Place Over'.[6]

Liverpool is a city built on contradiction, non-conformity and paradox. English, but not English; quintessentially cool, but mawkishly senti-mental; catholic, protestant, red, blue: Liverpool defies definition and positively revels in its enigmatic resolve. From the second 'City of Empire' to the pariah city of the 1980s, Liverpool and its people have adapted to its changing fortunes with resilience, humour and what John Belchem calls 'characteristic inverted pride'.[7]

A mistress of reinvention, the Madonna of the modern industrial city, contemporary Liverpool has continued to take the remarkable highs and lows of the last decade in its stride, from European Economic Commu-nity Objective One status to 'Livercool', from Liverpool Football Club as Champions of Europe in 2005 to Boris Johnson's accusation as 'self-pity City', from architect Will Alsop's 'The Cloud' that never was to UNESCO World Heritage status and designation as European Capital of Culture in 2008.

Ironically, for a city that continues to thrive on its 'exceptionalism' and difference, contemporary Liverpool still finds its security and sanctuary in its icons, shared beliefs and identity as a collective. The new Liverpool brand, launched in 2009, centres (once again) on the Three Graces at the Pier Head, further proof if any were needed that the sight of these build-ings presiding majestically over the Mersey can still melt the 'coolest' of Scouse hearts, just as the familiar tones of a fellow Scouser when in exile, as the *Echo*'s Peter Grant describes, can be 'like an aural postcard from home'.[8] And while the influence of the Church may well be less pronounced for many of the new generation, ask about that other communal mass of creed, worship and unwavering faith – football – and you will still be hard pressed to find a neutral answer to the eternal question: 'Red or Blue?'

Perception – the 'bad cop' to identity's 'good' – varies dramatically depending on audience, as Arabella McIntyre-Brown captures in *Liverpool: The First 1,000 Years*:

> No matter where you go in the world (outside Britain), say you come from Liverpool and peoples' faces light up with big smiles. It's almost certainly going to be one of two things that people associate with Liverpool: football or music ... In Britain, the image is rather different. You'd think that Liverpool sprang into being 30 years ago, fully formed as a depressed northern city populated by work-shy, bolshie trouble makers, comedians and criminals ... Everyone knows the docks are dead, the city is a hideous blot, Scousers are stupid and aggressive, and they wouldn't know culture if they fell over it.[9]

Well, we are full of surprises.

The relationship between perception and identity is central to unpicking the Scouse mentality. Often, this is less about the message than the source. Narrative voice is critical. Famed for self-parody and ready humour, historically the city has also collectively recoiled at misrepresentation, slur and slander, battening down the hatches to protect its own. Today's Liverpool will tell its own story, thank you very much. Externally, we may have been 'designated' Capital of Culture, but internally 'we won'. Liverpool has not been *regenerated*, but perhaps more than any other city is described as 're-generating itself'.

We prefer our narrative in the first person.

Voice is of course fundamental to the Scouse identity. From the stressed (out) 'glottals', adenoidal diphthongs and careless dental fricatives of its instantly recognisable yet ever-evolving accent to a unified voice against oppression for transport workers, suffragists and dockers and the unmistakeable Scouse grit of the Fab Four voices who shook the world, Liverpool is a city whose voice demands to be heard.

Much maligned, celebrated, imitated and satirised, the Scouse accent, as one might expect, defies clear historical or etymological definition, but is generally thought to have arrived on the boat from Ireland in the nineteenth century and to have taken hold in the social melting pot of the docks. Used both to establish a common identity and to assert a clear difference (principally from 'woollybacks', Lancastrians and Mancunians),

Liverpool's accent continues to mark out its people whenever and wherever they open their mouths.

And do we talk.

We talk good: 'In London nobody speaks to you and here everybody chats.'[10]

We talk bad: 'The 1970s saw strikes all over Britain – but Liverpool's strikers were more articulate than most and the media fed on endless images of strife and gloom.'[11]

And we talk ugly: 'They speak a bastard brogue: a shambling, degenerate speech of slip-shod vowels and muddied consonants – a cast-off clout of a tongue, more debased even than the Whitechapel Cockney, because so much more sluggish, so much less positive and acute.'[12]

Well. You cannot please all of the people, all of the time.

Ironically, a Scouser is only truly a Scouser when not in Liverpool. Away from the safety in numbers, each utterance carries with it the burden of one's forefathers, every guttural vowel torn up from the potato fields, every missed consonant tinged with unionism, sectarianism, militancy, every gargled 'k' dragging out comedian Stan Boardman and his 'Germans who bombed our chippy', and inviting yet another comic turn from a budding Harry Enfield.

But even our accent is getting soft. No longer that particular mix of 'Welsh, Irish and catarrh',[13] so beautifully described by John Kerrigan in his preface to *Liverpool Accents: Seven Poets and a City*, phonologists have attributed the change largely to cleaner air, better sanitation and more genteel working conditions rather than the 'notorious problems of public health which made Victorian Liverpudlians prone to adenoids and respiratory disease'.[14]

In his much-cited 1973 doctoral thesis, Gerald Knowles asserts that the distinctive nasal quality of the Victorian Scouse accent may well have had a physiological basis, but spread simply by becoming accepted over time as the group norm and adopted only through imitation by future generations.[15] Its characteristics certainly continued to be observed in the 1960s, with the celebrated accents of the Beatles and the Mersey poets (when arguably public health conditions had not seen too much by way of improvement), in early 1970s footballers (with their perms), the *Boys from the Blackstuff* and 'Gizzajob' (glossing over the portrayal of Yozzer Hughes by Bernard Hill, a confirmed 'Manc' in real life) and well into the 1980s with 'our Cilla', *Letter to Brezhnev* and *Brookside*'s 'our Ga', 'our Ba' and 'our Te'.

Through the nineties, naughties and teenies, the nose has continued to be the weapon of choice for both Scouse parody (see *Harry Enfield and Chums*) and dramatic representation (see Robert Carlyle's Albie in *Cracker*: 'L-I-V-E-R-P double O-L, Liverpool FC!'), but in reality there has been a marked softening of the prevalent native accent in the city, particularly in its city-centre and more central suburban areas, with the diehard 'adenoidals' retreating ever further to the outposts of the metropolitan boroughs.

Surely this is down to more than a good decongestant.

Exposure to outside influences through mass media and internet communications, increased opportunity for travel, social mobility, further education, inward and outward migration and latterly the particularly prevalent phenomenon of 'repatriation' have all brought their own influences to bear on the development of 'modern Scouse'. The need to operate in a globalised society and to communicate successfully not just with Brits but in an international forum has meant the modern accent has been required, in the great tradition of all things Liverpool, to *adapt*. As a result, the 'modern Scouser' about town often has several registers in his or her linguistic armoury, 'oo'ing out 'books' and cooks' with the best of them, but – even if quite subconsciously – saving one's highest register for occasions requiring the best china.

Perceptions too have changed dramatically over the last ten years. Perhaps the most celebrated example of this was in March 2003 when, to quote coverage in *The Times* of the event (because it *was* an event), *Tatler*, 'a magazine whose readers, you might imagine, would rather eat a septic pigeon than set foot in a place where a three-bedroom house costs less than the annual interest from their trust funds'[16] featured a twenty-three-page celebration of Liverpool's 'attitude, vitality and unashamed ostentation' under the banner 'Livercool'. So what if it featured the Countess of Derby, a Lady and an Honourable as its models? Atomic Kitten and 'WAG about town'/actress Joanna Taylor were IN for the proles. We had made it.

And we made the most of it. Riding high on our winning bid for Capital of Culture, still enjoying a 40 per cent subsidy from EEC Objective One funding and our 'Livercool' status certified in print, we set out on an intoxicating (and arguably intoxicated) course, testing the boundaries of just how cool we could be. If we said it was cool, it was cool, all right? – even if we were in pyjamas and Ugg boots.

Sadly, too often the kiss of death for the cool is being told that they are cool, thinking that they are cool and then – worse again – *trying to be cool*. Three years is a long time in showbiz and by 2006/07 we were stuck in never-ending roadworks, the Mathew Street Festival had been cancelled in the name of Health and Safety, our council chiefs were embroiled in a bitter feud, and we were facing the end of our twelve-year leg-up from Europe.

'Livercool' had gone distinctly lukewarm.

But we had heard there was another party just around the corner ...

2008 and All That

A European city of culture – and a city of European culture – should rightly be thought of as a place where a great deal of deflation goes on, a great deal of sceptical and unillusioned thinking that can penetrate the pretensions of all claims to final versions of the human comedy or tragedy; but a city will do this best when it recognizes, as this city has so powerfully done in its recent history, that the roots which nourish all this are Christian, the roots of a belief in change and growth, in the reality of hope in the heart of apparent failure, in the refusal to accept passively what others want to take for granted.[17]

Liverpool in 2003 was awash with stickers. Schools, buses, taxis, hospitals – if there was a bare surface, or something simply did not move quickly enough, it got stickered. All right, so not everyone was all that clear what 'this Capital of Culture lark' was all about, but we had been to Europe and liked it. Our airport had been transformed in no time from the tin shack on a Speke wasteland where we had been catapulted as children back over the Irish Sea for the annual Christmas visit to become the Liverpool John Lennon (with its slogan 'above us only sky'), Europe's fastest-growing airport serving 5.47 million passengers in 2007. 'European' felt right. Better than British or English anyway. And we had culture in spades. After all, we were the 'World in One City'.

So we laid our cultural wares before the eyes of Europe with a collective 'd'ye know worra mean?' backed with the full force of Scouse solidarity. And we won. 'If one had to say one thing that swung it for Liverpool', commented Sir Jeremy Isaacs, chair of the Capital of Culture decision panel, 'it would have to be there was a greater sense there that the whole city is involved in the bid and behind the bid'.[18]

No longer an Objective One poor relation, but a European *capital*, Liverpool set about preparing for its big year with characteristic single-mindedness, focus and determination – no pavement slab left chewy-ed, no Big Dig left un-dug. The iconic skyline rapidly became dominated by a new influx of cranes in full swing. Something was happening. Something good. Although once again we were not quite sure what, because now the council was 'doing culture', and, besides, you had to pay to use the sticker.

So began the love/hate relationship with 'ECoC'.

Opinion, as ever, was rarely neutral. The news from Dale Street sounded promising enough, Liverpool Culture Company's website heralding the forthcoming 2008 programme as 'Europe's biggest and most diverse celebration of culture, with more than 50 international festivals in art, architecture, ballet, comedy, cinema, food, literature, music, opera, science and theatre', but in the city that likes to talk, the years building up to 2008 saw little communicated from the ivory tower about the actual detail of the programme. Writing in 2006, the *Guardian*'s David Ward described Liverpool as 'The City of Tattered Dreams'. Recalling Sir Jeremy's comments about the winning bid in 2003, he wrote:

> But what did the whole city think capital of culture was about? A glorious high-art cultural festival, a kind of year-long Edinburgh? A community knees-up that would have them dancing in the streets of Toxteth and Speke? Or a chance to show the world that Liverpool, a bit later than several other British cities, was heavily into economic regeneration and dockside apartments?

> The message was never clear – and it still isn't. Today the euphoria has faded and, with 22 months to go, it is hard to say what – if anything – is actually going to happen in 2008.[19]

Certainly by 2006 the physical impact on the city centre was already tangible, with glossy apartment buildings being matched like for like (and arguably too alike) with even glossier hotels. But what about outside of the city centre? What about our neighbourhoods and communities? The council was accused of neglecting its 'bread and butter' responsibilities in its dogged pursuit of the 'culture' prize, of ghettoising the city by investing in a shiny city centre for the tourists while the then-Government's Housing Market Renewal programme started its unprecedented assault on homes and communities in Kensington, Toxteth and Anfield.

Then came Liverpool One.

Forty-two acres of straightforward, uncomplicated, capitalist pleasure; a chrome-and-glass playground of plastic-fuelled hyper-consumption; a veritable Mecca of shops, bars, restaurants and a fourteen-screen multiplex cinema. In one swoop of the Duke of Westminster's magic money wand, we had lost alternative shopping emporium Quiggins but gained the 'Bling Building' for Herbert the Hairdresser's.

For Liverpool, a city whose history, culture and – dare one say – whose very identity are so fundamentally intertwined with its physical form and architectural expression, the sweeping changes to its city centre felt nothing short of a whitewash. First, the seemingly unstoppable proliferation of faceless apartments, hotels and apart-hotels, followed by the all-conquering Liverpool One, which seemed not only to drag the centre of the city from Church Street to (ironically) centre-left but to shift the whole focus of the city away from its Three Graces and on to this new concrete monolith. Its delicate architectural balance and aesthetic symmetry momentarily upset, the city felt like ... it had lost its mojo.

Writing in 2006, John Belchem compares the process to the 1957 'clean-up' ahead of the city's 750th anniversary celebrations, which saw the hasty relocation of Paddy's Market and Professor Codman's Punch and Judy show and the decision made to abandon the Overhead Railway, commenting:

> Within the City Centre itself, 'official' culture is being prioritised in self-defeating manner, denying space to the alternative, diverse and challenging forms of cultural expression which have contributed so much to the city's cultural creativity and distinctive identity.
>
> As culture is commodified into corporate blandness, alternative and individual outlets cannot afford the regenerated rents, while public spaces in the city centre are being privatised and sanitised by developers (and their attendant security staff and CCTV cameras) at the expense of a diverse and vibrant street culture.[20]

Frustrations with 'the 2008 machine' grew quickly – with the Culture Company as the self-ordained ministry of culture, with the continued lack of communication, restrictive and inaccessible commissioning and tendering processes, and in particular with the perceived preference for 'external' contractors at the expense of local artists and organisations.

Refusing to sign up to 'the Corpy' version of culture, rejecting the sanitised version of itself and in essence vehemently objecting to *somebody else telling its story*, a counter-Capital of Culture was born, a celebration of a 'warts and all' Liverpool that refused to hide its dereliction behind multi-coloured neon hoardings; where the news was from nowhere, the poetry was confidential and the philosophy definitely tasted better in pubs. Led very much by artists, independents and the 'grass-roots', this was an avant-garde revolution, a cultural liberation front and a *résistance* where it was highly unlikely anybody would say anything *only once*.

This was real Scouse culture. And this was radical.

The outcome was a 2008 that managed successfully to capture the many faces of the 'Liverpool' of its time, seamlessly (or seemingly) incorporating large-scale 'arts for all' events with the edgy, the cutting-edge, the niche; the sentimental with the cool; the international with the local, the *glocal* and everything in between.

Despite being dropped as a tagline early on in the campaign, Liverpool 2008 arguably turned out to be the 'World in One City'.

But was that because of Capital of Culture or in spite of it?

A Radical Future?

PROTESTORS angered by proposals to increase university tuition fees brought violence and chaos to the streets once again tonight.

Westminster bore the brunt of lawlessness a fortnight after the Millbank riot as two police officers and 11 people were injured. At least 15 protesters were arrested for offences including violent disorder, theft and criminal damage as barriers were thrown and fires lit in the street.

Thousands also joined protest marches in Manchester, Liverpool and Brighton as pupils walked out of schools in Winchester, Cambridge, Leeds and London.

One protestor in Liverpool was arrested for throwing an egg.[21]

So which came first? The cultured chicken or the radical egg?

Liverpool is a City of Radicals. Unlike the 'Radical City' of Manchester down the road, its radicalism cannot be defined from above and confined within one catch-all label of homogeneity but is something intangible that comes from inside the guts of the city, from the bloodlines at its core and that is personified in those anarchic, revolutionary, 'bolshie' individuals who categorically refuse to accept the status quo.

From 1994, up to and including 2006, Liverpool lived under Objective One's roof and dutifully abided by its rules, filling in our endless ticky-box forms to meet European targets for 'cross-cutting themes', jobs and business start-ups, remediation of brownfield sites and creation of new floor space (in metres squared). By 2003, half way through the tranche of second funding, we were doing well. There was a buzz about the city centre. We had jobs, we had plastic, we were 'Livercool', and we had more city-centre loft apartments than Doddy could shake his ticklestick at.[22]

For once, we had nothing to shout about.

So 2008 was a radical moment. Not because of the billions, the 'cultural engagement' or the tourists. But because of the sheer frustration and indignation that brought the radicals screaming back out of their boxes, rested up and ready for a fight. Just as a Scouser is only truly a Scouser outside of the city, so the radical can only truly be radical when there is something to reject or rebel against, reforms to be made or injustices to put right: 2008 gave Liverpool its radicals back.

Since then, with our radical noses whetted, there has been a perceptible shift in thinking. Yes, we can all appreciate having somewhere decent to shop (especially without contributing any further to the Mancunian economy), but the focus for the city centre in recent years has been essentially to 're-Liverpool' Liverpool, shifting attention back to those parts of the city steeped in history and idiosyncrasy, with particular investment in the University District and the Hope Street Quarter and, latterly, in the city's 'bohemian urban village', The Ropewalks.

And 2010 has seen a political shift, with a change in administration to Labour after fifteen years of local Lib Dem council rule. Not particularly radical in itself, with Liverpool historically electing the party least allied to national power, this nevertheless points to a Liverpool leaning even further to the left, ready and waiting for change.

Certainly, the political landscape is ripe for revolt. Already this year, we have seen the start of the systematic decimation of the welfare state by the (un-elected) quasi-government of coalition, prompting mass protest and rioting, particularly in response to the rise in university-level tuition fees.

No doubt you would get good odds on Big Jim Larkin tackling the present coalition head-on. But what hope for Liverpool's 'Class of 2011' and their crystal-clear nasal passages? Are these really the rounded vowels that can lead a revolution?

In summer 2011, the doors will open to the new Museum of Liverpool. Its predecessor, the Museum of Liverpool Life, closed in 2006, along with its enduringly popular *Demanding a Voice* exhibition, which remembered (among other things) the suffragists, the unions and co-operatives, the Unity Theatre group, the Toxteth riots and the Meccano strike. Could it be that the new museum's tinted-glass facade is hiding similar revolutionary secrets, and that its forthcoming opening will act as a Pandora's Box through which radical Liverpool will once again find its voice?

And if that voice heralds a radical future, when exactly can we expect it all to 'kick off'? After all, it took us a good five years from the icy detachment of 2003's 'Livercool' to get warmed up enough to start the fireworks in 2008.

Fittingly, as part of an initiative led by LARC partners, 2013 – five years on from 2008 – has been designated 'The Year of Nothing'.[23]

If ever a year was asking for *something* to happen ...

Notes

1 As part of the 2008 celebrations, Liverpool Culture Company commissioned 125 mini-replicas of Taro Chiezo's iconic *Superlambanana* sculpture, which featured designs by local organisations and community groups, and were located throughout Liverpool and Merseyside. French performance art company La Machine showcased *La Princesse*, its fifteen-metre (fifty-foot) mechanical spider, in Liverpool city centre to crowds of thousands between 3 and 7 September 2008.

2 Beatriz Garcia, Ruth Melville and Tamsin Cox, *Creating an Impact: Liverpool's Experience as European Capital of Culture*, Impacts 08, 2010, The Liverpool Model, European Capital of Culture Research Programme, University of Liverpool. <www.impacts08.net>.

3 High-society magazine *Tatler* (Mar. 2003) contained a twenty-three-page fashion and lifestyle feature on Liverpool under the title 'Livercool'.

4 Founded in 1974, Liverpool's News from Nowhere bookshop is a not-for-profit worker's co-operative which seeks to support and promote equality, empowerment and social change. It is reputedly one of only six 'radical' bookshops in the UK.

5 Liverpool's Newz Bar features David Jacques' piece *Some Liverpool Radicals*: eight ceiling panels depicting radical figures and events in Liverpool's history, including the 1911 Transport Strike Committee, Liverpool-Irish conscientious objectors in the Second World War and the Liverpool Women's Suffragists.

6 Art Feast, 'Crustacean Communication, Declarations of Love and the Inside, Out'. Oct. 2010. <www.artfeast.co.uk/2010/10/crustacean-communication-declarations-of-love-and-the-inside-out/>.

7 John Belchem, *Merseypride: Essays in Liverpool Exceptionalism* (Liverpool University Press, 2000), p. xiv.

8 *Liverpool Echo* (9 Aug. 2008).

9 Arabella McIntyre-Brown, *Liverpool: The First 1,000 Years* (Liverpool: Garlic Press, 2001), p. 10.

10 Ruth Melville and Beatriz Garcia, 'Re-telling the City: Exploring Local Narratives of Liverpool', Impacts 08, 2010, The Liverpool Model, European Capital of Culture Research Programme, University of Liverpool (2007), p. 6. <www.liv.ac.uk/impacts08/Papers/Impacts08%28Dec07%29RetellingTheCity.pdf>.

11 McIntyre-Brown, *Liverpool: The First 1,000 Years*, p. 22.

12 Walter Dixon Scott, *Liverpool 1907* (Neston: Gallery Press, 1979), p. 144 (originally published as *Liverpool* (London: Adam and Charles Black, 1907)).

13 Peter Robinson (ed.), *Liverpool Accents: Seven Poets and a City* (Liverpool University Press, 1996), p. 2.

14 Belchem, *Merseypride*, p. 46.

15 Gerald Knowles, 'Scouse: The Urban Dialect of Liverpool', University of Leeds PhD thesis (1973), pp. 23–24.

16 'New Scouse Nous', *The Times* (11 Feb. 2003).

17 Archbishop of Canterbury Rowan Williams, 'Europe, Faith and Culture', lecture delivered at the Anglican Cathedral, Liverpool, 26 Jan. 2008.

18 Jeremy Isaacs, *Liverpool Echo* (4 June 2003).

19 David Ward, 'City of Tattered Dreams', *Guardian* (9 Mar. 2006).

20 Belchem, *Merseypride*, p. xix.

21 *Liverpool Echo* (25 Nov. 2010).

22 Ken Dodd, OBE is a comedian and singer/songwriter, born in Knotty Ash, Liverpool in 1927. Widely acknowledged as a much-loved Scouse institution, 'Doddy' is famed for his buck teeth, frizzy hair and feather duster (or 'ticklestick'). Bronze statues of Dodd and the equally venerated Liverpool MP Bessie Braddock were unveiled on the concourse at Liverpool Lime Street Station in June 2009.

23 Liverpool Arts Regeneration Consortium (LARC) is a partnership which includes seven of the City's leading cultural institutions. The designation in 2013 as 'The Year of Nothing' is FACT's response (as nominated lead partner for that year) to the LARC initiative to provide ongoing conceptual and thematic focus to the city's cultural offering.

Radical Soundings

In examining developments and key moments across the past one hundred years the previous chapters have attempted to articulate some of the strands in Liverpool's history that can claim radical significance. Some writers have brought their stories into the present, indicating how the past has informed radical impulses in the city today across cultural, social and political dimensions. This final chapter brings together other voices to propose what the city's radical prospects might be as we enter the second decade of the new century.

Such an exercise might be prone to indulging in unattainable crystal ball gazing, or evoking a nostalgic and unduly romanticised 'heritage' past in the formation of a radical future. Any set of possibilities, particularly for a city like Liverpool, with such a challenging, controversial and contested history, must therefore move beyond the familiar, however much it is enriched by it. In *Liverpool: Gateway of Empire* (1987), his masterful analysis of the shaping of Liverpool's identity, Tony Lane concluded that more than any other British city Liverpool 'needs a grand, even a grandiose, sense of a possibility' – critically, 'a future which does not look like an extension of the present', let alone of the past:

> It would be fitting for Liverpool to excel at cosmopolitanism, for that was exactly the character it had when it was last a city that mattered. If history was to be repeated in this respect too, a generous welcome would be essential for all settling strangers and not just those with enough personal and financial capital to become wealthy and influential. Successful global cities will be democratic places whose citizens are simultaneously intolerant of intolerance and captivated by creativity.[1]

Twenty years earlier, John Willett's prescient study of Liverpool's position and prospects in the field of the visual arts, *Art in a City* (1967), spoke similarly of the need to embrace creativity as a cornerstone of the city's reinvention. If less concerned with recapturing Liverpool's earlier cosmopolitan profile, his ideas for the future, laid out in a plan of campaign, embodied a 'straightening out' of the relationships between art and place, an integration of art at all levels of city life, from civic to community:

> In a world where communication has become so rapid and so relatively cheap, and geographical frontiers in art have been very largely swept away, this is the one hope of avoiding an ultimately cramping monotony.[2]

Since Willett and Lane envisioned a future Liverpool, the city has succeeded in retaining its distinctiveness in the face of encroaching cultural homogeneity, and the extent to which its present difference was shaped by radical forces has been interrogated by the previous chapters. In contrast to this largely retrospective focus, the following texts by a range of people from within and beyond the city – voices young and old, but all with a particular perspective on the challenges it faces – offer thoughts on what might constitute Liverpool's radical future.

Rogan Taylor, Director, Football Industry Group, University of Liverpool

Twenty years ago I wrote a book called *Football and its Fans*. It covered the period 1885 to 1985 in Britain, an account of the first chapter of an unfinished story. From the mid-1980s onwards, a new chapter began, with independent, radical supporters' groups emerging – and fanzines to match – taking an active role in the 'political game', and even taking on the government over specific issues like the infamous identity card scheme. The first national fans' organisation that individuals could join was also born here in Liverpool, in 1985 – the Football Supporters' Association. These innovations changed the format and discourse of football-reporting across the media. Back in the day, you *never* heard ordinary fans engaged in discussions about football issues; on television the only fans you ever saw were creating mayhem at home or abroad. These days, listeners and viewers expect to hear from articulate fans in media discussions. Today, we may be beginning a third chapter: the minority or majority ownership of large football clubs by the fans themselves. There is increasing dissatisfaction – even despair – at the vulnerability of these great cultural institutions to the passing interests of the super rich (or deeply leveraged). The government may respond with legislation that opens the gates to fan ownership. It could happen first here in Liverpool, where the 'radical' has real roots.

Jon Tonge, Professor of Politics at the University of Liverpool

Politics in Liverpool was riven with internal division for much of the twentieth century. First, the city's religious divide led to the most eclectic range of representatives of any English city: 'Irish Nationalist', 'Protestant', Conservative, Liberal, Labour, Independent. Then a divisive capture of the council by Militant, as the city fought back during the grim Thatcher years. The century was characterised by disorderly non-management of decline. Yet the twenty-first century looks much more promising. Always aesthetically dramatic and culturally exciting, Liverpool is now more united, prosperous and outward looking. Confidence has replaced internal strife. So what is still to be done? There are two political priorities. First, although national constraints will still shape local council actions, let us see a serious effort to end the north–south divide – within Liverpool, that is. Far too much unemployment, poverty and deprivation remain across large swathes of north Liverpool. Government and council must concentrate resources on those struggling wards. With commitment and political will, Anfield can become Aigburth, Walton transform into Woolton. Secondly, the biggest single change for Liverpool's youth to develop their potential would be entrance to higher education. Last century, poverty of ambition and university exclusivity meant many young people never remotely considered higher education, removing themselves from intellectual satisfaction (and financial reward). Political will, financial help and cultural change should combine to ensure university is the norm, not the exception, for all Liverpool teenagers.

Ron Noon, Labour Historian and Love Lane Lives Project Coordinator

How many people go around the streets and bars of our former European Capital of Culture fully conscious of the Beatles legacy but deeply unconscious of an inheritance bequeathed by a socialist stonemason and buried in June 1904 under the Anglican Cathedral's foundation stone? Fred Bower was born in Boston, Massachusetts in 1871 but reared in a Liverpool described ten years later as 'the New York of Europe', a 'World City'! Our city's merchandise has never just been commodities and the contents of ships' holds, but people and ideas, music and movement, and the cosmopolitan exchange of cultures as well as things. As a thirty-three-year-old, on the threshold of another trip to New York, scheduled for the maiden voyage of Cunard's SS *Baltic*, Fred wrote a 'short hurried note' to a future socialist society. Together with his pal Jim Larkin they clandestinely buried the message 'that you will own the trusts' and leave 'the world the better for your having lived in it' below the massive Gothic edifice that imperiously looms over our world heritage waterfront. For Liverpool radicals the 'message in a Bower' at the end of Hope Street is to 'dream, plan and achieve' precisely that.

Jane Davis, Director, the Reader Organisation

Public libraries do not serve the public enough, so I do not want to save them. I want to start again with a New Readers' Library: people and books and comfy chairs, open sixteen hours a day, seven days a week, a home for the voiceless and the aimless. The New Readers' Library will have excellent coffee and be run as a trust. It will have a neon sign calling 'You can be at home here!' and those who think the world holds nothing for them will be tempted in. It will have corners and lamps and a learning kitchen so we can eat something fantastic and cheap for lunch, and the world's cookbooks will be stacked up there. We will go to the New Readers' Library to learn, reading Aristotle together and working out what he means, joining the knitting class. The New Readers' Library will be a place where we can read with others, browse the shelves, talk to Mariam, be silent, watch Niall feeding tropical fish (and all the fish books shelved right there). My mum-in-law will do t'ai chi. There will be volunteers but we will think of them as our friends. It is a place in the future. Come with me.

François Matarasso, Researcher in Community Cultural Practice

Ports exist to enable transitions. Uniting the utterly different worlds of earth and water, they allow people and goods to move from one place, one life, to another. And many other things catch an unseen ride on those living and dead packages moved across gangplanks and hoisted by cranes: bacteria, viruses, ideas, cultures and values cross boundaries to plant themselves in new worlds that they change and by which they are themselves changed. Whatever else it may be, art is a carrier of ideas, meanings and values, enabling transactions between people that change them in unforeseeable but enriching ways. It is not the parcels ferried by dockers or the objects in galleries that matter. Both would be hollow without the intangible spirits that move with them. Liverpool's great days grew from the myriad transactions channelled through its port. They opened the city to the world and the world to the city: neither has been the same since. But that greatness does not depend on a port: a culture in transition, a culture of exchange, can do as much and more. Look outward, Liverpool: give and receive your cargoes of art. And remember to take a coin for the ferryman.

Alexandra Harris, Lecturer in English, University of Liverpool

Perhaps it is odd to seek Liverpool's radical future in a building that looked out of date long before it was finished. But the sheer red cliffs of the Anglican Cathedral always give me a shiver of hope. Designed by Scott at the age of twenty-one, it has that audacity of youth that usually lives in dreams and is rarely translated into stone. And yet its courage is partly in its conservatism, its amplification of Early English style, its conviction that our future involves a confident embrace of the past. If the building is an essay in belatedness, it is also out in the lead. 'Welcome to the Great Space', say the posters. To the non-believer there is a brave note of irony: is this the space left by God? But the Cathedral brilliantly demonstrates the possibilities of a place that needs to be Godly and Godless at once. In 2008, the theatre company Dreamthinkspeak filled it with echoes of the Divine Comedy, climbing through labyrinths before showing us, from the tower, Liverpool laid before us, a possible paradise. Tracey Emin's neon sign over the West Door seems, to me, supremely apt in this building that knows how to experiment. It is big, bold, and anonymously electric; it is intimate, subtle and written by hand in the oldest way we know. It is one of many recent intimations of what Liverpool can be.

Hans van der Heijden, Architect

Is Liverpool a city of radicals? Yes and no. Yes, in the sense that the city has been the habitat of uncompromising artists, and not just the Beatles. No, in the sense that such radicalism has failed to make contact with the political and economic world. Liverpool, virtually a third world economy, has gratefully to accept any sort of investment without asking questions. A world of cheapness. Old and underused edifices only left there because the land they sit on is worth money. Imagine if Liverpool were radical enough to put a ban on constructing new edifices and another on the demolition of buildings. The city would then possess millions of square metres of vacant buildings with limited land value. Newness happened everywhere else, while Liverpool played a card of oldness. One could expect all these square metres to become more readily available to Liverpudlians. Large families would live in two houses instead of one. Students would work in spacious studios and sleep in palaces. It would be easy to start companies and even easier to stop them again. The city's impressive reservoir of fine old buildings would become desirable. And Liverpool would come to terms with its own shortcomings as well as its strengths.

Ian Wray, Writer, Planner and Visiting Professor, University of Liverpool

The idea that Liverpool might become a major tourist destination was floated in 1981 by Whitehall's think tank. The Cabinet received their paper with disbelief. Ministers made jokes about the Costa del Scouse. But it does not seem so crazy now, does it? So I want to make another bizarre suggestion: Liverpool can become a global Oxbridge. It is already happening. This year 50 per cent of students at my university are Chinese; next year it will be 60 per cent. They do not have prejudices or preconceptions. They see Liverpool has a great, world class university, fantastic architecture and powerful associations with popular culture. They probably like the night life too. Consultants McKinsey's recent report on the future of the UK sees higher education as a huge opportunity for export earnings. It is something we are good at in Liverpool. So what needs to happen? Nearly all government research institutions are in the south. Let us move five to Liverpool. Let us identify our top ten university departments and get government to double their funding. In 1898, a great battle was fought between Liverpool and London about the location of a new national school of tropical medicine. Liverpool got its school, and now it is a jewel in the crown of international medical research. They did it then.

Mandy Vere, News from Nowhere Bookshop

The Female Eunuch, The Communist Manifesto, Soledad Brother, The Ragged Trousered Philanthropists – every progressive movement has had its 'Bibles', rallying cries for liberation. And every progressive person can cite a book that changed their outlook forever. As such, the best books are not passive, but in informing and educating they can act as catalysts for change. How important then is a place where books of this nature are gathered together, where we can find information on previous struggles for change, theories of how to organise society, practical solutions to climate change, critiques of global finance and power? Not to mention fiction that opens our eyes to other worlds or books that celebrate the art, music and creativity of new worlds envisaged. Such a place is a radical bookshop. There were once more than sixty in the UK. Every major city and most towns had one; Liverpool had nine. Now only three remain outside London, of which Liverpool's News from Nowhere is one of the oldest, biggest and the only one run by a women's co-operative. For Liverpool, one of the toughest cities economically, to have managed to sustain a radical bookshop must say something about its anti-authoritarian nature ... and, equally, the necessity of News from Nowhere's survival as a beacon of radical thought.

Dinesh Allirajah, Poet

Just at the moment we were scouring the backs of our wardrobes and riffling through our Doc Marten shoeboxes to retrieve our old 1980s animosities; in the week Liverpool opted out of central government's showpiece Big Society policy; just when that clear red water between this city and Westminster rippled as Cameron denounced multiculturalism, and my six-year-old was called a Paki at school, I was asked to write my vision of a radical future for Liverpool. It does not take a visionary to work out that some of us do not belong in the futures business. We imagine the future the same way we fillet the past for the fictions we live by today. There is no consensual progress to a radical future. How do we radicalise a teenage Edward Rushton without the colossal spike of the slave trade? He could join the Yellow House and go to Eastern Europe to be heard, while the Liverpool section of Waterstone's pushes the memoirs of drug barons. There is a renegade, mongrel aesthetic here, but when our dirty realism is sold back to us as fetish wear that is the time to uncork our heads from our arseholes and look around: we hold no patent for radicalism.

Ciaran Varley, Writer and Editor for Television and Online

Liverpudlians have long traded on their outsider status. Whether this constitutes a 'radical' outlook or not is up for debate. The 'Spirit of Shankly' movement has shown that Liverpudlians can still come together when they feel their interests are being threatened. However, it is interesting that there has been no such response on the same scale to the announcement of massive government cuts, despite the fact that Liverpool will be one of the hardest hit councils in the country. This contradiction seems to give the lie to the theory that Liverpool is still a radical city. Is football simply the modern opiate of the masses then? Or perhaps this inactivity comes down to the fact that the industrial landscape of the city has changed over time. There is one more thing worth observing. Recent protests against tuition fee rises and the abolition of Education Maintenance Allowance (EMA) have shown that young people are beginning to find a voice. What has been particularly interesting is the way that these young radicals have used social networking sites, bypassing the traditional forms of mobilisation. As the cuts make more impact it will be interesting to observe whether we see any more of this kind of behaviour.

Councillor Joe Anderson, Leader of Liverpool City Council

Liverpool and innovation go hand in hand. This is a city that does not stand still and, as a result, will always be classed as radical. The docks, so many times described as the lifeblood of Liverpool, are a great example of this. In its heyday it was a busy port, importing and exporting goods. While it is still a very successful port, the docklands are dramatically changing – from the new look of the Pier Head to the creation of the cruise terminal facility and of course the newest addition to the waterfront – the new Museum of Liverpool. But the most radical change, and one that will make a massive difference, not just to the city but to the north west, will be the creation of Liverpool Waters – an ultra-ambitious scheme that has the potential to revitalise the north of the city. It will be controversial, thought-provoking, cause endless debate and argument and provide a stream of headlines for the media. Just like Liverpool has over the last hundred years

David Jacques, Artist

It is always useful to revisit examples of cultural activity that might be termed 'radical', if only for the purpose of weighing up their component parts and how they would relate to/contradict each other – those evidences of 'resistance', 'imagination', 'experimentation', 'autonomy', 'solidarity' etc. But any attempt to prescribe or re-enact for the future – going off such events – would just feel *wrong*. Thinking back, the most interesting radical phenomenon often burnt brightly for a short time before expiring – and it is OK for that to happen. Because in that continually regenerating radical firmament, comparable occurrences will re-emerge (often quite unexpectedly) and disappear again, re-emerge and disappear … Something could even surface today, for example, *despite* or potentially *because* of the homogenising property development projects pushed locally by Peel/ Grosvenor. Either way, I am personally holding out for an equivalent to the *End* fanzine from the 1980s to show, easily the most radical cultural high spot of my time. No contest.

Lizzie Nunnery, Writer and Musician

Under the jurisdiction of the Liverpool Society for the Fair Distribution of Beauty, the most magnificent homes will be laid open to the public one week each year: the Georgian mansions where the grand pianos sit silent and the lawns yawn tidily will become sites for mass table tennis tournaments and impromptu gigs, debate societies and book exchanges. Year round, William Morris prints will adorn the insides of taxis and be projected onto building sites. There will be free music tuition for every child in the city on any instrument – tubas and sousaphones, penny whistles and piccolos flooding the schools. Adrian Henri's poetry will be engraved into the paving stones of Mount Street. The crime of building a shoddy, unacceptably dark or painfully cramped house will be taken extremely seriously, with high fines for perpetrators. Everyone who lives anywhere will have a tree outside their window. Every inch, every tone of the city will be named and traced: the cracks in the walls of the bombed-out church, the particular note of a drunken shout on Hardman Street at night, as the homeless are welcomed into St George's Hall, and the Liverpool Philharmonic busk on the street.

Tayo Aluko, Actor, Singer, Playwright, Nigerian

Bloody Nigerians. They'll be the ones to start it. Maybe at the Liverpool Women's. Or the Royal, perhaps. The African NHS Walk-Out. Consultant gynaecologists, cardiologists, haematologists and other '-ologists'. Nurses, midwives, GPs, cleaners and the invisible ones, like cooks, lab technicians and whatnot. Two weeks they'll say it'll last. Then the others will join them – Ghanaians, Kenyans, Rwandans, Ugandans, South Africans. Even Egyptians (and you know what *they* are like). Then the Indians, Pakistanis, Singaporeans and Malaysians will see that the Africans have a point, and walk too. For two weeks! How are we to cope? And what will they be saying? Of course, they're getting paid more here than they'd get at home, but what they want is for our government to divert at least 75 per cent of military 'aid' to health. They'll say that would make their health services so good they'll all go back home. Heck, when our own workers hear that, they'll demand the same too, and call for the billions we are spending in Iraq and Afghanistan to be spent on our own health service. We can't have that, can we? There's no money in 'peace'. It's not macho or sexy. Who came up with that dangerous idea? Let's bury it before it gets out. Bloody Nigerians.

Mike Storey, Liberal Democrat Peer,
Leader of Liverpool City Council, 1998–2005

The history of education in Liverpool shows a radicalism probably not seen anywhere else in the country, with remarkable pioneering institutions not only shaping education here, but also nationally. In 1970, two teachers set up Scotland Road Free School. The principles behind this and the subsequent Liverpool Free School were that they would be part of the community – run by parents, teachers and children, with no hierarchy or central authority control. I foresee education revisiting this concept. The next decade will see a proliferation of different types of schools and schooling. There will be no single, 'one size fits all' school system, as education is gradually tailored for individual children's needs. Other developments will take place: schools offering provision from nursery through to secondary, on purpose-built campuses, ensuring that issues surrounding children today over transition and continuity no longer pose a barrier to learning. And we will see the 'reinvention' of boarding school provision, not just for the wealthy and those working abroad, but for children who will benefit socially and emotionally from such a school. The stigma attached will evaporate owing to social and parental inclusion, ensuring a safe, nurturing environment to provide our communities with the future workforce to encourage cities to grow and develop. Liverpool will also establish an international school within the city.

Ed Vulliamy, Journalist and Writer

Liverpool may have been chosen as prototype for Britain's politically didactic de-industrialisation, but it does not have to follow where the rest of this sinking country is headed. If there is one place that can exit the political system, sack the financial barons and their whores in parliament and the city halls, and explore new notions of convivial citizenship, new forms of participatory democracy, experimental forms of co-operative *re-industrialisation*, it is Liverpool. The city could and should mobilise politically to test the bounds of what is legally and constitutionally possible (and go beyond them if necessary), to go its own way rather than be dragged down with the rest of the country. This can be done within Europe – with the likes of Germany, Sweden, Holland and even France, who have not gone the post-industrial way, and kept their maritime traditions. Not as a slavish limb of the UK, but independent of it. 'The Leaving of Liverpool' needs a whole new meaning: not migrants headed for the Atlantic's far shore, but the city and its citizens of the ocean leaving Fool Britannia altogether, to do something better – in that same cause of liberty and the pursuit of happiness. Scousers were always good at telling people who tread on them to f*** off. Now Liverpool urgently needs to put its brain and brawn where its gob is.

Notes

1 Tony Lane, *Liverpool: Gateway of Empire* (London: Lawrence & Wishart, 1987) republished as *Liverpool: City of the Sea* (Liverpool University Press: 1997), pp. 141–45.

2 John Willett, *Art in a City* (London: Methuen, 1967; repr. Liverpool University Press, 2007), pp. 250–51.

Index